Laurie Keller

Reasoning Guide 125
Reaction Guide 127

# TEACHING
# READING
# IN
# CONTENT AREAS

*second edition*

# TEACHING
# READING
# IN
# CONTENT AREAS

Harold L. Herber

*Syracuse University*

PRENTICE-HALL, INC., Englewood Cliffs, New Jersey 07632

*Library of Congress Cataloging in Publication Data*

Herber, Harold L
    Teaching reading in content areas.

    Bibliography:   p.
    Includes index.
    1. Reading.   I.  Title.
LB1050. H437  1978        428'.4'07        77-18013
ISBN   0-13-894170-X

Printed in the United States of America

10   9   8   7   6   5   4   3   2   1

PRENTICE-HALL INTERNATIONAL, INC., *London*
PRENTICE-HALL OF AUSTRALIA PTY. LIMITED, *Sydney*
PRENTICE-HALL OF CANADA, LTD., *Toronto*
PRENTICE-HALL OF INDIA PRIVATE LIMITED, *New Delhi*
PRENTICE-HALL OF JAPAN, INC., *Tokyo*
PRENTICE-HALL OF SOUTHEAST ASIA PTE. LTD., *Singapore*
WHITEHALL BOOKS LIMITED, *Wellington, New Zealand*

# Contents

v

# *appendix b*

# Preface

Those who are familiar with the first edition of this text will see that this one is similar but, at the same time, different.

The similarities are the emphasis on the functional teaching of simplified reading and reasoning processes; the emphasis on the simultaneous teaching of reading and course content; the emphasis on strategies for showing students *how* to do what we require them to do. Chapters on levels of comprehension, organizational patterns, reasoning, and vocabulary development remain the heart of the book. The preliminary and follow-up activities related to each chapter still focus on establishing a context and purpose for reading and a means for interpreting and applying what has been read.

The differences are many. Two new chapters (one and two) set the *background, purpose,* and *definitions* of reading instruction in content areas. A third new chapter (seven) presents the use of *prediction* as an important instructional strategy. The concept of *assessment* is in a separate chapter (ten) rather than being only one part of a chapter. The idea of *simulation* was expanded into a significant part of the chapter on grouping (eight).

The chapters carried over from the first edition were completely reorganized: new procedures for demonstrating the processes being discussed; new explanations of those processes; new materials to illustrate those processes. The appendix was changed to include all new materials to serve as examples of what can be developed to guide students' reading and reasoning while simultaneously learning course content. The chapter on the *Instructional Framework* (nine) was shifted from the beginning to near the end of the book. In this new position it serves both as a review of the entire text and more clearly demonstrates how all of the instructional strategies presented in the book can fit together in a lesson or series of lessons.

Finally, because of the increased opportunity to work with content teachers throughout the country since the publication of the first edition, and because of the research that has been conducted during that time, much has been learned about this aspect of reading instruction. This learning has made possible a greater clarity and precision in the presentation of the information and ideas in this text.

As one can see, the text was almost entirely rewritten; but not because the first edition was insufficient or inappropriate. Being the first of its kind, it could not contain the experimental and experiential evidence that its advent stimulated. Thus, this second edition builds significantly on the first.

I hope you find the reading of this edition a rewarding and useful experience. Writing it was such for me.

HLH

# Acknowledgments

It's an enlightening experience to develop a statement that acknowledges all those who have contributed to one's work. If nothing else, the task refreshes one's perspective on the value of one's colleagues and friends.

But, where to start? Where to end? A full list of the contributors to this edition would seem endless. I concluded that I should acknowledge categories of contributors for the sake of efficiency: teachers, graduate students; secretaries and typists; and one special person.

Hundreds of content-area teachers have contributed to this text. After the publication of the first edition, I was privileged to work with such teachers all over the country. This work contributed greatly to my own thinking as I observed their teaching and discussed various instructional strategies with them. I owe much to these professionals.

I have been fortunate in the graduate students who have chosen to study with me at Syracuse University. Even while maintaining their individuality and creativity, they have worked cooperatively over the years to create a series of interrelated dissertation studies on reading instruction in content areas. Frequent references to their work are found in this text. You will recognize many of them as persons who are contributing significantly to this aspect of reading.

I also have been fortunate in the nature and quality of secretaries and typists who have worked with me over the years that this edition was developing. They kept me organized and enabled me to meet my objectives. My thanks to Virginia Beecher, Debbie Elliott, Bonnie Macklin, Barbara Murphy, and Madeline Rathbun.

With no apology to any of the others, I saved the best until last. Joan Nelson was the most significant contributor to this text as advisor, colleague, and friend. What makes it the best is that she is also my wife—a fact which makes me both proud and happy.

To all these good people, my gratitude and thanks.

HAROLD L. HERBER

*Homer, New York*

# TEACHING
# READING
# IN
# CONTENT AREAS

# one

# Rationale and Definitions

The first edition of this book was published in 1970 and was the first textbook devoted exclusively to the concept of teaching reading in the content areas. Since 1970, interest in this aspect of reading instruction has steadily increased and has been reflected in many ways, not the least of which is through a variety of publications: major textbooks, special bulletins, numerous monographs, many articles. Two obvious reasons for this interest are the failure of special reading programs instituted in the 1960s and the continuing need for reading instruction at all levels.

The failure of programs has received much attention nationally. Several millions of dollars were spent in the sixties on materials, equipment, and personnel. Relatively little was accomplished to help the millions of students who experienced difficulty trying to read the materials required of them throughout their school years.

Two assumptions are basic to this failure: The first concerns where reading instruction is provided and by whom; the second, the lasting effect of reading instruction.

Most expenditures for reading instruction in the sixties were for programs which were separate from the regular school curriculum. That is, students were given special reading instruction in a setting different from that in which the reading skills were really required. Separate reading classes were formed, and rarely was attention given to coordinating that instruction with what was being read by the students in their subject areas. It was left to the students to transfer what they learned in the reading classes to what they needed to learn in the content-area classes. Most people were disappointed because, even though students improved their reading scores in the reading classes, they did not progress proportionately in their reading performance in other subjects. Therefore, when the federal and state money for reading was withdrawn, the problem remained. School personnel began to cast about for intelligent alternatives and, logically, concluded that the appropriate place to provide reading instruction is in the setting in which the reading is required. Such instruction could be provided by the regular classroom teacher within the regular class through materials normally used in the subject areas being studied. This alternative offered enormous economy of personnel, materials, and special programs. There was only one problem: content-area teachers needed training to provide reading instruction simultaneously with instruction in their course content. Thus, the need continues for this—and similar—texts.

Assumptions about the lasting effect of reading instruction also contributed to the failure of reading programs. To the uninitiated, it seems logical to assume that once a person has learned "how to read," there is nothing left to learn. If you can read, you can read. Why should more instruction be necessary beyond the period when learning has taken place?

The answer is simple but often overlooked. Like any other skill, reading skills are applied at many levels of sophistication. As students progress through the grades, they encounter increasingly sophisticated material. The concept load is heavier. The ideas are more abstract. The information load is increasingly more concentrated. The basic skills learned in early reading instruction contribute to a student's ability to handle such requirements, but they are not sufficient. Students must learn how to adapt these skills (and even learn some new ones) to meet the demands of increasingly challenging materials. Left on their own, most students make the adaptations necessary for real success only with great difficulty. Some do make the adaptations, but more by chance than anything. Consistent instructional intervention is necessary for students to experience maximal growth through the grades.

School personnel experience great frustration as they note the lack of sufficient progress in students' reading performance as they move through the grades. Early reading instruction often is blamed, and in response more money and personnel are spent at that level in an effort to solve the problem. Over and over we have proven that this does not work. But finally we seem to be moving toward a sensible alternative: providing instruction at each successive level of education so that students learn how to apply their skills at the level of sophistication demanded by the materials they are required to read.

## RATIONALE

Having learned from the past, it seems logical to assume that the way is now clear for providing sensible reading instruction for all students in all grades and in all subjects. Not so. As reading instruction in content areas has gained popularity, other problems have emerged. With many reading personnel advocating such instruction, it was inevitable that differences of opinion would arise as to what constitutes teaching reading in content areas.

The differences seem to turn on the preposition "in" in the phrase "teaching reading *in* content areas." To some, it means to do in the content-area classroom what used to be done in the reading class. Past failures, they feel, were caused by the location of the instruction, not by the instruction itself. Therefore, they shift the location to subject-area classes and provide traditional instruction in reading in that setting, calling it teaching reading *in* content areas.

Such a view is held by those strongly oriented toward the clinical and/or elementary model of reading instruction. Students are tested for strengths and weaknesses in their reading skills, and instruction is prescribed for overcoming the weaknesses and enhancing the strengths. Believing that there is no other way to teach reading while acknowledging that the approach has not produced students who experience success in reading content material, they blame the location, not the instruction. Thus, although the reading class is abandoned, the content-area classroom becomes the locale for the same old instruction. Content-area teachers resist; because they do not want to become reading teachers nor do they want to divert time from their curriculum to teach reading. Because they are coerced into it, little comes from their efforts.

In an alternative approach, reading teachers go into the content-area classes to provide the reading instruction while the content teacher watches (or goes to the teachers' lounge). Such an approach preserves the reading teachers' position and satisfies the administration and community that something "new" is being done about the reading problem. But because the subject-area teachers are not involved through their curriculum and because the reading skills being taught are not necessarily those appropriate to the course content, the program is usually not successful.

There is another variation on the application of the preposition "in" in the phrase "teaching reading in content areas." The past failures were caused not only by the location of the instruction but also by the materials used for instruction. The skills taught and the method of teaching were all right. To these people, teaching reading in content areas means using "content-type" material as the vehicle for teaching reading skills. Reading selections drawn from representative subject-area texts become the basis for lessons which develop specific content-related reading skills. The content of the materials used is consistent with the subject area in which the reading instruction is taking place. Since the purpose of the instruction is to develop a set of reading skills rather than a set of concepts related to the curriculum, the content of the reading selections may or may not be related to what is being studied at the moment in the curriculum. Frequently the content is different, creating a dichotomy between the reading instruction and the content instruction, even though both are occurring within the same class.

Though one step closer to the most logical solution, this alternative—and the resulting program—still falls short. Students still have to adapt the skills learned in one setting to the requirements imposed by materials in another setting. The subject-area teachers still see this as an imposition on their time, on their curriculum, on their students. They do not see it as a direct answer to the needs evidenced by their students. It adds to a burden they feel is already more than they have the training and time to handle.

The position taken in this text goes a step beyond the two views mentioned. Failure of past programs and past reading instruction involved all three elements: the location, the materials, the skills taught.

A basis has been clearly established for advocating that reading instruction be provided in each content area, at all grade levels. One can logically argue for using basic texts and resource materials as vehicles for teaching and reinforcing subject-related reading skills. Why not use material the students are required to read for teaching them how to read it successfully? Why waste time teaching reading skills with other material and assuming (or hoping?) they will transfer what they have learned and apply it to what they must read in their subjects? How this can be done is developed later in this text; now we are just discussing the logic of doing so.

The *fundamental* difference in the four positions lies in the instruction provided. What skills are taught? The first three programs described are organized around a list of skills to be taught. As noted above, the question of content becomes secondary. In contrast, the position taken in this text is that the curriculum content in each of the subject areas should be the organizing element for the reading instruction: It is the set of concepts that comprise the curriculum and it is the information imbedded in those concepts that the student should master.

Having established the importance of the curriculum, the reading instruction is then based on the principle that "content determines process." That is, implicit in the content of what you want to be read are the skills needed to read it successfully. The information presented, the concepts developed, the very organization of the material—these will determine how one should read the text. Those are the reading skills to be taught in the content areas *as* the students read what they are required to read. Reading skills and subject content can thus be taught simultaneously. There need not be a dichotomy between the content of a subject and the skills for learning the content. Such a view of reading instruction requires one to change traditional views about how to teach reading. But when such instruction does take place, its efficiency and effectiveness are apparent. When it continues up through the grades, it meets the challenge of increasingly sophisticated material by showing students how to apply the same skills at increasingly sophisticated levels. *How* this is done is the subject of this text.

## Curriculum as Context

The context for this approach to reading instruction is the curriculum normally taught in each subject at each grade level. There is no need to design a special curriculum in order to include reading instruction. Materials with sufficient information to convey the concepts that comprise the curriculum can serve as the vehicle for instruction in both the concepts and the related reading skills. The subject-area teachers need not abandon their curriculum to teach the reading skills related to their subject. Reading instruction becomes as natural a part of the curriculum as are the information sources themselves.

## Content as Vehicle

The curriculum is comprised of content. Since reading skills are learned only in reference to the material being read, the content of the curriculum serves as the vehicle for the reading skills to be learned. Again, since content determines process, the skills taught are those essential to understanding the material. When reading skills are taught as means to an end, that end being an understanding of the content of a curriculum, they are more likely to be learned than when they are taught as ends in themselves, taught for their own sake without regard for the content of the curriculum or the material they ultimately will be applied to.

## Sense of Process

Reading skills are the means by which one learns the content of the material being read. In their aggregate, these skills can be called the reading process. The objective of reading instruction in content areas is to help students develop a sense of the reading process. Most of this text is devoted to identifying what this process comprises and determining how one teaches the process simultaneously with course content. When students acquire a sense of process, when it becomes second nature to them, when they see its appropriateness to the content of their required reading, their pleasure and success in reading will be such that they will want to read as much as they are required to read and more.

## Sense of Structure

There is—or should be—an organization within, around, and about everything students study and learn. When students develop a sense of this structure, they are better equipped to become independent learners; they have a better grasp of both the content and the process related to the subject. There is a structure implicit in most factors related to instruction, ranging from lessons to materials to interaction among students and to the curriculum itself. Once the structure is perceived, it more readily can be reproduced. For example, when students perceive the structure of the lessons presented by their teacher, they are more able to anticipate new learning activities, as well as the content of those activities. The various kinds of structure and how to develop an understanding of them are dealt with more implicitly than explicitly throughout the text, given its purpose. However, due note is taken throughout to call your attention to these elements so that, in your own instruction, you can provide for your own students a sense of process combined with a sense of structure within the content of your curriculum.

### Showing How

This book makes much of the need to show students *how* to read. The thrust of the book is an application of the principle that "the essence of good teaching is to show students how to do what they are required to do." Chapter 8 goes into detail on this matter of "showing how," and most of the other chapters also develop the same principle. If teaching is not showing how, then it is really just a combination of assigning and testing. Assignments are given, identifying what has been learned. In between as well as within these two points is where teaching can and should take place. If students experience difficulty in reading, then the instruction which takes place between assigning and teaching should include showing them how to read the assigned material.

This text is organized around that principle in two ways. First, it contains materials designed by teachers for use with students. These materials, properly used, show the students how to read the selection in a textbook so as to develop an understanding of the content and a sense of the process implicit in the selection. They are not the final word in materials, only illustrations of what you can do for your students. They are examples from full lessons, not full lessons in themselves. But they do illustrate what can be done to show students *how* to read what they are required to read.

The second way in which the text is organized around this principle of showing how is through the materials within the chapters which guide your reading of this text. The same reading skills you will want to teach your students are required for the reading of this text. The level of sophistication is no doubt higher, but the process is essentially the same. Many adult-level sample materials are included. Go through them and you will have a better sense of what you can provide to your own students and what happens in their minds as they respond. Material at the end of each chapter is designed to help you develop a sense of the reading and reasoning processes implicit in the content of the text. As you carefully go through these end-of-chapter materials and discuss them with your colleagues, you will develop a better sense of the message of the text and a better understanding of how to put into practice the ideas it presents.

## DEFINITIONS

### Teaching Reading in Content Areas

There is much confusion about the responsibility of content teachers for teaching reading. Pervading the literature is the feeling that content teachers just do not understand—they are ignorant of—what they can and should do for their students. Bruner (1965) makes a significant point about "understanding":

Let us recognize that the opposite of understanding is not ignorance or simply "not knowing." To understand something is, first, to give up some other way of conceiving it. Confusion all too often lies between one way of conceiving and another better way.

The "better way" of conceiving reading in content areas generally has not been made clear. There is a definite difference between teaching reading in a reading class and in a content class. When this distinction is made clear, confusion fades and content teachers are more inclined to teach reading, to the benefit of students and of their own peace of mind.

The most satisfactory way to define "teaching reading through content" is to compare the responsibilities of a reading teacher to those of a content teacher. Each has a specific set; each has a curriculum to teach.

A reading teacher's curriculum is a set of reading skills. Certainly the teacher hopes to develop students' inclination to use these skills to enlarge their interests, appreciations, and understandings of life around them, but his or her primary responsibility is to teach the skills. He arranges the skills in logical sequence, following a pattern prescribed by a manual or one he has himself established. He analyzes the students' needs and this analysis determines where he enters the sequence for a given student and his level of sophistication in teaching the skill (or skills).

He selects reading material through which he can teach the skill and through which the students can practice the skill after they have received the initial instruction. He is not primarily concerned about the content of this material, as long as it is interesting and informative. The content can be related to any curriculum area in the school or it can be general material that has no bearing on a specific content area. He is not teaching *content*; He is developing an understanding of the *processes* being applied to these materials.

The content teacher has a set of ideas as his or her curriculum. These ideas have order; definite relationships exist among them. The teacher establishes a sequence for these ideas based on logic, study, and experience. Either the basic text for the course or the curriculum guide may determine the sequence.

The teacher analyzes the students' needs, decides where in the sequence of the curriculum they require instruction, and plans a teaching program accordingly. Students are weak in specific concepts; they need exposure to specific ideas; they need to see relationships among various principles; they need to enlarge the base on which they have established their own points of view. The content teacher finds materials (or identifies selections from the textbook, if that is all that is available), which contain the information and ideas the students should encounter, understand, and use. The teacher is not primarily concerned with the skills students must use in reading materials. When teaching the students *how* to acquire the information and ideas from an assigned selection, she has to be aware of the skills inherent in the selection. But those skills are *not* the reason for using that material. She teaches students only the skills needed to understand the ideas that the curriculum calls on them to understand. She does not teach a reading skill for its own sake, as does the reading teacher.

She is concerned not with the sequential development of reading skills, but with the sequential development of ideas. Skills are developed functionally, not directly. The skills to be taught are determined by the content of the material assigned for a given lesson, never the reverse.

Again, to state the difference in a somewhat different way, the reading teacher says: *I have to teach these skills. What materials can I use to give instruction and provide practice on these skills? I don't care what the subject matter is, as long as the students must use these skills to understand what they read.*

And so the reading teacher finds the material, teaches the skills, and has the students engage in reinforcing practice. She hopes, of course, that the students will transfer these skills to their subjects and that the instruction they receive in reading class will help with assigned readings in each of their courses.

In contrast, the content teacher says: *I have these ideas to get across to my students, and this text—or these texts—develops the ideas quite well. I'll assign this material for homework so that students, through their reading, will develop some understanding of these ideas. Now, to develop and use those ideas, the students must use a specific skill. It isn't "main idea," because the mere apprehension of the central thought is not the key to understanding this concept; nor is it "inference," because the author is rather straightforward in his statements; nor is it "recognition of assumption," because the author has identified his premises and has not relied on assumptions. No, in this particular selection the students have to read for "cause and effect," and so I will discuss organizational patterns briefly before they begin reading the selection. They will need assistance so I'll have to provide some guidance for them. I'll have them working together as I guide them so that they learn both the content and this reading skill simultaneously.*

This is the difference between the reading teacher and the content teacher who also teaches reading. The cliché "every teacher a teacher of reading" has been interpreted by content teachers in light of the reading teacher's role and responsibility for teaching reading. Content teachers have rejected that role, and rightly so. Moreover, there has been a concerted effort to force on all content teachers the direct reading instruction properly engaged in by the reading teacher. This is unfortunate. There is no place for reading instruction as reading teachers generally employ it in content areas. There is a need for a whole new strategy in teaching reading through content areas, a strategy that draws from what we know about the direct teaching of reading but adapts that knowledge to fit the structure of and responsibilities for the total curriculum in each content area.

Regular curriculum materials—basic and supplementary texts—can be the vehicles for reading instruction in each content area when teachers show the students how to successfully read the required materials. There is no wasted time, no separate emphasis, no risk to the curriculum. The strategy *does* require modification in teaching behavior and changes in the role of both teacher and learner, but the modifications and changes are realistic and practical.

## Reading

The view that reading instruction should be part of the curriculum in each content area necessarily implies a broad definition of the term "reading." Though there are many definitions, most agree that reading is not a unitary act, that reading comprises several functions. For example, ". . . the complete act of reading has four dimensions—word perception, comprehension of stated and implied meanings, critical and emotional reaction, and application of perceived ideas to behavior" (Artley, 1966).

In this book, "reading" is defined as a thinking process which includes decoding of symbols, interpreting the meanings of the symbols, and applying the ideas derived from the symbols.

**Decoding** There are those who hold a very restricted view of reading, defining it only as a decoding process. For them, reading is simply a matter of associating symbols with sounds. A student viewing a symbol—whether a letter or a word—internally compares that symbol to all other symbols he is familiar with, searching through his experiences with sound and symbol relationships to associate a sound with that symbol. If he makes the association, he can read the symbol. If he cannot, he must learn the sound or, if he applies an incorrect sound to the symbol (incorrect perception), he must learn the correct variation or the new sound.

Meanings associated with this kind of decoding are rather restricted; they generally relate to what the symbol "says," not to what the symbol "means." Thus it is possible for a person to decode a word and associate sounds with that symbol so as to "pronounce" it, yet have little or no understanding of the concept represented by that word. Such decoding is important but, standing alone, it has limited usefulness.

Others (Goodman, 1970, for example) believe that this view of decoding is too restrictive. Decoding also involves the use of the context in which the symbols appear. Students can at times deal successfully with an unknown symbol by using the context to hypothesize what that symbol logically must mean. Depending on the student's experience background, the new symbol, thus decoded, can carry rich meaning or only superficial definition.

Though there seems to be a logical sequence among decoding, interpretation, and application, these three elements of reading probably interact and occur almost simultaneously as one develops reading proficiency. Thus, interpretation is involved in decoding.

**Interpretation** The second aspect of reading is interpreting the meanings of the symbols. Readers should not only associate sound with the symbol but also associate meaning with the symbol, drawing on ideas they have developed in relation to the symbol. If the symbol is a word, they associate it with an experience they have had—real or vicarious—in connection with it. That is the meaning for the symbol. If the symbol is other than a word—perhaps a formula, an equation, a sentence, or a paragraph—the process is the same; only the degree of complexity differs.

Many students successfully decode words but fail to find meaning in what they read; their failure reflects lack of experience associated with the words or longer units of language. Such reading is a rather futile exercise, particularly when viewed in light of the reading demands placed on students in content areas. Students are expected to derive meanings from what they read. Failing to do so frequently means failing the course.

Associating meaning with successfully decoded symbols does not complete the total act of reading. There is yet a third factor.

**Application** It is important to use the ideas that are developed through the decoding and interpretive processes. "For learnings to become the full property of the learner, he must *use* them. So long as his knowledge is a passive thing, it is immature and impermanent. Its maturation depends on its active use in new situations" (Smith and Dechant, 1961).

In what manner are these ideas used? They are applied to previous ideas and experiences to determine if there is corroboration or contradiction. If the former, then specific ideas are strengthened; if the latter, specific ideas may be modified. Ideas acquired through decoding and interpretation may not be immediately applicable and therefore may be "stored" and used later when they have particular bearing on an activity or other idea that is considered. Teachers can show students how to organize ideas and keep them readily accessible for appropriate use.

Reading cannot be narrowly defined when associated with instruction in the content areas. Proper reading of resource materials requires that students interpret what they decode and effectively use the ideas they acquire.


## HOW TO USE THIS BOOK

Depending on your own needs or on how your mind deals with new information and ideas, you may want to go through the chapters in this book in a different order than the one in which they are presented.

You may be very anxious to start using tomorrow whatever it is that this book has to offer you for help in your classroom. If so, you might turn to Chapter 3 for specific, practical ideas that you can apply immediately. Then you can go on to Chapters 4-7 for more of the same, or back to Chapter 2 to study the purposes which underlie this kind of instruction. The rest of the book can be studied to develop refinements in your understanding.

You may want to start with an overall picture of how everything in the text fits together into an instructional program. You can then study the details. If that's your way, read Chapter 9, Instructional Framework, first, then Chapter

2. Within this framework, you can then study the other chapters to see where they fit.

Some people believe strongly that vocabulary development should be the first consideration in any program of instruction designed to improve students' reading skills. If you agree, you may well want to start with the section entitled "Selection for Emphasis" in Chapter 6, then move in whatever direction you wish.

The sequence of chapters presented in the book is obviously the one I find most comfortable. As I have conducted workshops and taught courses over the years, this sequence seems to allow me to communicate to my students and colleagues most clearly and efficiently what I want them to know and understand. The sequence identifies the problems, then shows how to deal with them. It shows how the suggestions fit together, how need and achievement are assessed, and what can come of such instructional programs.

But regardless of the order in which you read the chapters, it is important that you do the activities within them. You will be tempted to skip them, or to do them superficially by yourself. To gain maximum benefit from the book, you must do the activities. And to gain maximum benefit from the activities, you must work with a small group of persons similarly interested in reading instruction in content areas.

The preliminary information for each of Chapters 2-10 should be carefully read. Its purpose is to prepare you for the information and ideas in the chapter and to give you a sense of how to deal with them.

The reaction guides at the end of each chapter also are important. Their purpose is not to test your comprehension of the chapter, but to guide you in developing understandings of the significance of the information, ideas, and suggestions in the chapter. These reaction guides also should be discussed with others in a small-group setting. The discussions allow you to compare responses among members of the group on the items in the guide and to clarify reasons for differences when they occur. Always be ready to provide evidence for the position you take on an item or an issue. In most cases this evidence will be drawn both from the text and from your own experience. Sometimes it will be only the former or the latter.

Since there is no right or wrong answer in almost all cases, there is no answer key to the reaction guides. Where answers are necessary to accomplish the purpose of the activity, suggested answers are located at designated places in the text. I have opinions on each of the items in the guides. If you are particularly concerned about some of them, I would be happy to share that opinion with you. I can be reached through the publisher of this book, who will forward your letter to me.

*     *     *     *     *

## REACTION GUIDE

*Directions:* Read each of the following statements. Each has some bearing on the content of the chapter. Place a check on the numbered line before each one with which you agree. Discuss reasons for your decisions with your colleagues. Then circle the numbers of statements with which you think the author would agree. Discuss the evidence from the text on which you based your decisions.

_____ 1. The true measure of the value placed on an instructional program is what happens to that program when the money runs out.

_____ 2. You can expect failure from people when you add to their obligations but don't show them how to meet those obligations.

_____ 3. Ideally, instruction in reading should never end; practically, reading instruction should last at least through high school.

_____ 4. Sensible alternatives for failing reading programs require changes in location of the instruction, materials for the instruction, and personnel who provide the instruction.

_____ 5. When traditional programs do not meet students' learning needs, it is reasonable to question a response which is to continue doing the same thing—only faster and harder.

_____ 6. In content-area classes, content determines process; in reading classes, process determines content.

_____ 7. Implicit in content are both structure and process.

_____ 8. Availability of money seems to reinforce the traditional in education; scarcity of money seems to stimulate creative alternatives.

_____ 9. Telling is not teaching; assigning is not showing.

_____ 10. Without content, curriculum has no substance; without process, content has no life.


## REINFORCING ACTIVITIES

A. Using blacksmithing as an analogy, relate the fire, the metal, the hammer, and the anvil to the student, the content, the process, and the material. (Feel free to add components.)

B. Write the following words on slips of paper or on 3"x5" cards—one word per slip or card. Working with at least two other people who have read this chapter, arrange the words so they represent the issues raised and/or ideas developed in the chapter.

| | | |
|---|---|---|
| hope | despair | promise |
| deliverance | action | dollars |
| results | logic | alternatives |
| intelligent | separation | insufficient |
| consistent | intervention | fusion |
| synthesis | dichotomy | tradition |
| content | process | |
| practical | theoretical | |

You may want to add other words to this list as you engage in the activity.

\*      \*      \*      \*      \*      \*

## REFERENCES

ARTLEY, STERL. "Influence of specific factors on growth in interpretation." In H. Alan Robinson (ed.), *Reading: Seventy-five years of progress.* Chicago: University of Chicago Press, 1966.

BRUNER, JEROME. "After John Dewey, What?" In *On knowing.* New York: Atheneum, 1965.

DECHANT, EMERALD V. *Improving the teaching of reading* (2nd ed.). Englewood Cliffs, N.J.: Prentice-Hall, 1970.

GOODMAN, KENNETH. "Behind the eye: What happens in reading." In *Reading process and program.* Urbana, Ill.: National Council of Teachers of English, 1970.

SMITH, HENRY P., & EMERALD V. DECHANT. *Psychology in teaching reading.* Englewood Cliffs, N.J.: Prentice-Hall, 1961.

# two

# Significant Problems / Promising Solutions

---

## VOCABULARY

The following terms are important to an understanding of this chapter. Each is defined in context. Read through the list to identify those for which you have uncertain meanings. Then as you read the chapter, pay particular attention to their definitions. Also make certain that the meanings attributed to the remaining words by their context in the chapter correspond to the meanings they hold for you.

readability formula
student interaction
intraclass grouping
student-centered curriculum
intellectual investment
emotional investment
concept development
transfer
transformation
colearner

tolerance for ambiguity
functional teaching of reading
fragmenting reading
simulating reading
sequencing
independence
sophistication
caring
expectation

The following terms also are important to an understanding of this chapter, but they are not defined in context. A brief definition of each follows:

*Resource materials:* sources used in a curriculum area to communicate its content to students

*Information sources:* media which contain basic data about the content of the curriculum, most frequently textbooks or other printed material

*Content:* the substance of an information source and/or a curriculum

*Process:* the means for acquiring the content of an information source

*Curriculum:* the body of knowledge making up a subject area studied in school

## IDEA DIRECTION

This chapter identifies the purposes of this book. First, problems faced by most subject-area teachers are identified. They relate both to teaching in general and to the teaching of reading in particular.

Second, solutions are identified. These solutions may appear to be theoretical and philosophical in nature. To a certain extent they are, but they are rooted in practicality. As noted throughout the chapter, the purpose of the book is to show you practical ways to apply the proposed solutions to the specific problems in your classroom.

You will want to give close attention to how well the solutions match the problems.

## READING DIRECTION

This chapter is a preview of the rest of the book in that the remaining chapters explain how to apply the solutions to the problems this chapter identifies. Therefore, you should read the chapter carefully so that both problems and proposed solutions can be recalled and applied as you read the rest of the book.

---

## SIGNIFICANT PROBLEMS

Ask several groups of teachers what their most pressing problems are and you will probably get as many sets of answers as you have groups. But a close examination of all those sets probably would reveal certain problems common to all. They are problems with direct bearing on teaching—problems which prevent teachers from realizing the full potential of their teaching skills and prevent students from realizing the full potential of their learning abilities. Interestingly enough, most of these problems, in one way or another, have a direct relationship to reading.

Several such problems are listed below. They are discussed, even though they may be familiar to you, because it is important for you to realize that this book is addressing these problems. You may find it comforting to know that other people have the same problems as you.

### Use of Difficult Texts

Reading instruction in content areas is possible only when it is responsive to the needs of both students and teachers. Teachers are responsible for communicating a given body of knowledge and the understandings and applications of that knowledge. Students need help in learning and applying the skills that are essential for acquiring that knowledge, developing those understandings, and making those applications.

Further, reading instruction in content areas is possible and practical only when that instruction is an integral part of instruction in the course content. The integration of these two instructional emphases is possible when both are provided through basic resource materials commonly used in a given subject area.

The reason often given for not integrating reading and content instruction is that the basic resources to be read are "too difficult" for the students. This argument is based on either objective or subjective data, or both. The subjective data usually are the teachers' observations of their students' performance on reading assignments, expressed as, "They just can't read that material." The objective data come from two interrelated factors: the readability of the texts and the students' reading ability.

**Readability-Reading Ability: Objective Data**   Readability formulas can be applied to texts to determine their level of difficulty, usually stated in terms of grade level. Many formulas are available for such purposes (Klare, 1974).

Students' reading abilities generally are assessed by means of standardized tests; results are frequently reported in terms of grade level. Many tests are available for such purposes (Buros, 1965).

A mismatch between a student's reading ability and the readability of the text is taken as objective evidence that the text is "too difficult." A match of the two factors is taken as evidence that the text is "right for the student" (Bormuth, 1974).

One can be led astray, however, by the rather naive notion that the solution to textbook difficulty lies in the interrelated application of these two grade-level factors. A student's reading grade-level ability can be determined and matched with a text written at the same grade-level of difficulty. But unfortunately, such a match does not insure that reading will take place. The text, very likely, may still be "too difficult" for the students, and there are a couple of reasons for this.

First, students' grade-level reading scores really represent an average of their performance over the specific reading tasks which make up the total test. This means that they really have a range of reading ability: some skills fall below, some at, and some above the grade level indicated for the total test performance. Thus, depending on the specific reading task required by the basic text, their performances may be poor, adequate, or superior.

Second, the readability level of the text usually represents an *average* of sample passages drawn from across the entire text. This means that the text has within it some sections below, some at, and some above the grade level assigned to the total text. Thus, the problem is compounded. A given student's success will depend on whether there is a match between the difficulty level of a given passage in the text and the performance level of the student on the particular reading task required by that passage.

**Readability-Reading Ability: Subjective Data**   The subjective observation that the students "can't read the textbook" is based on the incorrect notion that they should be able to read that material independently. Assignments are given; students do poorly in their attempts to read the material; the teacher is disappointed; the students are frustrated.

Students often have difficulties with resource materials because they are reading about information and ideas that are new to them. If the information and ideas are not new, at least in their level of sophistication, then a teacher should question whether the text is appropriate for instructional purposes. But if they are new, or more sophisticated, or both, as they should be if the material is to be instructionally useful, then the students' problem with the text should come as no surprise. Even with a perfect match between the difficulty of a passage and the students' performance on the reading tasks required by that passage, they would have a problem. This is because reading performance in content areas involves more than just ease of reading. Reading in content areas primarily is a means through which students encounter and deal with *new* knowledge and *new* ideas. If they are not properly prepared for the reading and are not guided through it, the students will be frustrated by this newness. Students should not be expected to read such new material independently.

Because of evidence drawn from both objective and subjective data, as described, teachers frequently avoid having students read their basic texts. Substitute methods, principally the lecture, are used for conveying information and ideas. Obviously the lecture is an appropriate instructional procedure, but used as a substitute for students' reading, it is actually detrimental to learning. This book deals with ways to avoid the need for such substitutions and ways to use a text even though it is "too difficult."

## Accommodating a Range of Competence

A teacher will be with a class only a short time before discovering a considerable range of ability and achievement, regardless of the criteria used for grouping students into classes. If a reading grade-level score is the criterion for homogeneous grouping, the teacher will find a range of ability among the students. The correlation between IQ scores and reading scores is not sufficiently high to be certain of homogeneity of the latter when the former is used as the criterion for homogeneous grouping. Moreover, even students with identical scores will vary considerably in their reading performance. *Reading* is too complex a process to be expressed in a single score. The procedures for deriving the single scores that designate reading achievement reflect this fact. Reading scores are generally derived from several subscores; therefore, different combinations of strength and weakness can produce the same reading grade-level score. It is quite possible for two students to have the same reading grade score with the areas of strength for one being the areas of weakness for the other. For example, the advanced form of the *Iowa Silent Reading Test* has nine subtests; the total test score is computed by using the median score from among the nine. Student A might be relatively strong in subtests one through four and relatively weak in subtests six through nine, his median being subtest five. Student B, then, might be relatively weak in subtests one through four, relatively strong in subtests six through nine, her median being subtest five, and her score identical to Student A. Although both would have identical total scores, they would have opposite strengths and weaknesses.

When *ability* is used as the sole criterion for grouping, one will find a range of *achievement* in reading. The relatively low correlation between IQ and reading again is evident. Moreover, because ability scores are also composites, as they are in reading, comparability is similarly limited. Composite scores mask differing strengths and weaknesses in intelligence just as they mask differences in specific reading skills.

Frequently students are grouped by two criteria: reading achievement and intelligence. Even so, there is still a range of actual ability and achievement among students within the class.

The need is not only to admit to the existence of differences in ability and achievement, but also to discover how to accommodate this range. Teaching to individual differences can be workable, within the framework of the curriculum as it now exists and the present organizational structure of schools, and can have sufficient flexibility to meet the demands of new educational developments. Each student can understand the content and can experience success in reading the required material at his or her level of competence.

## Active Student Participation

An informal survey of classroom activity in a substantial number of school districts would show students in a relatively passive role, or at least, more passive than is generally advocated. As any experienced teacher knows, student activity or action or interaction is no guarantee that learning is taking place or that the classroom environment is productive. But any experienced teacher knows that passivity is no guarantee either!

Promoting students' active involvement in learning experiences is a problem of major significance when reading becomes part of the instruction in content areas. The concern is not with mere physical activity, but rather, with the students' intellectual involvement in the learning tasks. Students can be quite active physically, be thoroughly engaged in tasks requiring various kinds of motion, but be simultaneously passive intellectually. The question for teachers is how to promote the desired intellectual activity.

In the teacher-dominated classroom, students can remain anonymous and intellectually passive if they "behave" so as not to become objects of attention, if they do not offer to recite, or if they do not raise questions with the teacher. The probability of their being called on is minimal. The real intellectual activity often is between the teacher and those students who either volunteer their participation or are "volunteered" by the teacher. The rest of the students may learn the basic information in the course, but they often miss the beneficial effects of an intellectual interaction with other people: clarification of ideas, synthesis of new and old ideas, hypothesizing, confirming, and so on.

The very strong movement toward individualizing instruction falls into this error also. Students are active, moving through materials at their own pace. But because of time pressures and organizational format, a given student may have little intellectual interaction with either the teacher or other students. As a consequence, the student is rather passive intellectually and also misses the beneficial effects of consistent intellectual interaction.

A very constructive possibility for solving the problem of students' real involvement in learning is the use of well-structured intra-class grouping. Suggestions for accomplishing this are examined in detail in Chapter 8.

### Student-Centered Curriculum

Adults often observe that students seem to have no interest in learning. But as Hogan (1971) argues, ample evidence shows that most students have considerable interest in both learning and teaching. He refers to the "nook and cranny curriculum" as evidence of this interest. This curriculum is what occurs among students between classes and before and after school. Observers of students dealing with this curriculum—in reality, the "stuff" of their world—are convinced of their interest as well as their skill in its communication. But when students enter the school world, as opposed to their own "real" world, they lose interest at best, becoming antagonistic at worst.

Like reading, "interest" should have an object. "Interest in what?" is the question. *Their* curriculum? Yes. *Our* curriculum? frequently not.

Some suggest new, relevant curricula more attuned to students' interests. But given the caprice of their interests and the rapidity of their change during school years, any curriculum reform tied to such criteria would be chaotic indeed. Abandoning the curriculum and letting students study anything they want can lead to chaos unless the schools and the teachers are unusually well-equipped and gifted. The more open and free the curriculum, the more organized the teacher must be and the more well-equipped the school must be in order to provide for the multiplicity of options students might decide to pursue.

For teachers who acknowledge the importance of students' interests in learning, the problem is how to develop a student-centered curriculum without abandoning what they believe to be valuable in the curriculum in their particular subject area.

**Investment** This is the key word in a discussion of interests. Two types of investment are important: intellectual and emotional. When students make both investments in a task, they will stay with it to its logical conclusion. As is true with any kind of investment, intensity of interest is highly correlated with the amount invested. Getting students to invest deeply is the key, but how?

The assumption operating in this suggestion is that students already have prior knowledge and experience concerning nearly everything we study in the curriculum, if we treat that curriculum broadly enough. For example, students in American History may know little about trade unions, but they do know a lot about the broader concept of protest. Introducing the lesson on unions through the concept of protest allows students to contribute to the lesson out of their knowledge and experience—to invest, if you will. Through this investment they contribute the basic stuff of the lesson: information, ideas, feelings, concerns. Their contributions become the central ingredients of the lesson and the curriculum becomes student-centered. As they study the development of unions as a form of protest, they see it as a commentary on and qualifier of their own ideas and experiences—a student-centered curriculum.

Thus, without abandoning important parts of the curriculum, a teacher can deal with students' interests, helping them capture and make use of what they already know. That's what relevance is about. Both intellectual and emotional investments are realized.

Specific illustrations of how to engage in this process are presented later on in this book.

## Concept Development

The definition of reading established earlier includes the need for the development of ideas from reading and, subsequently, the application of those ideas. The formation of concepts (ideas) and their use is of critical importance to students who wish to be successful in their studies, but students frequently lack facility in handling concepts.

A concept is defined as "a generalization drawn from particulars" (Webster, 1963). As students read, they gather specific information (particulars), which they attempt to organize in some fashion so as to identify relationships among them. A relationship that they identify and subsequently use is a generalization. "The learner originally makes specific responses to specific stimuli. When he learns to apply these responses in other situations, he has generalized his behavior. This generalization of behavior is a most important kind of transfer . . . Studies on transfer have stressed the value of generalization. Generalization provides for applications to new learning situations." (Smith and Dechant, 1961).

A physics teacher once observed: "It seems apparent that we are training good memorizers rather than good thinkers." What gave rise to his comment was the inability of his students to make use of information acquired from their texts. They could recite details and interpret the significance of some information, but when asked to analyze interrelationships or to generalize from the information, their achievement was far from satisfactory. They had not learned how to make good use of the information they had acquired. When given instruction on the development and use of concepts, they improved significantly in their achievement in the subject (Herber, 1964).

This problem is not unique to above-average students in physics classes. Less able students, poorer readers, rely extensively on identification and memorization. They have as much need to develop and use concepts as more able students have, and they should be shown how.

There appears to be more retention and better learning when attention is focused on development of concepts rather than on identification and memorization of detail. However, teacher-made examinations and standardized tests have fostered the latter procedure. Being test-wise, students reject concept-centered instruction because "it won't be on the test." Education perpetuates generations of students conditioned to view learning as the storing of information rather than the development, evaluation, and use of ideas. Gardner (1964) comments on this kind of instruction:

> All too often we are giving our young people cut flowers when we should be teaching them to grow their own plants. We are stuffing their heads with the products of earlier innovation rather than teaching them to innovate. We think of the mind as a storehouse to be filled when we should be thinking of it as an instrument to be used.

## Transfer and Transformation of Skills

"Transfer is the application of our previous learnings to our current problems" (Smith and Dechant, 1961). The great hope in education is that what students learn in one situation can be transferred and applied to comparable situations. On development of this ability we predicate much of our teaching. Were it not possible for students to transfer knowledge from one subject area to another and one grade level to another, we would have to reteach continually everything that students need to know. This is impossible, impractical, and unnecessary.

The need to develop the ability to transfer has been a basic consideration in reading instruction. Skills are taught in elementary grades with the assumption that children can transfer them to the reading of content materials in these and succeeding grades. It has been widely assumed that skills taught in the elementary grades are sufficient for the needs of students entering junior and senior high schools. We need only witness teachers "passing the buck" from secondary to elementary levels to realize that the *assumption* of transfer is true even though the *fact* often is not.

Teachers can provide instruction in how to read the content materials so that students are not dependent on this assumed transfer. Content teachers will find it helpful to think of a factor *beyond* transfer when they consider ways to help their students read the materials in their courses. This important factor is *transformation,* or adaptation, of skills. Skills taught in reading classes are applicable to content materials, but students must adapt the skills to meet the peculiarities of each subject they study. There is "horizontal transformation" as students adapt reading skills to various subjects within a grade level. There is also "vertical transformation" as students progress from grade to grade within a subject and adapt skills to meet the increased sophistication of content materials at successive levels. Transformation is discussed in more detail in Chapter 9.

### Teachers as Co-learners

When you reflect for a moment on what might be called the teaching-learning ritual, you discover that one common ingredient is "guessing what's in the teacher's mind." Teachers ask questions and students respond. Teachers give all sorts of signals to indicate whether or not the students have responded "correctly," meaning that they have produced information or ideas which conform to what the teacher anticipated when asking the question.

These signals include body motions such as hand gestures that encourage further comment or indicate that the comment was satisfactory; they include turning away from students when the wrong response is given or toward them when the correct answer is supplied. The signal may be a tone of voice that encourages further explanation: the "yeeeeesssss . . . " with the voice rising indicating that more should be forthcoming as compared to the firm "yes" which indicates that the answer is appropriate. The signaling of a wrong answer might be the teacher's eyes rolling heavenward; the correct answer might be signaled by a smile. No matter the medium, the message is the same: See if you know what I know and if you can give it to me correctly and without embellishment. If you can, you are a success; if you can't, you're a failure.

No doubt you will think that this is overstated, and for you it may be. But in many classrooms across the country one can find this ritual in operation.

One of the problems basic to providing reading instruction in content areas is to move away from this ritual and toward developing a classroom environment that encourages more independent thinking, more exploration of alternatives, more awareness of the validity of differences, more concern with the process by which answers are developed than with whether or not the answers conform to someone else's preconceived notion of what is "correct." Teachers who create this stimulating environment are usually so knowledgeable about their subject that they realize clearly just how much they do not know. And they are secure in this ignorance. They know that it is not necessary always to be right, always to have all of the answers. They know that even their students may discover information about a topic that they have not yet encountered. Acknowledging that fact is not troublesome to them; meanwhile, it is bolstering to the student who makes the contribution.

Such teachers know they need not fear the words, "I don't know." When students ask a question and the teachers confess ignorance, no great problem results. The teachers and students can discover the answer together. With this security, teachers don't have to cover up the ignorance either by faking an answer or by ruling the question irrelevant and moving the discussion back to their "comfortable" area of knowledge. And such teachers derive genuine pleasure from students who come up with ideas, with insights, which the teachers themselves had not previously considered. The words "I never have thought of that before" or some such, are beautiful to the ears of students, especially when they come from teachers whom they respect. The teachers are not diminished in the eyes of the students; instead, respect is enhanced as students discover that their teachers also are learning and that they can contribute to the teachers' knowledge even as the reverse is true.

Everyone knows that teachers have an advantage over students in terms of knowledge and experience. Yet even that is relative and depends on the specific area of concern and the backgrounds of the students in the course. More than likely, some students will have an advantage over some teachers and other students in certain areas of study, merely because of experiences they have had.

In such an environment students develop respect for their own ideas as well as for the ideas of others. The classroom is seen as a place where they can test ideas, where they can risk error with no fear of being punished if they actually err; where they have the right to be wrong. For it is out of the exploration of viable alternatives that learning is enhanced; if alternatives are never entertained by the teacher, the learners' learning will be limited. This is not to say that viable alternatives must always come from the students. Certainly not. But they will never come from students unless they see the teacher as receptive to alternatives, as a "co-learner."

Conducting your classes so that your students view you as a colearner takes great patience, good organization, tolerance for ambiguity, openness to other ways of viewing the world, and a great deal of self-respect. Patience is needed because it takes time to help students develop their thinking to explore the ideas that are evolving in their minds. You cannot routinely plod through the curriculum nor can you be too concerned that you may not cover all that is in the plan book for the day. Helping students develop ideas is more important than following that arbitrary plan. You are helping them develop skills they need to be able to educate themselves.

Good organization is required. The more receptive you are to the ideas of the students and the more willing you are to incorporate their experiences and ideas into the lessons, the clearer must be your objectives and ultimate goals. If you don't have a clear picture of the concepts you are trying to develop, then all the exploration probably will lead nowhere. If you have a clear content objective, there is purpose to the exploration and you have criteria for determining the value and contribution of the alternatives. As stated earlier, the more receptive teachers are to the ideas and experiences of their students, the more organized they must be. In contrast, the more regimented they are in their instruction, the more they expect given responses, the more intolerance they show for divergent thinking, the less organized they need to be—because there are no deviations from the ritual.

Tolerance for ambiguity is difficult to attain, but it is essential both for teachers who wish to be co-learners with their students and for the students who learn in that environment. Because answers are evolved rather than imposed, finding answers takes longer; therefore, judgments must be suspended longer. Anxiety for the resolution of differences may short-circuit the process of evolving the answers. Many issues have multiple answers, depending on background knowledge and experience of the persons involved. None of the multiple answers is the "right" one; what is "right" is the process by which the answers are evolved and their justification provided.

The procedures suggested in this text in large part require this kind of tolerance for ambiguity. Such tolerance is not a vagueness or uncertainty that comes from lack of knowledge; rather, it is a holding back on the imposition of authority and a delaying of closure to allow students to pursue their own lines of reasoning and to develop, justify, and share conclusions from that reasoning.

### Balance Between Content and Process

Sometimes a genuine concern for the development of students' reading skills can jeopardize their study of the content of the various courses in which they are enrolled. For example, some programs organized for teaching reading in content areas require all teachers to devote one class period per week to reading instruction and the other four to instruction in the content of the curriculum. This means that twenty percent of the instructional time is devoted to reading and eighty percent to content.

Because most teachers believe that one hundred percent of their time is not sufficient for dealing with the content of their curriculum, they logically will resent devoting twenty percent to reading instruction, especially when they have not been educated to do so. A dichotomy is thereby created in the minds of students and teachers between the content of the subject (the substance of the curriculum) and the process implicit in the subject (the means by which the substance is to be learned). When taught as two separate entities, content and process rarely interact to enhance one another, rarely are brought together into the delicate balance that is possible between the two, the balance that is necessary if reading is to be taught efficiently for all students at all grade levels.

On the other hand, a genuine concern for students' acquisition of knowledge and understanding of the content of their subjects can jeopardize the development of their reading skills. For example, teachers and administrators often say of their subject: "Yes, this subject requires a great deal of reading and students are expected to be able to handle it. If they have difficulty reading, they should not be in this course. They should have developed those skills before they enrolled in my course." Such an attitude perpetuates the idea that a dichotomy exists between reading instruction and content instruction and that the reading skills taught in one setting are sufficient for use in all other settings.

As suggested in Chapter 1, a dichotomy need not exist between content and process. When basic texts and other resource materials normally used in the subject areas are used as the vehicles for teaching the information and ideas related to the curriculum as well as the reading and reasoning skills implicit in that information and those ideas, then reading skills and course content can be taught simultaneously. Neither has to be sacrificed to the other; a dichotomy need not exist.

The problem most teachers and administrators face is how to develop and maintain the very delicate balance that exists between content and process. The what and the how of each curriculum area can be combined instructionally for the enhancement of both and the neglect of neither. One of the major purposes of this book is to present practical ways to develop and maintain this balance.

### PROMISING SOLUTIONS

Developing answers to the problems identified in the preceding section of this chapter is the purpose of this book. The solutions can be identified and explained rather succinctly. However, to synthesize and assimilate the solutions into one's own teaching so that they are a natural part of one's instruction takes time and practice and further elaboration. Thus, the next section of this chapter identifies and briefly discusses the proposed solutions to the problems; the balance of the book elaborates and illustrates them further and provides opportunity for synthesizing practice.

## Teaching Reading Skills Functionally

Reading is taught functionally (1) when the skills being taught are those which must be used by readers in order to understand the content of an information source they are assigned to read, (2) when those skills are taught *as* the students read that information source, (3) when that information source is assigned in order to teach the content it contains rather than to teach the reading skills it requires.

Functional reading instruction is based on the principle that "content determines process" (Parker and Rubin, 1966). That is, both the concepts which are developed and the manner in which the related information and ideas have been organized and presented in the information source will dictate the reading/reasoning processes a reader must apply to that source in order to read it successfully. This principle encourages, even requires, that the criterion for assigning a reading passage in an information source be that it contains the content which the teacher wants to teach. It is only *after* making the selection for that purpose that the passage is examined for its implicit processes so that appropriate reading instruction can be coordinated with instruction in the content.

For example, a teacher will first establish the content objectives for a lesson: the knowledge to be gained; the understandings to be developed. He or she will then determine what is to be read to attain those objectives. The teacher will examine the reading selection to determine how students should read that material to gain the information it contains and to develop the concepts it supports. By noting the technical vocabulary, the organization of the material, the levels of abstraction, what is said as well as what is implied, the teacher identifies the reading process which the students must apply to understand the material. And this is the process the teacher will teach to the students *as* they read the material.

That's functional teaching of reading: teaching the process students need if they are to understand what you require them to read, *as* they actually read it.

This seems so obvious that one might wonder if it's worth mentioning, let alone worth writing a book about. You only have to consider how reading is usually taught to see why this emphasis is being made.

Most reading instruction can be classified as direct rather than functional. That is, skills in reading are taught for their own sake. Certainly the reading skills will be used for acquiring information and ideas. However, in the immediate concern for helping students learn to read, teachers give comparatively little regard to the content of what students are reading while they are being taught to read. The organizing element is a set of skills to be taught, not the content of a subject area nor the concepts of a specific curriculum.

Students are tested and then programmed for instruction in specific skills according to the data. These skills are taught through whatever material is handy, as long as it is organized to serve as the vehicle for teaching the needed skills. Thus, a specific reading passage is used to develop specific skills; if students happen to learn some of the content that's a bonus, not a primary purpose. The direct focus on reading skills perpetuates the dichotomy between content and process; reading skills are taught virtually in isolation; the content is unrelated to what they study in their courses or is unexplored.

In contrast, the content teacher neither searches the material for the presence of a specific skill that must be taught nor twists the material to fit a skill that should be taught. That would be teaching reading skills directly rather than functionally and would perpetuate the dichotomy we hope to eliminate.

The functional teaching of reading is not neat and tidy; it cannot be fitted easily into scope and sequence charts. Skills are taught as they are needed, as they are required by the material being read. Because functional teaching of reading is different from the usual, direct teaching of reading skills, it is less understood and less popular. Functional teaching of reading in a sense is contrary to our society's "Mr. Fix-it" impulse. Whenever anything goes wrong with anything, the impulse is to take it apart, work on the parts, and put it back together again so that it will run better. Carried over to reading, the impulse is to take reading apart and teach the various subskills one at a time, expecting the *student* to put them all together whenever they are required to read. As discussed in Chapter 1, this direct approach has not produced acceptable results; it's time for a change and that change is gradually taking place.

But there's more to the change than just accepting the notion of teaching reading functionally rather than directly. Clarifying just what skills ought to be taught is equally important to solving the problems identified earlier in this chapter.

### Simplifying Reading Instruction

One reason that subject-area teachers are reluctant to teach reading is that reading instruction has been made too complicated to be appropriately included in the various curriculum areas. Tradition has much to do with this.

Traditionally and logically, reading instruction is initiated at the elementary level. The major emphasis on reading instruction over the years has been in the primary grades. This instruction develops early reading skills, which are basic to word perception and acquisition as well as to comprehension. There is a similar emphasis in remedial programs because most students classified as remedial seem to lack many of these initial reading skills. Since the education of most reading personnel focuses principally on the teaching of these skills and since most reading programs are elementary and/or remedial in nature, there has been perpetuated the strong impression that reading instruction means teaching these early reading skills. This, of course, is a very narrow and limiting view of reading instruction.

There are two logical consequences of this impression and actuality: (1) teachers who know little about reading but are asked to teach it in their subjects believe that they are being asked to teach these early reading skills; (2) because these early reading skills lend themselves to division into multiple subskills, reading has been fragmented into isolated bits and pieces. Consider this last consequence first.

It is relatively easy to identify specific subskills, so called, within the whole concept of early reading skills. The general skill of associating sounds of letters with the symbols or letters themselves can be subdivided into as many subskills as there are sound-symbol relationships. If one likes to formulate behavioral objectives, one could easily develop an objective for each of these subskills. If one likes programmed instruction, one could easily establish programmatic materials for each of these subskills. If one likes scope and sequence charts that delineate the various relationships among the skills, one could easily design beautifully descriptive charts for this purpose. But to what end? There are those who say that such a breakdown of early reading into logical subskills is reasonable, efficient, and effective. There are others who say it's not so; reading is not that way at all. Reading is related to language and one does not learn to speak or use language in a fragmented fashion. Such skills are best taught in a context where natural language is read by the student and, through a monitoring interaction with a teacher, the student has an opportunity to discover how to deal with his language in printed form in its natural flow and development (Goodman, 1970).

The purpose of this book is not to debate this point or to try to determine which of the two positions is correct. However, the issue must be raised because it does have a bearing on reading in the content areas.

Recall the first of the two consequences mentioned above. When this narrow and limiting concept of reading instruction is imposed on subject-area teachers, particularly when they know little about the field of reading improvement, disasters occur. They reject reading instruction because it is complicated and time-consuming and, more important, because it seems inappropriate for inclusion in the content areas for two reasons:

First, *most* students in most subject areas in grades four through twelve already possess these early reading skills. Many teachers will debate this point, citing evidence of many students ". . . who cannot read." But one needs only to watch these students between classes or before and after school to discover that indeed the students *can* read. They are "won't" readers rather than "can't" readers. What they need is a practical review of the skills they already possess and the motivation to use them to study what the curriculum requires. This can be done without elaborate instruction that is so specialized as to be beyond the knowledge of the subject-area teacher, and without separating the instruction in reading from the content of the course. To be sure, there are students who, for some reason, have not acquired the early reading skills and need remedial instruction. The purpose of this book is not to discuss how to provide that remedial instruction, but rather how to help this kind of student, along with all other students, be more successful in reading the regular subject-area materials.

So subject-area teachers needn't worry about teaching these early reading skills as they are taught in remedial and/or early-grade classrooms.

Second, most reading done in the content areas in grades four through twelve requires comprehension and study skills of a much more sophisticated nature than those found in the early reading instruction. Unfortunately, so much time, energy, research, and money have been spent on the early reading skills that relatively little has been done to study these more advanced aspects of reading. Thus, subject-area teachers have not learned how to teach students how to read the required materials in their subjects, nor have reading personnel had much to say to the content-area teachers as to what skills should be taught and how they should be taught. National Institute for Education (NIE), in its documents related to reading instruction, refers to this more sophisticated aspect of reading as "skilled reading," as distinct from "early reading," discussed earlier (NIE, 1976).

In an effort to discover more about the nature of "skilled reading," reading personnel have imposed on that process the procedures that generally have been advocated for early reading instruction. That is, they have made an effort to identify the various subskills which make up this more sophisticated reading. As a result, a multitude of skills have been identified that are supposed to develop competence at the higher levels of comprehension implicit in skilled reading. But virtually no research evidence has validated these subskills. Reading comprehension has been fragmented for instructional purposes by what might be called authoritative opinion rather than by empirical research. Because the authoritative opinion often comes from persons who are oriented toward early reading instruction and who have had reasonable success in providing early reading instruction, their suggestions for applying the same methods to reading instruction in the content areas are listened to carefully. Unfortunately, such opinions have been perpetuated in spite of ample evidence that they are not applicable in the content areas and for that reason are resisted by most subject-area teachers.

There is one further extension of the erroneous imposition of the early reading instruction model on reading instruction in the content areas. The "authoritative opinion" suggests that not only are there multiple subskills which make up comprehension, but that these subskills are different in each content area. This means that the set of subskills each subject-area teacher teaches differs from the set other subject-area teachers teach. This opinion, too, has generally been accepted as correct, representing what must be taught if students are to learn how to read successfully in the various content areas.

What is imposed on subject-area teachers is a compounding of error. The subskill approach to early reading instruction, itself an object of strong differences of opinion, is applied to the skilled reading required in later grades, particularly in the content areas. This results in a complicated fragmentation of the reading process. The fragmentation occurs both within and across subject areas: within, by separating out the subskills that supposedly are included in comprehension and teaching them one by one until mastered by students; across, by identifying discrete skills appropriate for comprehending the materials peculiar to each of the subject areas which require reading.

Subject-area teachers are faced, then, with a seemingly impossible, unnecessarily complicated job: combining the teaching of this complex process with the teaching of their sophisticated content. They say it cannot be done. And they are right! There is ample evidence that it doesn't work.

What is the answer? Simplicity. Simplification. One of the purposes of this book is to discuss and demonstrate that the reading instruction appropriate for skilled reading, for the reading required for success in the various content areas, neither is nor need be complicated. It is exceedingly simple; thus, it is exceedingly manageable both by subject-area teachers and by their students.

Chapter 6 shows how one can simplify reading instruction as it pertains to vocabulary acquisition and development, even when the instruction includes some early reading skills. Chapters 3 and 4 show how one can simplify the comprehension skills appropriate for reading the materials required in the various subjects in grades four through twelve. Chapter 5 shows how one can simplify the reasoning skills required for responding to the curriculum materials presented in all subjects at all grade levels, regardless of their medium.

When the reading process is thus simplified for instructional and learning purposes, it can be taught functionally in combination with the content of the courses in which it is being taught. Though not to be viewed as a panacea, nor is it suggested as such, this simplified approach to the development of skilled reading in the content areas will satisfy the needs of most subject-area teachers and their students. But much has to be understood before that goal can be realized. The rest of the book will help develop that understanding.

### Simulating the Reading Process

So far there have been two interrelated suggestions for how to respond to the basic problems facing the content-area teacher who seriously wishes to provide reading instruction as part of the curriculum: (1) to teach reading functionally; (2) to simplify the reading process so that it is more manageable for teachers and students. There is a third interrelated suggestion: simulating the reading process so that as it is taught, students experience it and learn how it works.

Simulation, for our purposes, can be defined as "an artificial representation of a real experience; a contrived series of activities which, when taken together, approximate the experience or the process that ultimately is to be applied independently" (Herber and Nelson, 1975). A classic example of simulation occurs in astronautics. Prior to actual space flights, all the anticipated activities of the astronauts during space flights were simulated so that the astronauts could experience them ahead of time and develop their skills. The experiences did not involve actual space flight, but they approximated it so closely that when the astronauts actually were in space they felt as though they had been there before, had experienced the sensations and had done the work hundreds of times. In driver training, simulators that approximate actual driving conditions are used. Potential drivers are trained to respond to a variety of road conditions and a variety of situations while they learn how to handle the controls of the automobile and develop appropriate physical and judgmental responses. When the trainees actually drive an automobile in traffic, it is as though they have done it dozens of time before.

The principle is applicable to teaching in general, to reading in particular. One of the main purposes of formal education is to develop students' abilities to educate themselves. We expose them to areas of knowledge and we challenge them with the development of new ideas so ultimately they can use that knowledge and those ideas to expand beyond our present horizons. The development of skills is the same. Formal education equips students with skills so they ultimately can educate themselves. The task of formal education is to teach students *how* to learn and to do that, we need to consider carefully the lessons available to us from the process of simulation.

Too often our skills instruction is not based on the principle of simulation, the idea that students must be shown *how* to use specific skills. Rather, it is based on the assumption that students already possess the skills we are supposed to teach them. Take, for example, the process of comprehension.

The usual tool used to teach students is *questioning.* The Socratic method is venerable and useful, but it assumes that students have the skills needed to answer the questions. When applied to teaching reading comprehension, questions become a problem. Suppose a teacher wants to teach students how to interpret. She usually does so by asking students interpretive questions to guide their response to the reading selection. Now, if the students already know how to interpret, the questions provide reinforcing practice. If, however, they do not know how to interpret the material, asking questions that require them to interpret does not teach them how to interpret. Rather, it only tests to see if they *can* interpret. Since the teacher already knows they can't (that knowledge is the basis for asking the questions in the first place), it seems useless to further test them and even more useless to try to teach them by requiring them to use the skill they don't have, the skill which supposedly is being taught.

If questions aren't the answer to the problem, what is? *Simulation.* We must take the reading process which we have simplified, the process which we intend to teach functionally, and analyze how it works. Then we must create situations—conditions—which approximate the operation of that process and then walk our students through that process over and over again until they develop a feeling for it and it seems natural to them every time they read a passage. Then they are ready to respond to questions which require the use of that process because it has become part of them.

One of the purposes of this book is to examine ways that subject-area teachers can simulate the reading process for their students, showing them how to read what they are required to read. Chapter 8 discusses simulation in more detail. Chapters 3 and 4 deal specifically with ways to simulate the comprehension process. Chapter 6 relates to the simulation of vocabulary acquisition and extension. Chapter 5 shows how to simulate the reasoning processes appropriate to all resource materials found in various content areas.

### Sequencing for Independence and Sophistication

If you subscribe to the "authoritative opinion," which supports the fragmentation of the reading process into a multiplicity of subskills, you will also be concerned about scope and sequence charts. In what order should these subskills be taught? There is no research evidence which clearly establishes the superiority of one sequence over another. Any recommended sequencing is based on logic and/or "authoritative opinion" (not necessarily synonymous criteria). Since the subskills themselves were generated in that fashion, it is consistent to use the same criteria to justify the teaching sequence.

If you subscribe to the "authoritative opinion," which simplifies the reading process (though supported by good evidence; see Chapter 3), then your concern for sequencing should have a different focus. First, you should be concerned about sequencing for increased sophistication in the use of the reading process.

This simplified view of reading instruction suggests that the same reading skills are required across all subject-area materials. Some subjects may involve a few special or unique skills, but such differences are due primarily to the nature of the materials to which they are applied. The skills are the same; they are adapted to fit the content of the various subject-area materials. You will recall the discussion of transformation of skills earlier in this chapter. What we are dealing with here is the horizontal transformation of skills.

As students progress through the grades, the skills remain basically the same. But because the materials become more and more sophisticated, the reading process becomes more and more sophisticated. When reading is taught through subject-area materials at increasing levels of sophistication, the students' skills increase in sophistication. This involves vertical transformation and a sequencing which is practical and possible.

You should also be concerned about sequencing for students' independence. Independence is a relative term, one which describes a concern most teachers have about their students' ability to perform. There is a natural concern that if you simulate the reading process for students in order to teach it, when and how do they ever operate on their own? How do they develop independence?

A sequence to follow to help students achieve independence is suggested in Chapter 8. At this stage it has not been researched carefully. However, its practicality has been demonstrated in various programs for teaching reading in content areas. You probably will find it useful and satisfying, and if nothing else, it is much more manageable than trying to develop students' independence with a multiplicity of reading subskills.

## Expectation and Caring

Much has been written about the influence of teachers' expectations on students' performance. There is ample evidence to indicate that when a teacher expects high-quality performance from students, that performance is often forthcoming. When that expectation is coupled with careful instruction in how to do the tasks expected of them, students are even more likely to fulfill the expectations. When the expectation and careful instruction are coupled with a caring about the students' success, fulfillment seems almost certain.

Naive, you say? Not at all. One can observe it happening in schools across the country. But one can observe the opposite too: teachers who expect students to fail, and they do; teachers who not only expect them to fail but teach in such a way that the students are certain to fail, by never showing them how to do what they are being required to do; teachers who seem not to care that their students are failing, blaming both the students and their previous teachers for the students' lack of skills, knowledge, and understanding.

Interestingly enough, one can observe the effect of both kinds of expectation on the very same students. In one subject a student will have a teacher who expects success from her—and that student succeeds. The next period the same student is in a class with a teacher who expects her to fail; and, sure enough, the student fails.

This point is raised not to assign blame, but rather to identify the powerful influence of the teachers' attitude on students and the relationship between the teachers' expectations for and caring about their students and the successes those students experience. Teachers with a positive attitude toward their students have well over half of what is needed to succeed. Knowledge of the subject and ability to teach it clearly make up the balance of the teachers' competence.

The purpose of this book is to provide the positively oriented teacher with practical ways to help students learn how to read within the context of the subjects taught from grades four through twelve. These suggestions will not be at all useful to teachers who do not expect their students to be successful (though sometimes students do succeed in spite of a teacher's negative expectations). If you really doubt that anything can be done for your students, close the book. Don't bother to continue reading. You'll not find the ideas successful. But if you sincerely believe that students can be successful if you help them and if you are looking for ways to help them, then this book is for you. Read on. Apply the ideas. You and your students will be delighted with the results.

Now to the specifics.

*　　*　　*　　*　　*　　*

## REACTION GUIDE

*Part I*

*Directions:* Listed below are the problems and solutions described in this chapter, each set in a separate column. Demonstrate, and discuss, your understanding of the chapter by matching solutions to the problems they are supposed to solve. A solution may relate to more than one problem.

_____ 1. Difficulty of text

_____ 2. Range of competence

_____ 3. Active student participation

_____ 4. Student-centered curriculum

_____ 5. Concept development

_____ 6. Transfer and transformation

_____ 7. Teachers as co-learners

_____ 8. Balance between content and process

a. Teaching reading functionally

b. Simplifying reading instruction

c. Simulating the reading process

d. Sequencing for independence and sophistication

e. Expectation and caring

*Part II*

*Directions:* Listed below are ten statements which represent ideas related to this chapter. Place a check on the numbered line before those statements you believe are supported by the chapter. Be ready to cite evidence to support your decisions.

_____ 1. Not every problem has an apparent solution.

_____ 2. Most problems are solved through a combination of solutions.

_____ 3. In problem-solving, the familiar (concept, practice, material, etc.) often is a deterrent to discovering a solution.

_____ 4. In problem-solving, simplicity often is thought to be naive and complexity, sophisticated; yet in actual experience often the simplicity is sophisticated and the complexity, naive.

_____ 5. Priorities are revealed by what is made the center of interest.

_____ 6. Without tools, skills are nonfunctional; without skills, tools are inoperable.

_____ 7. Among the people in any given group, there is represented a range of independence and sophistication on any factor you care to mention.

_____ 8. Actions that are not instinctive are learned through instruction and problems arise when there is a failure to identify which are which.

_____ 9. Expectancy without caring is insensitive; caring without expectancy is undisciplined.

_____10. In the performance of tasks, more is accomplished by adaptation of the old than by development of the new.

### REINFORCING ACTIVITIES

A. Read the following pairs of words. Check those pairs that stand for relationships you find expressed or implied in the chapter. Discuss your decisions with your colleagues.

| | |
|---|---|
| simple - complex | problems - solutions |
| responsive - insensitive | difficult - easy |
| test - teach | information - ideas |
| intellectual - emotional | ability - achievement |
| evidence - opinion | relative - absolute |
| rigid - flexible | active - passive |
| dichotomy - unity | functional - direct |
| questions - statements | |

B. On 3"x 5" cards, write out the pairs of words, or each word from the pairs, with one pair or one word per card. Working with at least two other people who have read the chapter, arrange the words and/or pairs so that they represent issues raised and/or ideas developed in the chapter. Compare and discuss your arrangement with those of other groups.

C. Using the relationship among the concepts of *worker, tool, expectation,* and *product,* draw an analogy between the following two sets of concepts. Decide what the problems might be, what options are available for solving the problems, and what options you would select.

   1) carpenter; saw; cutting a board on a straight line; a board cut crookedly

   2) student; text; read to secure information; partial information secured with some inaccuracy

*   *   *   *   *   *

## REFERENCES

BORMUTH, JOHN R. "Reading literacy: Its definition and assessment." *Reading Research Quarterly*, 9, no. 1 (1973-74).

BUROS, OSCAR K. *The sixth mental measurement yearbook*. Highland Park, N.J.: Gryphon Press, 1965.

GARDNER, JOHN W. *Self renewal*. New York: Harper & Row, 1964.

GOODMAN, KENNETH. "Behind the eye: What happens in reading." In *Reading process and program*. Urbana, Ill.: National Council of Teachers of English, 1970.

HERBER, HAROLD L. "Teaching reading and physics simultaneously." In *Improvement of reading through classroom practice*. Newark, Del.: International Reading Association, 1964.

HERBER, HAROLD L., & JOAN NELSON. "Questioning is not the answer." *Journal of Reading*, 18, no. 7 (1975), 512-517.

HOGAN, ROBERT. "You'll like it. It's caneloni." *Phi Delta Kappan*, 52, April (1971), 468-70.

KLARE, GEORGE R. "Assessing readability." *Reading Research Quarterly*, 10, no. 1 (1974-75) 62-102.

National Institute for Education. RFP for *A center for the study of reading*. Washington, D.C.: National Institute of Education, 1976.

PARKER, J. CECIL, & LOUIS J. RUBIN. *Process as content*. Chicago: Rand McNally, 1966.

SMITH, HENRY P., & EMERALD V. DECHANT. *Psychology in teaching reading*. Englewood Cliffs, N.J.: Prentice-Hall, 1961.

GOVE, PHILLIP B., ed. *Webster's seventh new collegiate dictionary*. Springfield, Mass.: Merriam, 1963.

# three

# Levels
# of Comprehension

---

## VOCABULARY

The following terms are important to an understanding of this chapter. Each is defined in context. Read through the list to identify those for which you have uncertain meanings. Then as you read the chapter, pay particular attention to their definitions. Also, make certain that the meanings attributed to the other words in the list, by their use in the context of the chapter, correspond to your own meanings for them.

| | |
|---|---|
| comprehension | principles |
| levels of comprehension | concepts |
| literal | details |
| interpretive | content analysis |
| applied | declarative statement |
| simulate | intrinsic concepts |
| | extrinsic concepts |

The following words are not defined in context; therefore, a brief definition of each is given for your reference.

*Construct:* (noun form) a set of individual items which have an inter-dependent relationship

*Levels guide:* a set of materials designed to guide a reader through the three levels of comprehension as applied to a specific passage in some information source

*Content objective:* the information and/or ideas to be derived from a study of a specific selection in an information source and/or a particular part of the curriculum

## IDEA DIRECTION

The examples and illustrations presented in this chapter are drawn from full lessons. As you examine the material and participate in the activity, assume the following: (1) that before assigning students any reading in the information source, the teacher will have established the overall concept to be learned as a result of the study of that material; (2) that the teacher will have worked with the students in reviewing previously covered material so as to set a context and purpose for the study of the new material; (3) that the teacher will have worked with the basic, essential vocabulary, which students will need to know to succeed in their reading of the passage.

You should assume that the lessons in which these illustrative materials are used are well-organized and structured. Further, assume that they were prepared because students need help in reading the required material. Finally, assume that the teacher was aware of the problem and was willing to help.

If you should wish clarification on any of these assumptions, you might want to read Chapters 9 and 6 first. Chapter 9 discusses lesson structure; Chapter 6, vocabulary development.

## READING DIRECTION

This chapter presents a way to help students improve their reading comprehension in various content areas. It involves you in an example of how to do this and then presents additional illustrations for you to study. To get the most out of the chapter, you should follow the directions for the various materials presented. These experiences will provide a basis for translating the ideas and suggestions into practice in your own subject at your own grade level.

## EXPERIENCING LEVELS
## OF COMPREHENSION

This chapter presents a simplified view of reading comprehension which is instructionally applicable in most subject areas by most classroom teachers. In this form, comprehension can be taught functionally; it can be simulated so that students are shown *how* to comprehend the resource materials in their subjects.

Before you examine this view of comprehension in detail, you should experience how it works instructionally. The following activity is designed to serve that purpose. Please go through the activity as the directions indicate. You should work with two or three other people in this activity; it is not as effective if you work alone.

I. *Directions:* Listed below are three statements. Read the first statement with others in your group. Look in the following reading selection to see if it contains the same information contained in the statement. Place a check on the numbered line if the statement does so. It may use either the exact words or may paraphrase, as long as it says the same thing. You must be able to give evidence to support your opinion. If any persons in the group have a problem with words in either the statements or the reading selection, be certain to help them develop an understanding of those words. React to all three statements.

_____1. Seagulls have seriously damaged Swedish crops and gardens.

_____2. Seagulls laid eggs faster than the experts could destroy them.

_____3. Experts boil the eggs and the gulls keep trying to hatch them until it is too late.

For years millions of hungry seagulls have flown inland and seriously damaged Swedish crops and gardens. Experts at first tried to reduce the number of gulls by destroying their eggs but found that the gulls merely laid more eggs.

Now, armed with saucepans and cooking stoves, the experts boil the eggs and carefully replace them in the nests. The gulls, not knowing the eggs will never hatch, sit on them hopefully until it is too late to try again.

II. *Directions:* Read through the following statements and think about how they relate to the information you discussed in Part I of this exercise. Place a check on the numbered line before each statement which expresses an idea that can be reasonably supported with information from the reading selection. Be ready to discuss the supporting evidence with others in your group.

_____ 1. Swedish people place more value on vegetable life than animal life.

_____ 2. Seagulls don't recognize hard-boiled eggs even when they are sitting on them.

_____ 3. The Swedes have found a way to control the seagull plague.

_____ 4. A good way to keep seagulls from multiplying is to make it impossible for their eggs to hatch.

III. *Directions:* Read through the following statements. Think about ideas and experiences you have had which are similar in principle to what you found in the reading selection. Check each statement which you think is reasonable and which you can support by combining ideas contained in the reading selection with your own related ideas and experiences. Be ready to present evidence from both sources to support your decisions.

_____ 1. Man's ingenuity insures his survival.

_____ 2. If at first you don't succeed, try, try again.

_____ 3. Destruction can be peaceful or violent.

_____ 4. Appearances can be deceiving.

**Overview**

Reading comprehension can be simplified by defining it as a three-level process. First, the reader examines the words of the author and determines what is being said, what information is being presented.

Second, the reader looks for relationships among statements within the materials, and from these intrinsic relationships derives various meanings. The intrinsic relationships the reader perceives are colored and influenced by previous knowledge of and experience with the topic in question. However, the reader is confined by the text and determines meaning primarily as perceived in intratext relationships.

Third, the reader takes the product of the literal—what the author has said—and the interpretive—what the author meant by what he said—and applies it to other knowledge she already possesses, thereby deepening the understanding. At the applied level the reader selects intrinsic relationships produced at the interpretive level of comprehension and synthesizes them with concepts that are the product of previous knowledge and experience. Out of this synthesis the reader perceives a new relationship—an extrinsic relationship—that has a scope larger than the meanings imposed by the context of the reading selection, producing new ideas which extend beyond those immediately identifiable in the reading selection.

**Comparisons**

For purposes of comparison on the *Seagull* activity, you and members of your group should examine the following responses to the statements in each of the parts of the exercise and see if—and why—you agree.

**Part I** In Part I, Statements 1 and 3 were checked; Statement 2 was not. Evidence for supporting Statement 1 comes from the first sentence of the first paragraph. Except for the elimination of the first five words plus words seven, eight, and nine from that sentence, the first statement is an exact repetition.

Statement 2 does not say what the authors say. One might infer the statement as a possible fact, but the paragraphs do not give that information. The directions were to determine whether the information in the statements was the same as that in the paragraphs, to determine whether the statements said what the authors said.

Statement 3 paraphrases the second paragraph, presenting the essential information. Though words are rearranged, the information remains the same and, therefore, the statement says what the authors say.

**Part II** Now, consider Part II. Compare the consensus of your group with these responses. Statements 1, 2, and 4 were supportable by evidence drawn from the paragraphs. Statement 3 represents an idea the authors seemed to imply, but the supporting evidence was thin, so it was accepted with reservation.

Statement 1 seems reasonable, supported by reference in the first sentence of the first paragraph to the crop damage by the gulls and to the Swedes' consequent effort to destroy the gulls, as noted in the second sentence. Thus, the statement represents an idea which probably would be supported by the authors of the reading selection.

Statement 2, although a weak attempt at humor, nevertheless expresses an idea implicit in the combination of information contained in both sentences of the last paragraph. Thus the statement is a reasonable representation of an idea the authors might have had in mind.

Statement 3 is more difficult to judge. The first paragraph indicates that previous methods were not sufficient to control the plague. The second paragraph presents the alternative method devised by the experts and the gulls' response. The "too late to try again" seems to imply that the gulls are deterred from laying more eggs. One can reasonably infer that this deterrent will solve the problem and the plague will be controlled. Thus Statement 3 can be seen as a reasonable inference drawn from the information presented.

Statement 4 probably is so obvious that one need not refer to the reading selection to find support for it. But one must remember that the task is not to determine the truth of the statements. Rather, the task is to determine the *reasonableness* of each statement as a reflection of an idea which can be supported by information provided in the selection. The question here is, does the text support this idea? When one examines the information in the paragraphs, one finds that this statement is a conclusion one can validly draw from the evidence, but it must be qualified. In the first paragraph, the experts made it impossible for the eggs to hatch by breaking the eggs; that did not seem to solve the problem because more eggs were laid, and the gulls multiplied. In the second paragraph, another approach was used with different results. This statement, therefore, is a qualified conclusion one can draw from the evidence and, as such, probably deals with the author's meaning.

**Part III** Now consider the statements in Part III. All represent broad principles that can be supported reasonably by combining ideas drawn from the text with ideas previously held by the readers or drawn from other sources.

Statement 1 certainly is reasonable. The text supports it, since the experts' imagination was tested to evolve a clever scheme to outwit the gulls and to protect the crops. Other experience suggests that man constantly is having to find ways to control his environment and overcome those forces that would destroy him if they were left unhindered. The whole history of medicine is an example of this, as are the food, the clothing, and the housing industries. These examples combined with ideas from the text amply support the reasonableness of the statement.

Statement 2 has double meaning, depending on the reader's point of view. In either case, whether referring to the experts or the gulls, the statement reflects an ethic of persistence and determination. The principle is that effort is required for success and that success is not always forthcoming on the first attempt. Both the experts and the gulls illustrated this principle. Examples from other sources are abundant: Edison's persistence in pursuit of the appropriate material for the filament for his light bulb is but one classic example. The combination of evidence from all sources supports the principle.

Statement 3, although somewhat abstract, finds support from ideas in the text and from other sources. Whether smashed ("destroyed") or boiled, the eggs are rendered useless for producing offspring. There is ample evidence in our society of both quiet, unobtrusive destruction and violent destruction of people, places, and things. Evidence from the text and experience couple to support this principle.

Finally, Statement 4 refers to ideas from the reading selection implying that the gulls were unable to discern that the eggs had been tampered with and were not hatchable. The outward appearance of the shell apparently was sufficient to satisfy their nesting instincts. Most people have ample experience in encounters with facade and the surprise or disappointment which occurs when the facade is exposed. Both the text and experience seem to support the principle here.

## EXPLANATION AND RATIONALE

What you have just experienced in the preceding activity is a simulation of reading at the three levels of comprehension. Its purpose was to serve as the basis for explaining what the three levels are and how they work. This chapter will show you how you can make them work in your own subject for your own students.

Each part of the activity based on "Seagulls" involved you in reading at one of the levels of comprehension. Part I of the activity had you reading at the literal level of comprehension. Part II of the activity had you reading at the interpretive level of comprehension. Part III of the activity had you reading at the applied level of comprehension. As you made decisions about the acceptability of each statement, you were actually reading the material at the level of comprehension to which that statement belonged. As you justified your acceptance or rejection of the statements by citing evidence from the text and from other sources, you were reading the text in the same way as the person who created the statements that guided you. The only difference was that you had to *react to* the statements rather than *create* them. In supporting the statements, you engaged in the same mental process that he did in creating them.

You were thus guided in reading at the three levels of comprehension so that you began to develop a "feeling for" comprehension. You could get a sense of how you mind works, how it interacts with information and ideas to apprehend and elaborate on meaning. With such experiences repeated over time, students could develop a sense of independence in the comprehension process.

## Literal Level *Identify Information*

Literal-level comprehension is determining what the authors are saying, what information their words convey. Students have difficulty reading at this level of comprehension. This may be because they do not understand the definitions of words; therefore, the information is not obtainable. Work on vocabulary development (see Chapter 6) will properly prepare them for reading at this level. Guided practice in reading selections at the literal level will reinforce the vocabulary development skills. It also will develop a sense of how to identify essential information in the text.

Other students may have trouble at this level because they read "too well." That is, they have no trouble reading the words, so they proceed immediately to interpretation before they are sure of what information has been provided to serve as the basis for the interpretation. Being guided in reading the selection at this literal level provides reinforcing practice on the essential quality of accuracy in the acquisition of information. Experience repeatedly bears out the worth of guiding students' reading at this level of comprehension.

Part I of the activity was a literal-level guide to assist you, the reader, in identifying the basic information in the reading selection. Notice that you were asked to read the statements *before* you read the paragraphs. This was to guide you in reading the paragraphs for specific information. You carried to the paragraphs specific information from the statements and determined whether or not that information was present in the paragraphs. You gave evidence of your decision by reading from the paragraphs the sentences or sentence fragments which contained the same information as the statements themselves did. This "carrying and confirming" occurred when the statement was "literally literal," that is, almost a word-for-word reproduction of information presented in the paragraph, as in Statement 1. It occurred when the statement did not accurately represent the information contained in the paragraphs, as with Statement 2. And it occurred when the statement was a paraphrasing or translation of information presented in the paragraph, as with Statement 3. In all cases, your reading of the paragraphs was focused on the essential information, triggered by the need to support your decisions about the three statements with information from the paragraphs. Thus, you were being guided to read at the literal level of comprehension.

Please recall once again that you read the statements *before* you read the paragraphs. You brought the statements to the paragraphs rather than the reverse. This is an important point. The purpose is to *show students how* to read at the literal level of comprehension.

It helps your students if you assume that they need help in reading the selections you assign. It is logical to assume, then, that it does *not* help to ask them to read the selection before they read the statements. Doing so assumes that they can read the text with little or no difficulty. And if they are able to read the selection prior to reading the statements, they do not need the statements to guide their reading. To use the statements following the reading of the selection does not guide their reading; rather, it merely tests their recall. If your purpose is to show them how to read at the literal level of comprehension, then do so; don't test to see whether or not they can. You already know that.

In spite of the logic of this point, many teachers will use such materials incorrectly, first having students read the selection, then having them read the statements to confirm the presence of that information in the passage. These teachers are so conditioned to the read-question-answer-discuss sequence of activities that it almost seems like "cheating" to have students read the statements first.

Other teachers reject the recommended procedure of reading the literal statements before the selection, fearing students will read only that portion containing the same information presented in the statements. That, of course, is exactly what happens initially. But if we are guiding students because they are unsuccessful in reading on their own, then reading only a portion of the selection in this fashion places them far ahead of where they would be without such guidance. Because of the teacher's care in identifying information to be stressed in the literal-level guide, when students respond to the statements in groups and cite evidence from the selection to support their positions, they are initially identifying the essential information contained in the passage. Then, as the students progress through the interpretive level of comprehension, their grasp of this basic information is enhanced as they use it for evidence of ideas presented in the text.

Showing rather than just telling is the key here. In Chapter 8, in the discussion of simulation, you will find additional rationale for this kind of guidance.

### Interpretive Level

At the interpretive level of comprehension the readers determine what the authors mean by what they say. They develop intrinsic concepts from the relationships they perceive in the authors' information. The concepts are "intrinsic" because they are formulated from information presented in the information source.

At the literal level readers identify the important information. At the interpretive level readers perceive the relationships which exist in that information, conceptualizing the ideas formulated by those relationships, and expressing those relationships in either written or oral form. The result is the development of an idea that is not explicitly expressed by the authors. It is an expression of the meaning the authors seem to intend. It is implicit in what they say, even though they haven't said it. But it can be supported with evidence, by referring to what they have said—to the basic information.

Information in isolated bits and pieces is of little use to readers unless their purpose is merely to accumulate isolated bits and pieces of information. The minute readers begin to try to fit all of that information together into some kind of message, they go beyond the literal to the interpretive level of comprehension.

What you did in Part II of the activity for "Seagulls" is basic to showing students how to read at the interpretive level of comprehension. Refer back to the statements in Part II. Their purpose was to guide you in responding to the selection at this level of comprehension. You were asked to determine if the statements were reasonable expressions of ideas contained in the paragraphs. And you were asked to cite evidence from the paragraphs to support your decisions. In finding support for the statements you found reasonable, you were engaged in a mental process similar to what it took to create the statements in the first place. You looked for relationships among the details and found that the statements gave expression to those relationships. You experienced the process of interpretation in a highly structured, carefully guided experience. This experience serves as the basis for more independent work later on. Chapter 8 discusses in more detail the implications of this procedure, which can be called simulation.

Recall that the purpose of the interpretive level of comprehension is to discern the *authors'* meanings, the authors' ideas. The meanings, the ideas, can evolve only out of the information the authors provide to the reader. Thus, the reader must read objectively, carefully avoiding insertion of his own knowledge and experience and bias. That is why some, like Smith (1963), label this level of comprehension as "critical," requiring carefully objective reading.

But in spite of the best efforts of students and teachers to be objective at the interpretive level, prior knowledge and experience do have an influence. Ideas derived by this interpretive process will vary from student to student many times. One student will perceive one set of relationships within that literal-level information and will evolve a certain idea or combination of ideas. Another student will perceive a different set of relationships and might possibly come up with a different combination of ideas.

These differences often can be attributed to prior experiences. Because of a specific experience, one student will see certain relationships while other students without that experience will fail to perceive them. Thus, meanings will differ, even when both groups are reading objectively. The process still is interpretation, focusing on relationships within the information provided by the authors and not on the development of ideas external to that information which would involve the next level of comprehension. The ideas are still implicit in the reading selection, but they are perceived only by those who have the background to cause them to see the relationships that produce the ideas. To those without the background, it is as though the ideas did not exist.

The consequence of all this is that you can expect a wide range of responses to material at the interpretive level among students in a given class. Unless the teacher requires students to find the same meaning she perceives, this range of responses is not a problem. This relates to the discussion in Chapter 2 concerning the teacher's role as a colearner and the need for a tolerance for ambiguity on the part of both students and teachers. It enhances opportunities for students to learn from one another, for teachers to learn from students, and for students to learn from teachers.

Students need help in learning how to function well at this interpretive level. They need to develop a sense of how one sorts through information, searching for logical relationships, and a sense of how to express clearly the idea or ideas inherent in that set of relationships. If students are having difficulty with their reading comprehension, their problems may be at the interpretive level. They need to be shown how to read successfully at this level. Merely asking them the question, "What does the author mean by what he says?" is not sufficient. They must be shown how to perceive the possible meanings.

### Applied Level

As already stated, prior knowledge and experience have a bearing on the relationships perceived within the information provided by the author. Hence, those factors influence the meanings you perceive in what you read. But in still another way prior knowledge and experience relate to what you read: that is when you see a relationship between the ideas acquired from other sources and the ideas derived from the reading selection. Out of that perceived relationship, you evolve broad generalizations or principles which embrace both sets of ideas, but which represent something more than just the sum of the two. The applied level of comprehension is the process of taking what has been known and applying it to what has just been learned, then evolving ideas which encompass both *extrinsic* but extend beyond them. These ideas can be called extrinsic concepts, since they are external to the text, even though they embrace ideas in the text.

Gagné (1970) refers to this combining of information and concepts to develop broader ideas and generalizations as a "chaining" process. Details (literal level) are chained together to form concepts (interpretive level), which are chained together to form principles (applied level).

If students are having difficulty perceiving the relevance of what they read, perhaps they are having problems reading at the applied level of comprehension. Merely asking them, "How can we relate our own ideas and experiences to the author's ideas?" is not sufficient. They must be shown how to relate the two.

Consider your response to Part III of the activity on "Seagulls." Each of the statements in that exercise was so general that you could have responded to it without even reading the paragraphs. So one might well ask, "Of what value is the exercise for developing reading comprehension?" To answer, you must recall what the exercise required of you.

You were asked to identify supporting evidence for each of the statements in Part III which you found acceptable. The evidence was to come *both* from your own experience and knowledge *and* from ideas derived from the reading selection. If the statement could not be supported with evidence from the reading selection, then it was not acceptable, even though it might have been supported by evidence from the reader's experience and prior knowledge. Thus, the applied level of comprehension is very much related to reading.

One value of instruction at this level is that it provides students with a systematic way to incorporate their own experiences and ideas from other sources into what they are learning in school. As discussed in more detail in Chapter 7, one reason students see school as irrelevant is that they have little opportunity to relate what they generally experience to what they study in school. The applied level of comprehension provides that opportunity. It is exciting to watch students' responses when they realize that outside-of-school experience does really have something to do with what they are studying.

An important caution: Emphasize with students that the criteria for acceptability of the applied-level statements include both prior experience *and* the ideas from the text. Don't let them just emote about a statement they cannot support with the text. Don't reject the experience; just point out that if they cannot also find support in the text, it is inappropriate in this context. If the readers cannot find support from both sources, then the statement should be rejected. It is through the exercise of this caution that respect for both the content resources and the students' own experiences are enhanced in the eyes of both students and teachers.

## Objections to Levels of Comprehension

Even before trying materials which guide students' reading through the three levels of comprehension, some teachers will raise objections to the whole idea. Happily, they are in the minority. Happily, also, most of them are convinced by their own experience once they do try such materials in their own classes.

But consider the objections. Many may have come to mind as you read through this chapter. Some say poor readers should not be expected to respond to statements at the interpretive and applied levels because they don't have the skills to read even at the literal level. Unless they can acquire the basic information needed for developing the concepts and principles, trying to work at the interpretive and applied levels will be too frustrating and out of their reach. Experience suggests otherwise—when the teacher organizes the class to make it possible for the student to acquire that basic information.

Chapter 8 discusses the advantages of having the class organized into small groups, guided in their discussions by the statements at each of the three levels and learning to help one another constructively. If some students are having difficulty reading at the literal level, the guide material, coupled with small-group discussions, shows them how to acquire the basic information. After all, that is the purpose of working at the literal level. If the students already were able to acquire the basic information independently, then they would not need such help. Once they have the help, they are able to become involved in the discussion of the important information. Even though some students might not be able to read much of the text, through these discussions they are able to acquire the information essential to the development of the concepts and principles in the interpretive and applied level discussions.

Most poor readers can reason with some adequacy, even though they are *not* skilled in reading. They should *not* be excluded from educational experiences that require them to use their reasoning abilities merely because they are having reading problems. Guiding students through all three levels makes the inclusion of such students possible.

An objection to including the interpretive and applied levels comes from some teachers of so-called "poor readers" or "slow learners" or "low achievers" or whatever label is applied to students whose interests and achievement do not correspond to the school's expectations. These teachers frequently state that their students are just not able to deal with statements "on such a sophisticated level." Again, experience suggests otherwise. Time and again these same teachers will express astonishment as they see, in a demonstration lesson, their own students responding very well to such statements. The students display a wisdom sometimes beyond the more academically inclined students and sometimes beyond the teachers' as they draw on experience to support the interpretive statements. Their insights are beautiful to observe. Their contributions help develop a positive self-image and contribute to an awareness that they have much to offer the class.

An objection to including the applied level is that the statements, or the principles they represent, are so abstract as to lead students off on nonproductive tangents. Of course that's possible, but experience suggests otherwise. The teacher who has a clear sense of the concepts and principles to be developed in a given segment of the curriculum will find them being expressed in the applied level guide in one form or another. As students discuss the statements and find support for them in the text and in their own experiences, they are involved in the content objective of the lesson. The teacher structures the material and, if the principles expressed in the statements are not reflective of the content being studied, the teacher need only edit them to make them more appropriate. No doubt, discussion time spent on statements of principles produces greater learning than an equivalent time spent in the memorization of a set of details. (Of course, that would depend on the criterion used—if the test measures details, learning how to deal with concepts and principles will not be particularly helpful. But more of that in Chapter 10.)

A related objection comes from teachers who believe their subject areas are not sufficiently "philosophical" to support a productive discussion of statements at the applied level. Teachers in math and science, as well as some of the career-education-curriculum areas, sometimes express this opinion. However, experience suggests that broad generalizations, or broad principles, are not the exclusive domain of literature or social science. Both the content being studied and the experiences students are having in our society deal with important principles of science and math, for example. When teachers identify these broad generalizations and principles beforehand and construct their lesson material accordingly, they will find a truly legitimate connection between the course content and students' experience. Chapter 7 discusses this point in more detail; illustrative materials demonstrate the potential for a variety of subject areas.

### Identification of Levels of Comprehension

This book presents a variety of ways to help teachers help students become better readers of content-area materials in the subjects taught in elementary and secondary schools. This particular chapter has dealt with a specific construct of comprehension, has provided an example of its application for you to experience, and has explained its rationale. Before you design materials based on this construct for your own students in your own subject, it would be useful for you to engage in two kinds of reinforcing practice. The first is presented in this section; the second in the following section.

This section is a logical follow-up to your experience with levels of comprehension. In that presentation you experienced this approach to comprehension as part of a lesson and discovered how it could guide your reading and reasoning about the content of a particular reading selection. In this section, you are being asked to examine a series of statements that were drawn from a three-level guide designed to accompany a particular reading selection. They are not organized by level but are randomly mixed, having been drawn from all three levels and placed in a single list. As you consider each statement as a response to the reading selection it is related to, decide what level of comprehension it represents. On the numbered line before each statement, indicated your decision by placing $L$ if the statement seems to be at the literal level of comprehension, $I$ if it is at the interpretive level, and $A$ if it is at the applied. Do this for each statement. Then compare your responses with colleagues in your group. Where you have differences, determine what they are, how they are supported, and whether you can resolve them. Where you have similarities, double-check the evidence to confirm the basis of this consensus.

Before you begin this activity, however, there are two more things you need. One of these is very obvious; to other, less so.

The obvious need is the reading passage. Unless you judge the statements in relation to the reading selection, it is almost impossible to determine which level of comprehension some statements represent. Therefore, the reading selection follows immediately after the next paragraph. After you read that paragraph and carefully consider the idea it presents, then read the selection in preparation for identifying the level of comprehension to which each statement belongs. Remember that this activity will provide experiential background in determining levels of comprehension, background that will ultimately prepare you to develop your own materials for your own students.

The not-so-obvious need is to know the content objective for the lesson in which this reading selection was being used. Establishing the overall concept to be stressed in teaching the content of a reading selection is an essential first step in the preparation of a three-level guide. Unless one knows what is to be taught, it is difficult to identify the essential information to be stressed at the literal level, to formulate the supporting ideas from that information for the interpretive level, and to develop at the applied level the generalizations which are consistent with and supportive of the content objective of the lesson. Knowing the overall concept being stressed will help you see the part it plays in the development of three-level guides. Also it will help you in the identification process which follows.

The overall concept drawn from the reading selection and stressed by the three-level guide was: Man's survival instincts are strong and he will find ways to overcome adversity no matter what form it takes.

Here's the reading selection. Read it first with this concept in mind.

# NEW LIFE FOR A DYING TOWN*

Craigsville, Virginia, was a little town with a big problem. Craigsville was dying.

Until the late 1960s, the only important industry in Craigsville was a large cement factory. Many of the townspeople worked there. But the cement factory began to run into trouble. The factory owners began to lose money. They closed the factory down. Suddenly, many people were out of work. What could they do? Where would they find new jobs?

Many of the unemployed workers had to travel as far as one hundred miles away to find new jobs. Although they wanted to live in Craigsville, they had no choice. They had to live close to their jobs. Soon, more and more workers and their families began to move away as they found new jobs in other places.

Everyone who stayed in Craigsville suffered when their neighbors left. Some stores had to close because they did not have enough customers. The movie theater closed. So did the railroad station. Craigsville was dying. People wondered what they could do to bring their town back to life.

"Garbage is our only hope," announced the mayor. And it was garbage that brought Craigsville its new life. The townspeople voted to convert the old cement factory into a garbage recycling center. "We can put up with a little smell if it means saving our town," said one resident. Many neighbors agreed.

Today, garbage is shipped from nearby towns and cities to Craigsville. The recycling plant turns this garbage into useful products, such as fertilizer and large solid blocks used for landfill. Some people doubt whether the project will work. But Craigsville now has a major industry again and her citizens have jobs. Craigsville is once again alive and well.

Many small towns in America face the same problem that nearly ruined Craigsville. Many people in Roundup, Montana, had worked for years in nearby coal mines. Then the mines ran out of coal and shut down. The people of Roundup felt hopeless until the high school principal studied the old mines. He found out that they were ideal for growing mushrooms. Today, the new companies are making a good profit by growing and selling mushrooms. Many former miners are making a good living again by working for the mushroom growers.

A country—or a town—can never really stand still. As people's needs change, industry and jobs must change too. Sometimes these changes hurt people by affecting their way of life or by leaving them jobless. Big cities offer many different jobs to the people who live there. But many people do not want to leave their homes in small towns. They like to know their neighbors, and say hello as they pass on the street. These people are working hard to keep the small town an important part of American life. They are learning new skills through job training. They are finding ways of helping their home towns to keep up with the changing times.

*Reprinted by permission from *GO Reading in the Content Areas* by Harold L. Herber, © 1973, 1974 by Scholastic Magazines, Inc.

Now, study each statement carefully and identify the level of comprehension it represents in reference to this reading selection. Use the coding system described earlier in this section.

_____ 1. Craigsville started a new industry.

_____ 2. The cement factory was losing money.

_____ 3. The mines in Roundup shut down.

_____ 4. The mayor of Craigsville liked garbage.

_____ 5. Industry changes as people's needs change.

_____ 6. It is hard to live if you do not have money.

_____ 7. Growing and selling mushrooms became a new way to earn a living in Roundup.

_____ 8. The people who moved away from Craigsville suffered as much as the people who stayed.

_____ 9. Many people in town had no job.

_____ 10. Change can hurt but it doesn't have to.

_____ 11. Craigsville has changed.

_____ 12. Some people in small towns are learning new skills.

_____ 13. The town was dying.

_____ 14. Some people would rather leave a problem than try to solve it.

_____ 15. Craigsville was at one time a dying town.

_____ 16. Something that is a problem for one may be a solution for another.

_____ 17. Some people like living in small towns.

_____ 18. Families began to move away.

_____ 19. Towns that lose their industries have to change or die.

_____ 20. Man's ingenuity insures his survival.

When you discuss your decisions with your group, draw on the explanation and rationale for levels of comprehension you studied prior to this activity. This will reinforce your understanding of the levels, their purpose, their function, their interrelationships. Of course, you will also want to refer to the reading selection for evidence to support your decisions on the level you assigned to each of the statements.

After your group has discussed its decisions about the statements, you might want to compare the group consensus with the following opinions.

**Literal level statements** Statements 1, 2, 3, 5, 7, 9, 12, 13, 17, and 18 are literal. No doubt you had strong differences of opinion on some of these. Only 18 is literally literal, in that it is a word-for-word duplication of what is in the reading selection; but even so, it draws from only part of a whole sentence, not the entire sentence itself. Statements 1 and 7 probably could be classified as borderline—either literal or interpretive depending on the competence of the reader. Statement 1 paraphrases the information presented in paragraphs 5 and 6. To a poor reader who has problems deriving basic information from a reading selection, such a statement would be interpretive. It requires the reader to put together information from several places in the text, even though the statement is only a restatement of that information with no interpretation of its meaning. To a poor reader, supporting the statement would be similar to what one does at the interpretive level. On the other hand, if the reader is reasonably skilled, a statement such as 1 would be literal since it is merely a recasting of information without change of meaning. If you were arguing that to be "literal," a statement must be a word-for-word duplication of the information in the text, then you would be correct in labeling it interpretive. If, on the other hand, you were arguing that paraphrasing or translating of information is also literal, so long as you are still just conveying information without interpretation, then you would be correct in labeling this statement literal. Obviously the recommended designation of this statement as literal indicates a leaning toward the more liberal definition of the word.

Experience has shown that flexibility in the concept of literal and interpretive is necessary if the needs of students functioning across a broad range of achievement levels are to be served. But in your real world of teaching, when you make use of guides for levels of comprehension, you needn't worry about such distinctions insofar as they would cause problems for your students. PLEASE NOTE: You would *not* do with your own students what you are now doing with these statements. That is, you would *not* ask them to identify the levels of comprehension a set of statements represent. *They* do not need to study the differences among the levels, but *you* do. *They* do not need to learn how to develop three-level guides, but *you* do. You are doing this because you must have a full understanding of the differences among the levels of comprehension so that you can guide your own students' reading. Well-constructed guides will give them the feeling of the total comprehension process, and that is the purpose of their use. Your students will experience the guides as you did when you read the selection on *Seagulls*. To repeat: Do not ask them to go through this step of assigning statements to levels. Your purpose is to teach them to *comprehend*, not *about comprehension*.

One of the reasons for giving you statements which could be either literal or interpretive, depending on the achievement levels of the students, is to help you become aware that such a variance does exist and can be accommodated. When you prepare your own guides for levels of comprehension, you will take into account the students who will be using them. If they are poor readers, you will develop statements for the literal level that are literally literal. Experience with such statements will build the students' confidence; based on that confidence you will be able to move them along to more sophisticated responses. But if they are reasonably good readers, needing help in attending to detail, you will probably want to prepare statements which are more like translations or paraphrasing for the literal level.

In either case, whether absolutely literal or a paraphrasing, the statements you would create for the other two levels would be consistent in their sophistication. As a consequence, in either case, the guide for all three levels of comprehension would help students develop a sense of the full process of comprehension. And, of course, that is its purpose.

To return to the analysis of the statements designated as literal, Statement 7 is much like Statement 1 in that it falls in this grey area, depending on the achievement level of the reader. The discussion presented with reference to Statement 1 could be applied to Statement 7 equally well. Based on the broader definition of literal and according to the considerations discussed previously, Statement 1 was designated literal.

The rest of the statements designated as literal are translations of a reasonably obvious nature; they require little, if any, pulling together of information for rephrasing. Statement 2, for example, says the factory was losing money; the text says the owners were. To a person sophisticated in economics and with a knowledge of corporate law, this statement could have interesting implications as it is contrasted with the text. To the rest of us, however, the statement says the same thing as the text and so seems literal.

Statement 5 is an interesting one. Reading it without reference to the selection, one could be almost certain that it is an interpretive statement. Examined in light of the text itself, one finds that it is a rephrasing of the second sentence of the last paragraph rather than a conclusion drawn from the incidents presented in the story. And yet, it is a conclusion drawn from the incidents presented in the selection, but because the *authors* drew the conclusion and presented it in the reading selection itself, its perception requires literal comprehension rather than interpretive. When the reader justifies his acceptance of that statement when it appears in a guide, he finds it so stated in the text, and, therefore, it's literal comprehension. But were you to ask the student to justify the authors' conclusion as presented in that paragraph with evidence from the entire selection, it would turn the statement into interpretive level.

Confusing and complicated? Not once you develop a sense of the purpose and operation of each of the levels, how they relate to one another, and how their operation depends on the content of the materials to which they are related.

**Interpretive level statements** Statements 4, 8, 11, 15, and 19 are interpretive, with 11 and 15 being *conclusions* that can be drawn from the evidence presented in the selection. Statements 4 and 8 are *inferences* one can draw when all the information is put together. "Liking" has many dimensions and a mayor probably would like anything that helped his town and its people survive. Similarly, "suffering" has many dimensions and degrees of intensity. Being forced to move out of a town they loved could well be a form of suffering equal to that experienced by those who remained through all the deprivation.

Statement 19 might have caused problems, with some people believing that this statement more properly belongs to the applied level than to the interpretive. Recall that the purpose of the interpretive level statements is to help the reader perceive the authors' meaning as constructed out of the information provided to the reader. Statements that guide the reader at the interpretive level of comprehension should be broad enough to encompass a combination of information presented in the text but narrow enough to clearly relate to the specific content or topic dealt with by the author. Statement 19 really meets these criteria. It is specific to the content of the reading selection, mentioning towns and industries, but broad enough to present an idea implicit in the incidents cited. When students decide if that statement is reasonable, given the information in the selection, and then justify their acceptance of the statement with information from the selection as supporting evidence, they are experiencing the process of interpretation.

**Applied level statements** Items 6, 10, 14, 16, and 20 are applied level statements. All have some bearing on the overall concept identified as the focus for the study of this selection. Each expresses a principle which is specific enough to be applied to the content of the reading selection and at the same time is broad enough to encompass other instances of man's drive for survival in the face of adversity. The reader, drawing from both sources, can justify the reasonableness of these statements and thus experience reading at the applied level of comprehension.

## PRODUCTION OF A GUIDE
## FOR LEVELS OF COMPREHENSION

The next step in the development of your skills in using levels of comprehension to enhance your students' reading competence is to develop a levels guide. For this activity, work together with your colleagues as you create the statements for each of the levels.

The passage for which you are to create the levels guide is on page 57. Probably only one group of participants will really be satisfied with this passage since it is a reading selection from a science text. Obviously it would be better if there were a separate passage for each subject area so that all participants would be learning on material they teach. However, there is not sufficient room in this book to accommodate everyone in this fashion. So, experience is provided through a common reading selection, this time related to science. You will have ample opportunity to apply your understanding to materials from your own subject area.

The purpose of this activity is for you now to apply what you have learned about the development of guides for levels of comprehension. There are several things you must keep in mind and do as you prepare your own three-level guide and subsequently compare it with the one that appears in Appendix A.

### Analyze Content

Establishing content objectives for the reading selection is an important preliminary step. A thorough discussion of the purpose, value, and procedures related to content analysis is presented in Chapter 9. It is important to note here, however, that before you can prepare material to guide students' understanding of a particular segment of your curriculum and the reading selections related to that segment, you have to establish in your own mind exactly what it is you want your students to learn.

Now, this admonition probably is very obvious to you. On the other hand, you may not realize that many lessons are taught and many assignments given by teachers who have *not* thought through clearly what it is they want their students to learn from the experience.

In any case, for *this* experience, please do the following: (1) read through the selection carefully and decide what the broad principle(s) is (are) or what general understanding could be taught through the study of the content of the material presented; (2) examine the material to identify the information that is essential to the development of that understanding; this is the information you will express as statements in the literal-level guide; (3) look for how the information you have selected fits together and for the ideas that come to mind as you consider the relationships; these are the ideas you express as statements in the interpretive-level guide; (4) examine the ideas you have expressed in the interpretive-level guide and think about other ideas that relate to the overall principle established for the central purpose of the lesson; expressions of ideas that come to mind as you consider the two sets of ideas will constitute statements for the applied-level guide.

### Use Declarative Statements

You may have noticed that in the guides for the two previous activities, no questions were used; only declarative statements were included. There is a very important reason for that, which is explained in detail in Chapter 8. But a brief comment about it is in order here.

What we are trying to do is to give students the feeling of what it is like to comprehend at each of these levels. The statements in the guide for each level really are the product of comprehension at that level. They were created by someone comprehending at that level and writing down the product of that comprehension as a set of declarative statements.

Think about the interpretive level as an example of this. Students determine the acceptability or reasonableness or appropriateness of a statement at this level and then cite evidence to support the determination. When they do this they are going through almost the same interpretive process as did the person who created the statements in the first place. The obvious difference is that they are reacting to the interpretation rather than creating it. As they find support for or against the interpretation they are reacting to, they are developing a feeling for the process of interpretation. The same holds true for the literal and applied levels.

If you are conditioned to always asking students questions about what they have read, writing statements may cause you problems. It may be satisfying to you for the moment if you ask *yourself*, rather than your students, the following questions as you prepare the statements for each of the levels as suggested above.

As you consider what to include in the literal-level guide, ask *yourself*, "What is the essential information? What important things did the author say?" The answers to those questions can become the items for the literal-level guide when written as declarative statements.

As you consider what to include in the interpretive-level guide, ask *yourself*, "What ideas is the author trying to communicate through all of this information? What does he mean by what he says?" The answers to those questions can become the items for the interpretive-level guide when written as declarative statements.

As you consider what to include in the applied-level guide, ask *yourself*, "What broad principles are illustrated both by the content of this selection and by other ideas I have already encountered? How can I synthesize the author's ideas with my own?" The answers to those questions can become the items for the applied-level guide when written as declarative statements.

### Apply the Process

Now you are ready to try your hand at developing your own three-level guide. Use the following reading selection for that purpose. When you have finished, compare your guide with the one in Appendix A. With your colleagues, discuss the differences and similarities between your guide and the one presented in this book and the possible reasons for these differences. You will find the rest of the chapter more productive and understandable if you complete this activity first. Go ahead and develop your guide; the rest of the chapter will be here when you finish! Be sure to compare your guide with the one in Appendix A.

### *USING A PUSH FOR A BRAKE**

A small spacecraft carries astronauts down onto the moon. This spacecraft is called a lunar module—LM for short. It looks like a big, heavy metal box with legs. It doesn't fly, like an airplane—it really just falls!

*From the "How Things Work" volume of *Childcraft—The How and Why Library*. © 1976 Field Enterprises Educational Corporation.

The LM falls from a bigger spacecraft, called the command module. It falls toward the moon faster than a jet plane flies!

But the LM must slow down to land. If it hit the moon at full speed, the astronauts would probably be killed. Even if they lived through the crash, they would never be able to get off the moon.

How can the astronauts land the LM?

They can't land it like an airplane. An airplane's wings only work in air, and there is no air on the moon. They can't float the LM down on a parachute for the same reason. A parachute can't work where there is no air. But they can use a push for a brake!

As the LM nears the moon, a powerful rocket engine is turned on. A blast of fiery gas shoots out of the bottom of the LM. The force of this blast pushes up as well as down. You can see for yourself how this works. Blow up a toy balloon and let go of it. The balloon will sail away. When the air pushes out in one direction, the balloon is pushed in the opposite direction.

So, when the fiery blast from the LM's rocket engine shoots down, it pushes the LM up. This upward push acts as a brake. As the engine keeps keeps firing, the LM falls more and more slowly. Finally, it lands on the moon with nothing more than a bump!

## VARIATIONS IN THE APPLICATION
## OF LEVELS OF COMPREHENSION

One of the problems posed in Chapter 2 was that of finding some application of the reading process that would serve the needs of students across a range of ability and achievement, across a range of subject areas and grade levels, and across a range of media. Levels of comprehension, applied to printed materials or even audio-visual materials through the use of levels guides, seems to be that process. That's a very strong statement, implying that the panacea for all reading ills finally has been found. The claim is not *that* strong, of course, because its usefulness depends on its application and that will vary from teacher to teacher and from student to student. However, the potential is there, and when teachers from a given faculty of a school combine their efforts first to learn the process through staff development programs and then to apply the process consistently in their own classes, then the reading needs of their students are met across this whole range of variables.

To accommodate the demands of all these variables, it is necessary to provide for variation in the basic construct of levels of comprehension. In this section of the chapter are presented a series of variations that have been found useful and necessary in order to meet these needs.

### Variations for Subject Matter

You already have seen guides for levels of comprehension as applied to reading selections in social studies ("New Life for a Dying Town") and science ("Using a Push for a Brake"). You have seen that the process of comprehension is essentially the same when applied to the reading selections through the use of the accompanying guides. This contrasts markedly with many opinions expressed in the literature on reading instruction in content areas. There are those who believe that material in each subject area requires a set of reading skills quite different from other subject areas. In contrast, as explained earlier, the levels-of-comprehension construct shows that the adjustments necessary for successful reading of material across subject areas have to do with differences in the content of the material more than with differences in the skills implicit in that material.

However, certain adaptations in the levels-of-comprehension construct have been found necessary for materials which are brief, precise, compact, and full of detail. Word problems in mathematics, lab experiments in science, recipes in home economics, and directions and patterns in industry-related writing are examples of such material.

*Word problems in math* are a constant headache to math teachers. It seems that most students can do the computations once they extract from the word problem what they are to do and what information they are computing. But that's precisely the problem: how to help them find out what goes into the problem and what operations should be applied.

In speculating on how levels of comprehension should be applied to the reading of word problems in math, it seemed clear that the literal level is important and appropriate. The reader must identify, in detail, the significant information in the problem. This information includes not only the factors that comprise the problem and the numerals related to those factors (such as six cows or two houses or eight records or one stereo) but also the operations to be applied to the numerals and factors (such as addition, subtraction, percent, estimation). So, literal level is literal level, in math as elsewhere. A sample word problem with an illustrative, literal-level guide is presented in Appendix A on page 256.

Statements at the interpretive level caused a problem in math. As applied to expository or narrative material, the interpretive level develops a sense of the author's meaning by drawing conclusions or inferences from the information presented. But in math word problems, what meaning can you derive? What inferences can be drawn from information about numbers of cows or records or stereos? The authors of word problems are not concerned about conveying a message; therefore, there is no "meaning" to comprehend. Clearly the concept of interpretive level of comprehension had to be adjusted to suit the needs imposed by the nature of the word problems.

After some speculation an answer to the problem seemed to emerge. True, ideas and meaning are not implicit in the content of the word problems. However, *ideas about mathematics* are implicit in the problems. It seemed reasonable to believe that solving a set of word problems would involve the application of specific principles and concepts in mathematics. That being true, it also seemed reasonable to think that it would be useful to construct a guide which would help students "interpret" the word problem in light of the mathematical concepts and principles which were operating as the problem was being solved. The interpretive-level guide for the sample word problem is also presented in Appendix A.

Speculation on how to adapt the interpretive level of comprehension for word problems in math carried over, naturally enough, to the applied level. The substance of word problems in math usually does not warrant the production and/or exploration of broad principles about life's values, opportunities, and obligations. It seemed clear that a modification in the applied level had to be made for word problems in math. The result of that decision was a redefinition of "applied" to mean simulating an application of the mathematical operations necessary to solve the problem. As you will note in the illustrative, applied-level guide for the math problem you have examined in Appendix A, the alternative statements for students to consider are expressions of how the problem might be solved. Students go through the alternatives and select the ones they believe valid. Usually several can be checked. Students must be able to justify their decisions with evidence drawn from their knowledge of mathematics.

The application of these three levels of comprehension to the word problem reinforces students' understanding of mathematics, which presumably is the purpose of having them do the problem. But that's not all. This procedure also provides direct, guided experience in learning how to read word problems. Students learn how to identify the important details in the problem, how to determine which math operations are appropriate, and how to determine which mathematical principles are being applied. Close work with math teachers over a considerable period of time has confirmed this observation over and over.

You probably have noted that the order among the levels in the illustrative guide for math in the Appendix is different from the order in guides for other subject areas. That change of order also came out of the speculation about the application of levels of comprehension to word problems in math. It was supported by formal studies conducted by Riley (1976) and by informal studies conducted by math teachers in District 11 in the Bronx during the 1975/77 school years.

It seemed logical that the order among the levels as redefined for word problems should be literal, applied, interpretive, rather than literal, interpretive, applied. Starting with the literal was sensible and necessary because the students need first to acquire the essential information which comprises the problem. The next logical step is the simulated operations for solving the problem. Consideration of the mathematical concepts and principles illustrated by the problem seems more the final step; therefore, the interpretive level is placed last.

Riley's pilot study confirmed the logic of this speculation and supported the literal-applied-interpretive (as redefined) order over the original literal-interpretive-applied order. Data on his main study did not show significant differences, but a tendency favoring this reordering was evident and, taken with the evidence from the previous study, seemed to support this procedure for mathematics. Moreover, experience with the math teachers in District 11 in the

Bronx supported this reordering; they also added other variations that seemed useful.

The math teachers who used these guides in their own classes suggested one other modification. They found it tedious and unproductive to have students respond to an interpretive level guide, as redefined, for *every* word problem read. They suggested that the guides for the literal and applied levels be prepared and used with each of several word problems which are similar in their mathematical requirements. A guide for the interpretive level can be prepared, which deals with generalizations and concepts about the mathematics illustrated by the entire set of problems. The math teachers found that this gave more meaning to the interpretive level of comprehension for word problems and the students were able to see more clearly the presence and operation of the generalizations in the problems with which they had worked.

This same variation in the use of the levels-of-comprehension construct can be applied to similar kinds of reading, such as lab experiments, recipes, and directions for construction.

## Variation in Order Among Levels

Although no data is available to confirm it, observation of both students and teachers in their response to the use of the three-level guide suggests that some people prefer to start with the applied level, then go to the literal and interpretive. Others seem to prefer starting with the applied level, going to the interpretive, then to the literal. Others seem to prefer starting with the literal, going to the interpretive, then to the applied, as the levels were originally intended and used. The differences probably have to do with preferences in "cognitive processing." You might want to experiment with varying the order in which you have your students go through the levels of comprehension.

Carl Frederiksen (1976) makes reference to differences among students in their preferences for "bottom-up" reasoning versus "top-down" reasoning. He indicated that some readers prefer to deal with the overall generalizations first, reinforcing them with details and ideas drawn from the passage and elsewhere. Others prefer to build logically toward the generalizations, first noting the detail (literal), then developing ideas and a sense of the author's meaning (interpretive) before trying to deal with the broad generalizations. The teacher's own teaching style and the students' own learning styles dictate the preferences. Generally, the "bottom-up" sequence has been useful; but you may want to explore variations for your students and yourself.

## Grade-Level Accommodations

If our educational programs are working properly, the concepts our students study will steadily increase in sophistication as they progress through the grades. Most educators would agree that this occurs.

That being true, it is logical to assume that information sources used to help students build those concepts also increase in sophistication through the grades. Students must become increasingly sophisticated in the application of their reading skills. Common educational experience confirms the logic.

Two concerns flow from this increasing sophistication of course content and reading process. The first concern is that students be taught *how* to deal with the new level of sophistication that they encounter at each grade. That is the purpose of this book: to communicate to teachers how to communicate the "how" to their students.

The second concern has already been expressed in this chapter and in Chapter 2: the need to realize that the reading process remains essentially the same across this range of sophistication. As Bruner (1960) suggests, the differences in intellectual endeavors across age, grade, and sophistication levels are differences in degree, not in kind. That is, the kind of reading process applied by a twelfth grader in science is essentially the same as that applied by a fourth grader in science. The degree of sophistication with which it is applied is different for each because of differences in the students' maturity and because of the complexity of the materials to which the process is being applied. But the process remains essentially the same.

Rather than establishing a new set of reading skills for successive grade levels, one can keep the same basic set of processes (levels of comprehension, for example) as a common tool across grade levels.

Thus there is a vertical transformation of the levels-of-comprehension construct across grade levels. Examination of the sample guides for levels of comprehension designed for use in various grade levels, (Appendix B) will illustrate this point.

As a faculty develops competence in teaching students how to read the required subject-area materials across the grades, they will find their students becoming more competent in handling such materials than they imagined possible. That is reasonable. If at each grade level the teachers make an effort to teach their students how to read what they are required to read, and if they use essentially the same process across the grades as well as across the subjects, then surely the students ultimately will be able to apply that process on their own.

### Variations for Individual Differences

The first edition of this book made the point that true and absolute individualization of instruction in content areas is almost impossible to achieve. Only if one has sophisticated materials and equipment, as well as a group of aides to assist in monitoring students and material, is fully individualized instruction possible. Since few content-area teachers have such support, truly individualized instruction is rare—though many schools purport to have an individualized program.

The first edition of this text also made the point, however, that individual-ization of instruction can be approximated, even though it cannot be fully achieved. To accomplish this, the text suggested that the levels-of-comprehension construct be used as follows: Identify in a given class students who are relatively poor readers and place them in one group. Place the best readers in a second group. Place the in-between readers in a third group. Then, with all students reading the same passage from the text, guide the poorest readers with a literal-level guide, the in-between readers with an interpretive-level guide, and the best readers with an applied-level guide. After each group has completed its work and discussed it, have them present their findings to the rest of the class so that, ultimately, all students are exposed to what everyone else did, and they learn the totality of the content.

Although that seemed to work and helped approximate individualized instruction, subsequent experience and experiments have shown rather clearly that such grouping was not as productive as having students randomly grouped and having all students read at all three levels of comprehension. When you analyze the revised grouping, you will find that nothing is lost in the approximation of individualized instruction.

Randomly assigning students to groups is relatively simple. You can have students count off by numbers (for example, by sixes if you have thirty in a class and want five students in each group), then have all the "ones" form one group, the "twos" a second group, and so on. The random grouping makes it probable that each group will have a range of ability, achievement, interest, motivation, knowledge, and experience that reflects the range for the entire class.

As you progress through the lesson, each group works together at each of the levels of comprehension, helping one another as they respond to the guide materials for the text. At the literal level, better readers help poorer readers as they need the help in identifying words and in confirming information. Experience has shown repeatedly that poorer readers also help better readers at the literal level by forcing a more careful reading of the material. Whereas the better readers might cover the material superficially, the poorer readers often attend to the detail and correct the better readers. This does not happen too many times before the better readers become aware of it and adjust their reading. But by then the better readers have developed a new respect for the poorer readers, the gap between them has narrowed, and there is a greater willingness to work together.

The greatest advantage of using all three levels with randomly assigned groups is that it gives poorer readers opportunity to deal with the interpretive and applied levels of comprehension. Once they have been exposed to the information, they can reason about that information and respond to the statements in the guide with intelligent insight. Many poorer readers have been exposed to experiences outside of school which are foreign to the better readers, and thus they bring insights to the applied level of comprehension, which are

instructive to the better readers. Merely because a student has difficulty reading
at the literal level, it does not necessarily follow that the student will have
difficulty reading at the interpretive and applied levels of comprehension. Poor
readers should not be cut off from instruction at the higher levels of comprehension. This procedure insures that they will not be; the other procedure almost
insured that they would be.

It is interesting that when guides for levels of comprehension are properly
developed and used with students in randomly assigned groups, there is an
almost automatic accommodation of those materials to the needs of individuals
within the groups. This individualization comes from the students themselves,
from their own abilities and experiences and insights, particularly at the interpretive and applied levels. It's almost an "automatic leveling" process. Because
of diverse experiences and insight, one student may infer meaning from a selection while another student without that background may not see the point at
all. Two people respond to the same material, but at different sophistication
levels; each learns from the other. It is not necessary to give each person a
separate set of materials to accommodate individual needs.

For essentially the same reason, experience has shown that in the development of guides for the interpretive and applied levels of comprehension, one
need not spend time devising "distractors" to insert among the "acceptable"
statements. Frequently students find ample justification for accepting statements which a teacher has included as distractors and, at the same time, cite
evidence for rejecting statements which the teacher has included as potentially
acceptable. As long as the task is to determine the acceptability of the statements and to establish the evidence for their decisions, then the comprehension
process implicit in the guides is being experienced; whether distractors are
accepted or not is of little importance. The *process* is what's important. Using
distractors is reverting to the old "right-wrong" mentality. The task is *not* to
identify the *right* statements; rather, it is to find evidence supporting both
decisions to accept and decisions to reject. Since different people find different
reasons, there is more room for developing personal insight than with the absoluteness of "right-wrong" responses.

Obviously this requires the instructional environment discussed in Chapter
2, created by teachers who are viewed as colearners by their students. The
teachers will usually have the advantage of more content-related knowledge and
experience, of course, but not always. And so teachers learn from the students
and students from the teachers. Student responses to the guides are not attempts
to feed back "what the teacher has in mind" nor give "what is on the answer
key," but to tell "what makes sense to me" and "here is the evidence for my
view."

Now, as you think of your real world, you may say that having all students
respond to all three levels of comprehension will not work. And you will think
the author is another impractical professor. Not so; it works, if *you* try it and if
*you* make it work. Students have to learn how to work with one another in

their groups to make the time together productive; and you may have to study how to form the groups, how to work with the students as they are in their groups, etc. Refer to Chapter 8 for specific suggestions about grouping and guiding students.

Your real-world perceptions may suggest a variation in the literal-level guide. If your students are indeed having great trouble reading at the literal level, you may need to work with the entire class just on that level for a short while. You can accommodate the range among the students at this comprehension level by providing statements across a range of sophistication. Some might be "literally literal," exactly word for word. Others might be paraphrasings— almost a summary, but without interpretation or changed meanings. Still others might be translations, putting essentially the same information into words that are closer to the readers' listening and speaking vocabulary (refer to the lesson on "Freedom," pages 183-86, for an example). As the students in a group go through the range of statements, each student responds to those he can handle with reasonable ease, but at the same time he learns from the work of others who respond to different items.

This is an extension of the "automatic leveling" process referred to earlier. It is not insulting to the student, because he seeks out the level of sophistication most appropriate; and, besides, everyone in the class—including the student— knows how well he reads. As long as the teacher does not try to cover up differences, nobody is embarrassed and no one minds. After students have completed the literal-level guide designed in this fashion, then all move to the interpretive- and the applied-level guides, which are of the same type as previously discussed. Collectively and across the range at the literal level, the students have encountered and apprehended the essential information and are prepared to search through it for meaning and to relate it to other concepts and experiences.

## Variations for Other Media

Comprehension is not restricted solely to printed materials. The comprehension process described in this text is as applicable to film or audio tapes as it is to printed texts. These two media present information, as does print. The media vary in how that information is presented, but the differences in processing the information for each medium are minimal. One can respond to film and tapes at the interpretive and applied levels just as one does to print, but the literal-level guide must be used differently, because the literal-level statements cannot easily be confirmed without rerunning the tapes or film. Since rerunning is often not practical, two procedures can be used.

The literal-level guide can be used as a checklist when viewing the film or listening to the tape. The guide is distributed to students before listening or viewing. Together, students review the statements in the guide to familiarize themselves with the information presented. Then, as they listen to the tape or view the film, they follow along with the guide and check those statements that present information contained in the tape or film. When they have completed the guide, they compare notes with others in their group. If there are serious differences, they may want to review the source; however, in most cases students from other groups as well as the teacher can serve as arbiters to resolve the differences. Once the students have completed their discussion of the literal-level guide, they can proceed to the next two levels of comprehension and deal with them as they would if the medium were print.

Another use of the literal-level guide with film or tape is as a predictor or hypothesizer. The teacher and students review what they have covered in their study of the topic so far. The topic of the film or tape is given and perhaps a synopsis as well. The teacher then leads the students in hypothesizing about what the author of the tape or the film logically should present about that topic. The literal-level guide is set up so as to direct this hypothesizing. Each statement contains information that the producer of the film or tape might possibly present. The students check those they believe they will actually encounter as they view the film or listen to the tape. They discuss their hypotheses or predictions with others in their group, citing the reasons for their predictions and attempting to resolve differences, or at least to clarify them. Then, as the tape is played or the film run, the students circle the numbers for those statements which represent information actually presented. They have a record of the accuracy of their predictions, and they can speculate on the reasons for differences, if any, that occurred between the predictions and the reality. They can then proceed to discuss guide materials for the interpretive and applied levels of comprehension, which are the same as for the printed medium.

All of this, of course, assumes that films and tapes are used in the classroom for other than filler and entertainment. In a study which employed the levels-of-comprehension construct with film, Thelen (1970) found that students apparently were not used to having films used instructionally; they thought of them more as entertainment. She found that when films were used for instruction in the classroom, even though students' achievement in the subject improved, their attitudes toward films became negative. You can draw your own conclusions from that.

## ALTERNATE CONSTRUCTS

You may want to compare the levels of comprehension presented in this text with other definitions of comprehension. If so, read this section. If not, go on to the summary and the end-of-chapter activities.

Gray (1960) described the comprehension process in terms that closely parallel the three levels of comprehension presented in this chapter. He said that comprehension involves: (1) reading the lines, (2) reading between the lines, (3) reading beyond the lines. The relationship between these three phases of comprehension and the literal, interpretive, and applied levels of comprehension seems clear. Indeed, as reported by Robinson (1966), Gray believed that comprehension

> includes, first, the literal meaning, that is, understanding what the author has said; and second, the implied meanings, that is, understanding what the author meant by the word sequences he used. The third aspect of comprehension is concerned with the significance of the communication, including an assessment of the author's purpose, frame of reference, assumptions, and generalizations.

There is also a relationship between Gray's model for reading and the levels-of-comprehension construct. Gray's model of reading included four major categories: (1) word perception; (2) comprehension; (3) reaction; (4) assimilation. Word perception has to do with identifying words and understanding their meanings. Comprehension, as he viewed it, already has been identified as a three-phase process. Reaction involved the application of judgment so as to evaluate what was comprehended. Finally, assimilation involved a synthesis or integration of what had been acquired from the reading with previously acquired, related ideas and experiences. What this comparison suggests is a precedent for operationally defining comprehension so broadly that it almost parallels a definition of the total act of reading. Except for the first category, word perception (its equivalent is covered in Chapter 6 of this book), the remaining categories have a close similarity to the three phases of comprehension as explained by Gray. His "reading the lines" could parallel the category of comprehension in his total model; his "reading between the lines" could parallel the category of reaction in his total model; and his "reading beyond the lines" could parallel the category of assimilation in his total model.

Consider this, then: the literal level of comprehension, as defined in this book, is parallel to at least the first aspect of comprehension as defined by Gray. The interpretive level of comprehension, as defined in this book, is parallel not only to the second aspect of comprehension as defined by Gray but also to the third category of his reading model, since the interpretive process does indeed require the kinds of activity included in what he calls reaction. Finally, the applied level of comprehension, as defined in this book, is parallel not only to the third aspect of comprehension as defined by Gray but also to the fourth category of his reading model, since the applied-level process does indeed require the kinds of activity included in what he calls assimilation.

This suggests, then, that when one guides student comprehension through the use of the levels, having preceded that instruction with preparatory emphasis on vocabulary acquisition as described in Chapter 6, the instruction has encompassed the whole reading process. Simplifying reading instruction to make it manageable in this fashion does not shortchange students in any way. They learn to handle the materials they are required to read. This simplicity makes reading instruction more manageable by content-area teachers. It also enhances the applicability of the same reading process across subject areas at any given grade level and across grade levels within any given subject area.

The theoretical base for the levels-of-comprehension construct presented in this book is further supported by the work of Carl Frederiksen (1976). He views comprehension as a psycholinguist and presents what he calls five "processing levels in discourse comprehension." As Gray did in his reading model, Frederiksen includes language acquisition activites as part of his comprehension model, referring to two levels which would parallel Gray's category of word perception: (1) sensory processing and (2) graphic decoding. His last three levels clearly correspond to the three levels of comprehension presented in this book: syntactic processing, similar to the literal level; semantic interpretation, similar to the interpretive; inference, similar to the applied.

Honeycutt (1971) found support for the levels-of-comprehension construct presented in this book by comparing it with Bloom's Taxonomy of Educational Objectives: Cognitive Domain (1956). Having done a lot of work with educational (behavioral) objectives, you probably know that Bloom's taxonomy is a theoretical description of various phases, or aspects, of thinking with the elements arranged in an hierarchical format. Bloom describes six phases:

1. Knowledge: acquisition of facts, details, information
2. Comprehension: translation and interpretation
3. Application: putting concepts to use in a real setting
4. Analysis: breaking things down into component parts
5. Synthesis: putting things together and naming the relationship
6. Evaluation: making judgments according to some criteria.

In his study, Honeycutt found the following relationships between the three levels of comprehension and Bloom's levels of cognition:

Literal level: knowledge
Interpretive level: comprehension
Applied level: application; analysis; synthesis; evaluation

Again, the implications are clear. When one uses the levels-of-comprehension construct to guide students' reading of basic resource materials in the content areas, one is providing instruction in what theoreticians perceive to be the full range of students' cognitive activity. To repeat, merely because the process is simple to apply, one should not fear that students are being shortchanged. They are not; they receive the benefit of being guided through a full range of intellectual activity as they read and react to their text materials.

## SUMMARY

In Chapter 2 of this text several problems faced by content-area teachers were examined along with their possible solutions. Consider how your use of the concept and construct of levels of comprehension relates to those problems and solutions.

Through use of guides for levels of comprehension, students can read a text even though it is "too difficult" for them. They are shown how to read what they are required to read but have not yet learned to read independently. A range of differences across such variables as ability, achievement, and interests among students can be accommodated by combining intraclass grouping with the use of three-level guides. Students are actively involved in the learning process, not only accumulating information but also developing concepts and synthesizing them with prior knowledge and experience.

Since students do not have to try to guess what the teacher has in mind or what is on the answer key as they respond to statements in the guides, they are consistently discovering that their own ideas are important, accepted, and respected. They discover that their teacher learns *with* them and *from* them, too, even as they learn from their teacher. Co-learner describes both the teacher and students. The motivation stemming from this discovery has a constantly positive effect on their learning.

The levels-of-comprehension construct is manageable both for students and for teachers. It is simple for teachers to learn. As a reading process, it can be taught functionally within any content area, allowing the attainment of the delicate instructional balance between content and process.

Finally, it is a process which can be simulated, so that students actually experience it. Being guided in its application, they learn how it feels, how it works. But more about this last point later—after the discussion of another way to help students read their texts more efficiently and effectively.

\*   \*   \*   \*   \*   \*

## REACTION GUIDE

*Directions*: Listed below are fifteen statements which relate, in some way, to this chapter. Place a plus sign before each statement you believe expresses an idea which is implicitly or explicitly supported by this topic. Place a zero before each statement you believe expresses an idea rejected by this topic. Be ready to cite evidence from this chapter to support your opinion.

_____ 1. Connecting the expression of an idea to some information source requires less sophistication than creating an expression of an idea drawn from an information source.

_____ 2. There are levels of comprehension which, themselves, have levels of sophistication.

_____ 3. The reading needs of each student in a heterogenous group can be met when all in the group are guided in reading the same passage at each of the three levels of comprehension.

_____ 4. An interrelationship exists among the levels of comprehension, whether they are approached from the bottom up or from the top down.

_____ 5. Connecting information from a source to support an idea expressed as a declarative statement is a simulation of creating the expression of an idea drawn from the combination of information.

_____ 6. Concepts intrinsic to the information source (as they pertain to the levels-of-comprehension construct) maximize the information source and minimize prior knowledge and experience, while concepts extrinsic to the information source emphasize both the information source and the knowledge and experience.

_____ 7. Students can be taught how to comprehend without being taught what comprehension is.

_____ 8. Complexity favors the theoretician; simplicity, the practitioner.

_____ 9. In the application of the levels-of-comprehension construct across subject areas and grade levels, differences are more in degree than in kind.

_____ 10. Assuring students' success in learning a process and/or a concept is a teacher's most important obligation.

_____ 11. Guiding students' levels of response to a reading selection is more critically important to learning to read than controlling the level of difficulty at which the selection is written.

_____ 12. Better teaching at the elementary level would insure better reading achievement in content areas at the secondary level.

_____ 13. When a literal level guide is used before the reading, it is a prereading organizer; when it accompanies the reading, it is a simulator; when it follows the reading, it is a test.

_____ 14. Since content determines process, the purpose and construct of guide material must remain flexible.

_____ 15. Overlap among categories in a classification scheme increases as the number of categories decreases.


### REINFORCING ACTIVITY

Write the following words on slips of paper or on 3"x5" cards—one word per slip or card. Working with at least two other people who have read the chapter, arrange the words to represent the issues raised and/or ideas developed in the chapter. Feel free to add other words.

| information | one | levels |
| ideas | two | comprehension |
| synthesis | three | evidence |
| experience | statements | prediction |
| intensive | questions | confirmation |
| extensive | concepts | accommodation |
| intrinsic | principles | differences |
| extrinsic | details | simulation |

\*    \*    \*    \*    \*    \*

## REFERENCES

BLOOM, B. S., Ed. *Taxonomy of educational objectives (cognitive domain)*. New York: McKay, 1956.

BRUNER, JEROME. *The process of education*. Cambridge, Mass: Harvard University Press, 1960.

FREDERIKSEN, CARL. *Discourse comprehension and early reading*. Unpublished paper. Washington, D.C.: NIE, 1976.

GAGNÉ, ROBERT M. *The conditions of knowledge*. New York: Holt, Rinehart and Winston, Inc., 1970.

GRAY, WILLIAM S. "The major aspects of reading." In *Development of reading abilities* ed. Helen Robinson. (Supplementary Educational Monographs No. 90). Chicago: University of Chicago Press, 1960, 8-24.

HONEYCUTT, C. DAVID. *An investigation of the theoretical construct of three levels of comprehension*. Unpublished doctoral dissertation, Syracuse University, 1971.

RILEY, JAMES D. *An investigation of the effects of reading guides and a directed reading method upon word problem comprehension, problem solving ability, and attitude toward mathematics*. Unpublished dissertation, Syracuse University, 1976.

ROBINSON, HELEN M. "The major aspects of reading." In H. Alan Robinson (ed.). *Reading: Seventy-five years of progress*. (Educational Monographs No. 96) Chicago: University of Chicago Press, 1966, 22-32.

SMITH, NILA BANTON. *Reading instruction for today's children*. Englewood Cliffs, N.J.: Prentice-Hall, 1963.

THELEN, JUDITH. *The use of advance organizers and guide material in viewing science motion pictures in a ninth grade*. Unpublished doctoral dissertation, Syracuse University, 1970.

*four*

# Organizational Patterns

---

The following terms are important to an understanding of this chapter. Each is defined in context. Read through the list to identify those for which you have uncertain meanings. Then as you read the chapter, pay particular attention to their definitions. Also make certain that the meanings attributed to the remaining words by their context in the chapter correspond to the meanings they hold for you.

| | |
|---|---|
| exposition | time order |
| comparison/contrast | simple listing |
| cause/effect | signal words |

Each of the following terms has been defined previously in this book. If you are not reading the chapters in sequence, you may need to examine the vocabulary lists for the preceding chapters for definitions of words for which you hold uncertain meanings.

implicit                    functional teaching
explicit                    vertical transformation
infer                       horizontal transformation
imply                       content objective

## IDEA DIRECTION

Many reading skills are inherent in content-area texts and the task is to make them manageable for both teachers and learners. This manageability comes through simplification. Using levels of comprehension, as presented in Chapter 3, is one way to simplify the reading process. This chapter presents another: organizational patterns. Think of how *patterns* fit with *levels* and add to your instructional options.

## READING DIRECTION

The discussion of organizational patterns assumes a knowledge of levels of comprehension. Thus, it is probably better for you to read Chapter 3 before reading this one. Even after reading it, you may need to refer back to specific discussions. Don't rely on recall at this stage. Make certain of your understandings.

---

## EXPERIENCING ORGANIZATIONAL PATTERNS

This chapter presents another dimension of comprehension to aid students in their reading of expository material found in many of the content areas. More specific than the levels of comprehension, this dimension provides students with an added tool. This aspect of comprehension can be taught functionally along with the content presented in any expository material. It can be simulated to show students how to comprehend the materials they read in this more specific manner. It is, as implied, instructionally applicable in most subjects by most classroom teachers.

Before you examine this dimension of comprehension in detail, you should experience how it works instructionally. Please go through the following activity as the directions indicate. You should work with two or three other people; the activity is not as effective if you work alone.

*Part I*

*Directions*: The author of the following article makes a variety of comparisons as he develops his point. Some of these comparisons are explicit, being directly stated; others are implicit, being only implied.

Listed below are twelve possible comparisons expressed by two words or phrases separated by a slanted line. The number in parentheses following each comparison refers to the paragraph in the article where the comparison might possibly be found.

Read the first comparison and then the paragraph identified for that comparison. If you believe the author made that comparison in the article at that location—either explicitly or implicitly—place a check on the numbered line. Do this for each of the twelve items.

_____ 1. New career/old career (1)
_____ 2. Empty/full (2)
_____ 3. Active evil/inactive good (2)
_____ 4. Easy activity/difficult nothingness (3)
_____ 5. Part-time/full-time (4)
_____ 6. Listening/hearing (5)
_____ 7. Expectations/reality (6)
_____ 8. Something/nothing (7, 12)
_____ 9. Advantages/disadvantages (12, 14)
_____ 10. Acceptance/excuses (9, 13)
_____ 11. Commitment/accommodation (14)
_____ 12. Long-range/short-range (16)

## THE ART OF DOING NOTHING*

1. Seven months ago, I quit a moderately well-paid, semi-respectable job as a newspaperman to embark on a new career: doing nothing.

2. Why did I choose nothing? Well, it voided a large fill in my life. I slowly had come to the conclusion that the world is in the terrible condition it is because people insist on doing things. Most of the things they insist on doing are awful, even if they don't seem that way in the beginning. Once it became clear that human activity is the enemy of all life, I was determined to see if it was feasible to stop doing doing. As I sat there thinking about it, I fell asleep. I knew then that I was ready.

3. I had dabbled in doing nothing on weekends and after work (and often during work) and felt I was well qualified. I knew that sustaining nothing twenty four hours a day wouldn't be easy, but then nothing worth

*"Nothing Doing," by Lewis Grossberger, March 8, 1972. © 1972 by The New York Times Company. Reprinted by permission.

doing ever is. And if anything is worth doing, nothing is. I succeeded beyond my emptiest dreams. I achieved absolutely nothing, which of course is what I set out to do. I got so good at nothing, I can do it with my eyes open.

4. Henry Miller once said that the ability to do nothing demands courage and intelligence of a high order, and frankly, he was right. Anyone can do nothing for brief stretches, but full-time nothing is more demanding.

5. For one thing, your friends and relatives will find it puzzling. They ask you what you're doing and you tell them and they can't believe it. Their eyes narrow and they say things like, "Huh?" You can repeat it 40 times—I'm doing nothing, you see, nothing, as in zero, you know, like naught, zip, 0—and they stare at you and say, Aw, c'mon, what're ya really doin'?

Nothing.

Aw . . .

6. People will believe anything but nothing. They're not programmed for it. It blows all the circuits. They can comprehend your being a sex criminal or a heroin addict or a defector to Albania, perhaps, but nothing? Nothing doing. The trouble is we've all had this curious notion ingrained in us that we're supposed to be out accomplishing something. Our lives are supposed to add up to something. We're supposed to be something.

7. Hi, I'm gonna be a fireman when I grow up; what're you gonna be? Nothing.

8. Nothing? How can they form an image of you in their brains? My son the . . . nothing?

9. So then they say, "But whatta ya do all day? I mean how d'ya spend the day?" You can tell them but they won't believe you. They'll all believe you're leading some kind of shameful secret life.

10. Here is what I did all day. Here is my official daily schedule for doing nothing:

    1. Wake up.

    2. Do nothing.

    (The first step is not absolutely necessary.)

11. It's difficult to go into great detail. I mean it's not easy to elaborate on nothing and besides, each person must find his/her own path to nowhere. But I can say with some assurance that:

12. Doing nothing is good for you. It really is. Nothing has it all over the other kinds of thing, such as some. It's a lot more relaxing. It keeps you out of trouble (and off the streets). It's quiet. It's dignified. It doesn't eat away at your integrity, like something so often does. It cleans out your system and calms your nerves.

13. But the idea of it, for some reason, terrifies people. They grow grumpy and defensive. They say: Well, I couldn't do that; I'd vegetate. (Ever see an unhappy vegetable?) Well, it must get boring after a while. (What doesn't?) But I have a family to support. (Tough.) But if everyone did nothing, what would happen to the world? (Nothing.)

14. Another nice thing about doing nothing is that it has enabled me to compose double-negative sentences such as this one: I'm not doing nothing anymore. I've quit temporarily (there's this annoying money problem), but I know I can go back to it whenever I want, because once you learn nothing you always carry it with you.

15. What I'm doing now is writing about nothing. That's the next best thing to doing it.

16. I'm convinced that almost everyone would be better off if she or he tried nothing, even if only for a while. People who are doing nothing aren't fighting wars, cheating, lying, exploiting, yelling, oppressing or littering. They're just resting, mostly. The more you do nothing, the easier it gets. After a while, you'll find you don't even feel guilty about it. You'll feel perfectly at ease with nothing.

17. There's really nothing to it.

Lewis Grossberger is, that is to say, was—oh, skip it.

*Part II*

*Directions*: Now that you have discussed the author's comparisons, react to the following statements. Think about how the author's information and ideas on this topic of "nothing" relate to your own ideas and experiences. Check those statements which seem to express those relationships. Be prepared to explain the bases for your choices.

_____ 1. Doing nothing can be hard work and even harder to explain.

_____ 2. Doing nothing is a great pastime and will keep you out of trouble.

_____ 3. You must have a strong self-image to consciously choose nothing as your career.

_____ 4. If you have to choose a thing, *no* is better than *some*.

_____ 5. When tempted to do, don't.

_____ 6. People do not accept what they cannot understand.

_____ 7. People do not understand what they cannot accept.

_____ 8. More problems are caused by action than inaction.

_____ 9. Escapism is a way of life for busy people.

## Comparison

For purposes of comparison you should consider the following response to the activities in Part I and Part II of this exercise. This is *not* an answer key by which you judge whether your response is right or wrong. It *is*, however, a point of view by which to judge the reasoning on which you based your own responses to the activities.

**Response to Part I** Undoubtedly you discovered that all of the comparisons listed in Part I could be found in the article itself either implicitly or explicitly. For only one item were both parts of the comparison explicitly stated in the referenced paragraph and that was item 8 as found in paragraph 12. For items 1, 5, and 8 (as found in paragraph 7), only one part of the comparison was explicitly stated in the referenced paragraphs. The other part of the comparison, as expressed in the item, was implied in the paragraph.

Items 2, 4, 9, 10, and 12 presented comparisons which were implicit in the reference paragraphs. That is, the reader had to infer both points of comparison from the information presented in the reading selection. The words used in the items were not actually used in those paragraphs. But these inferred comparisons were rather apparent because the words used to represent them were easily associated with the information from which the inferences were drawn.

Items 3, 6, 7, and 11 also presented inferred comparisons. These differed from the previous items only in the level of abstraction necessary to perceive the implication. The words used to represent the points of comparison are more abstract, not so clearly perceived as belonging to the information contained in the paragraphs. The process of drawing inferences is the same. The difference is in the *degree* of abstraction, not in the *kind* of process.

**Response to Part II**   The statements in Part II fall into two levels of abstraction. Each item can be supported by evidence and implications drawn from the article and by the experiences of most readers. One set of items seems more closely tied to the content than does the other. Items 1 through 4 make specific reference to "nothing" or "nothingness" even while presenting statements of broad generality.

Items 5 through 9 present broad generalizations which are illustrated by information and actions represented in the article, but which are not specific to the article itself. They express principles which are applicable to many situations, people, and times. Evidence for support of statements 1 through 4 would come more naturally from the text than from other sources. The tendency would be to immediately refer back to the text while discussing these items and afterwards, to draw on other sources (including experience) as supporting evidence. Evidence for support of statements 5 through 9 would come initially either from the article or from related external sources, with an almost immediate reference to the other source not initially used. This is because the items are more abstract in their language, presenting broad-ranging principles or generalizations. Depending on how an individual thinks, he might see the immediate application to ideas in the article while another might see a more immediate relationship to ideas from other sources and experiences. In either case, the reader is more inclined to synthesize ideas from a variety of sources when the guiding statements are tied to the content of the article indirectly through generalizations rather than directly through reference to the same topic or idea or information.

## EXPLANATION AND RATIONALE

The activity that you just completed focuses on one of four organizational patterns characteristic of expository material. These patterns describe how authors organize the presentation of their information and ideas. The patterns constitute the "internal organization" of the text. Awareness of this organization helps students develop an understanding of the author's information and ideas as expressed in that text.

The purpose of this chapter is to identify the patterns of this internal organization and to show you how to use your knowledge of these patterns to guide your students' reading. Through this guidance they will learn simultaneously both the content of the material and the organizational pattern as an aid to comprehension.

The other general type of organization, as it pertains to content-area textbooks, is the "external organization." On pages 97-98 this classification of organization is discussed in detail as it pertains to the development of students' study skills.

## Internal Organization

Most authors follow some organizational scheme as they write their texts. Some seem not to follow any scheme, but that in itself is a kind of scheme. The general consensus among writers of textbooks on reading and study skills is that there are four organizational patterns characteristic of expository material (Niles, 1970). Though there is not an agreement, nor concern, on which of the patterns is most important or useful, there is agreement on these four:

1. *Cause/effect:* Two or more factors (objects, events, or ideas) are presented with an indication, either explicit or implicit, that in any interaction among the factors, one or more takes action (cause) while the other reacts to that action (effect).

2. *Comparison/contrast:* Two or more factors (objects, events, or ideas) are presented to show likenesses (comparison) and/or differences (contrast) among them.

3. *Time order:* Two or more factors (objects, events, or ideas) are presented with an indication of a sequential relationship between or among them. The relationships are considered in light of the passage of time and/or the application of logic.

4. *Simple listing:* Two or more factors (objects, events, or ideas) are presented, one after the other. No significance is intended from the fact that one is mentioned before the others because to speak of two or more factors, one must be mentioned before the other. Authors may qualify the listing by such criteria as size, weight, or importance.

"Main idea" is sometimes identified as an additional organizational pattern. True, it is a pattern, but in a different sense. Its construct is so broad that it subsumes each of the other patterns. For example, a *cause* might be the "main idea" of a paragraph and the *effects*, the "details"; or a *comparison* might be the "main idea" and *contrasts*, the "details"; or a stated *objective* might be the "main idea" and the *enumeration* of steps leading to that objective, the "detail";

and so on. There are occasions, however, when the relationship between the statement of the central topic, or "main idea," and supporting information, or "detail," does not subsume one of these four basic patterns. In such cases, the broader label, "main idea/detail," is applied.

Each of the four patterns has a set of signal words that reveal the organization of a given reading selection. Vacca (1973) suggests the following:

*Cause/effect*: because, since, therefore, consequently, as a result, this led to, so that, nevertheless, accordingly, if . . . then.

*Comparison/contrast*: however, but, as well as, on the other hand, not only . . . but also, either . . .or, while, although, unless, similarly, yet.

*Time order*: on (date), not long after, now, as, before, after, when.

*Simple listing*: to begin with . . . ; first . . . second . . . ; next; then; finally.

Students can use the signal words to establish mind sets as they read, enabling them to follow the author better through development of the topic.

Organizational patterns characterize entire works as well as single paragraphs. For example, a full chapter in history may be organized in a time order, another in a cause/effect pattern. Single paragraphs within those chapters may be similarly organized.

It is important to know that there can be, and often is, a mixing of these organizational patterns within both single paragraphs and longer selections. For example, within a chapter organized sequentially, several paragraphs may have cause/effect or comparison/contrast organization. Though such a mixture is frequently found, one generally finds a predominant pattern within paragraphs or longer selections. While assisting students in the successful reading of expository material, teachers can focus on the most obvious pattern in the selection and ignore the others as far as that particular assignment is concerned. Students can be taught to focus on the predominant pattern, using it as an aid to understanding relationships within the material and as an aid for recall after the reading has been completed.

In Chapter 3 the point was made that content determines process. This principle is particularly important when you decide which organizational pattern to stress with a given reading selection.

As is true with the development of levels-of-comprehension guides, so it is true with patterns guides: you first must clearly establish the content objective for your instruction before you determine what reading process to teach. Having determined the concept to be taught, you next identify the pertinent information which contributes to the formation of the concept. Knowing that information, you can then determine the organizational pattern the author uses to present that information. Finally, you can prepare a patterns guide to help the students learn both the concept and the related organizational pattern.

Thus, developing your students' reading competence starts with the principle that "content determines process" and progresses systematically to the development of materials to guide their reading and understanding. Once again, reading is taught functionally as an integral part of the curriculum.

### Relationship Between Patterns and Levels

There is a logical, interacting relationship between organizational patterns and levels of comprehension. It suggests a convenient and sensible sequence in their use as the basis for guiding students' reading of materials in the various content areas.

It is clear from prior discussions of levels of comprehension that authors present information and ideas both explicitly and implicitly. Explicit information is usually discernable through literal-level comprehension; implicit information and ideas is usually discernable through interpretive-level comprehension.

Logically, if readers have become attuned to the difference between literal and interpretive levels of comprehension, they are sensitive to relationships among ideas, objects, and actions which are both explicit (literal) and implicit (interpretive) in nature. Since information and ideas are presented both explicitly and implicitly through organizational patterns, it makes sense first to guide students' reading through the levels of comprehension. After they develop confidence using the levels, they then can be guided in the application of organizational patterns when appropriate to the content objectives of the lesson. Prior experience with literal and interpretive levels of comprehension provides an appropriate reference for developing an understanding of how to perceive the explicit and implicit relationships within the patterns.

Recall your own experience with the comparison/contrast guide for the article, "The Art of Doing Nothing." Because you previously had been guided through the levels of comprehension, you probably were more sensitive to both explicit and implicit relationships in this article than had you not had that prior experience.

Part I contained both literal and interpretive items, in that they dealt with both explicit and implicit comparisons and contrasts. Part II was similar to the applied level, except it contained both interpretive and applied items, even as Part I contained both literal and interpretive items.

Both parts of the patterns guide are important, not only because they reinforce the relationship between levels and patterns, but also because they help students deal with the consequences of what they are studying. Part I deals with information and ideas that the author has to offer and with the specific organizational pattern in which the material is presented. But that does not seem to be enough. One feels compelled to ask, "So what? So what if they do have this information? So what if they do perceive these ideas? So what if they do have a sense of the organizational pattern? What are the consequences?"

Part II is really the "so what" section of the guide. It presents opportunity for students to connect their own experience with the author's ideas. These statements deal with the consequences of the ideas and information explored and explained through Part I of the guide.

Another reason for guiding students' reading first with levels of comprehension and then with organizational patterns is because the patterns are logically imbedded in the levels, particularly the interpretive level. You will recall from discussions in Chapter 3 that interpretation involves fitting together the information presented by the author.

When you guide students' interpretation with declarative statements, you help them make connections in the related information. Since, in expository material, those relationships fall into patterns (organizational patterns) as students cite evidence to support interpretive statements and discuss how the information fits together, they are indirectly sensing the organizational pattern in which that information is presented. Even without mentioning the patterns by name, the teacher is helping students develop a sense of organizational patterns through the interpretive-level guide.

This experience provides the basis for teaching the use of organizational patterns. Reference is made to searching for evidence to support interpretive-level statements and seeing how that evidence fits together, how those connections really fall into patterns of one sort or another, how those patterns have names, how the patterns can help both with the reading of the text material and the later recall of the information and ideas. The instructional sequence between levels of comprehension and organizational patterns does seem logical.

As implied above, this last point has bearing on the actual construction of levels-of-comprehension guides. It is useful to know the predominant organizational pattern of a reading selection before beginning to develop reading guides for levels of comprehension. Knowing the pattern, you can create items for the literal-level guide, focusing on information which contributes to the overall concept. By knowing the pattern, you have some objective way to select information for students to focus on in determining "what the author says." It is this information, then, that is connected within the pattern to develop the intrinsic concepts.

Without knowledge of the pattern, you may create random items for the literal level that may or may not contribute to the overall concept. With knowledge of the pattern, you can create items that not only focus on information contributing to the overall concept but also set the stage for developing an awareness of the process by which the concepts are formed. Thus, you make certain that process is not separated from content.

Similarly, awareness of patterns gives you a criterion to create items for the interpretive level of comprehension. The items in the guide should present possible relationships that occur among bits of information within the selection. And these relationships occur, as stated above, in one of the various patterns. As students respond to these items, they are functionally developing a sensitivity to the pattern, even though the pattern has not been labeled.

*Students* need not be aware of patterns to profit from guides that structure their response at various levels of comprehension. The patterns are exercised functionally. Nevertheless, the *teachers* need to be aware of patterns in order to create the guides for levels of comprehension. Patterns provide criteria for the creation of items for the guides for levels; they preclude arbitrary items that neither provide focus on important concepts nor allow the functional exercise of patterns.

### Review of Your Experience

Your experience with the activity at the beginning of this chapter demonstrated all of these factors, which have been presented with respect to organizational patterns.

This guide was prepared around the following content objective: to develop an understanding that what people become is influenced by (1) what they want to become, (2) how they use their talents, and (3) the firmness with which they hold to their ideals. The organizational patterns of *comparison/contrast* was identified as the predominant pattern among several. Both explicit and implicit comparisons were made between and among information and ideas which had bearing on the overall content objective. Thus, the guide was prepared to direct your response to the entire article through a focus on comparative relationships between and among specific objects, events, actions, and ideas. Part II was prepared by asking the "so what" questions and developing declarative statements which dealt with the consequences of these compared objects, events, actions, and ideas.

You experienced the relationship between Part I and Part II, and saw how the latter is a logical extension of the former. You experienced the relationship between patterns and levels. You saw that in Part I there were both literal and interpretive comparisons. You saw in Part II that there were both interpretive- and applied-level generalizations. You saw that in both Part I and Part II the comparisons and generalizations were formed at different levels of sophistication and abstraction, and you did not find that to be a particular problem. Whether concrete or abstract, the statements could be supported by the text and by related information and ideas. Thus, your experience in Chapter 3 with levels of comprehension was reinforced and you developed a sense of a more precise, specific reading process, which can be applied to expository material.

Finally, assume for a moment that not everyone reading this text with you has the same background of experience or the same achievement in reading. You probably observed that because the items represented a wide range of sophistication and abstraction, everyone was able to participate in the discussions.

Everything you experienced with this material your students can and will experience if you add to your repertoire the use of organizational patterns through specific guide material constructed for that purpose.

The balance of this chapter deals with how to develop these materials.

## Identification of Patterns

Before examining illustrative patterns guides, you will find it useful to practice identifying the organizational patterns in specific reading selections. To save space, the practice given in this test will be on short passages. Working with some of your colleagues you might want to extend the practice to longer passages.

Remember that more than one organizational pattern may be found in a given paragraph or longer passage. You should not try to use them all, but rather, you should identify the predominant pattern and guide students' reading accordingly. If you identify the content objective first, identifying the predominant pattern will be easier. Knowing the concept to be stressed, you can identify the related information, then the pattern that characterizes the organization of that information. This is the predominant pattern.

Read the six paragraphs that follow. In the space below each, list all the patterns you see in the paragraph. Then decide on a content objective (the concept to be stressed) for the paragraph and decide which pattern is predominant. Circle the name of that pattern on your list for each paragraph. Be ready to discuss reasons for your decisions with others in your discussion group.

1. The Calchona (kal-chō-nah) is a strange, hairy beast. The Indians of South America say it walks over steep mountain trails there. They say this beast is as big as a large dog, as white as snow, as woolly as a goat, and as nasty as a snake. People believe that on dark nights, the Calchona hides behind rocks along the mountain paths. Then it jumps out on travelers and steals their money. This is probably because the Calchona doesn't like anyone wandering through its land.

*S/C*

2. Some kinds of heels on shoes can be harmful. The thinner and higher the heel, the greater harm it can do. Scientists say this is because so much of a person's weight is put on the floor in one small spot. A thin heel can dent floors and rugs. It can also dent other people's toes!

*c/e*

3. In some ways, the food business is like the clothing business. In some ways it is different. People need what both businesses have to sell. But the things that each business sells are very different. One business sells products to eat. The other business sells products to wear. Which business do you think is more interesting to work in?

*c/c*

4. Tilly made a special punch for her party. First, she poured 1 pint of lemon juice and 1 pint of orange juice into a large bowl. Then she added ½ pint of grape juice and ¼ cup of sugar water. Finally, she poured in 2 quarts of ginger ale. Then, she poured the punch from the bowl into a large jar. The jar was filled to the top. How big was it?

*T/o*

5. Carlotta looked beautiful. She wore a long yellow dress and white shoes. A few curls showed below the edge of her yellow hat. She smiled

*c/e*

up at the man beside her. She seemed happy. It was her birthday. She was now six months old!

6. Soon some people will be able to grow crops for the first time in their lives. Scientists have discovered ways to turn sea water into fresh water. Because of this, new land will be able to be farmed. People will be able to grow wheat and other grains where they never could before.

**Comparison** Now compare your work with the following analysis of the paragraphs. This is not a definitive answer key, obviously; merely an opinion with which to compare your own analysis.

Paragraph 1: The predominant pattern is comparison/contrast, with the probable content objective focusing on the physical features of the beast. If a description of the behavior of the beast were the content objective, then the predominant organizational pattern would be cause/effect.

Paragraph 2: The predominant pattern is cause/effect, with the probable content objective dealing with the interactive effect of area, weight, and force. There is an implied comparison in this paragraph, also dealing with the same content objective; however, it is a secondary and subtle pattern and probably not the one to be emphasized.

Paragraph 3: The predominant pattern is comparison/contrast with the content objective being the understanding that businesses differ because their product and customers differ.

Paragraph 4: The predominant pattern is time order with the content objective being the understanding that the size of a container can be determined by the sum of all the ingredients placed in that container. In science, time order could be important if the ingredients had to be mixed in a certain sequence.

Paragraph 5: The predominant pattern is comparison/contrast with the content objective being to demonstrate the use of surprise in writing and to show how contrast between what is anticipated and what actually is found can create it. The contrast between the image established by the first six sentences with the image established by the last sentence is the stuff of surprise.

Paragraph 6: The predominant pattern is cause/effect with the content objective being an understanding of the life-changing effects of desalinization. The implied comparison/contrast pattern in the paragraph seems overshadowed by the cause/effect issues.

## ILLUSTRATIVE PATTERNS GUIDES

Presented in this section are four illustrative patterns guides: one for a reading assignment in science; two for social studies; and one for literature. Guides from three content areas are shown to call to your attention the fact that organizational patterns are present in materials across subjects at every grade level (horizontal transformation). The two patterns guides from social studies are shown to call to your attention the fact that organizational patterns are present in materials across grade levels within subjects (vertical transformation).

## Caution

Organizational patterns are not as generally applicable as are levels of comprehension. Since organizational patterns, as discussed in this chapter, are found in expository materials, they are rarely found in materials for certain subjects—for example, mathematics. Thus, math teachers need not be as concerned about organizational patterns as teachers of science, social studies, and literature should be. If, however, a math class includes reading expository selections which describe and discuss mathematics as a discipline, then students could benefit from the use of organizational patterns. The same would apply to other disciplines that normally do not require reading of expository material.

Organizational patterns should be applied instructionally only where appropriate to the material being used. Content determines process. Thus, if patterns are not appropriate for the materials your students will read, forget about them and use levels along with suggestions in Chapters 5 and 7. You might, however, study the following illustrative materials for your own information or so that you can help other teachers who are looking for ways to help their students.

## Assumptions in the Illustrative Materials

Each set of materials is drawn from complete lessons. You can assume that before developing the lesson materials, the teacher: (1) established content objectives; (2) assigned the reading selection because its content was relevant to those objectives; (3) decided to guide students in the use of the predominant organizational pattern because it seemed the most appropriate process to apply to the reading passage to accomplish the content objectives (content determines process); (4) prepared the guide to emphasize the information and ideas consistent with the content objectives, at a level of sophistication consistent with the students' ability and achievement levels.

You can assume that prior to guiding the students' reading with the patterns guide, the teacher prepared the students for the reading through appropriate procedures as described in Chapter 9. To save space, the related reading passage is provided for only one of the four illustrative guides. You will find it beneficial to complete and discuss the guide as would students in that class. This experience will reinforce the understanding you developed from the example at the beginning of this chapter and the subsequent explanation and rationale. It will also give you a sense of what students experience as they are guided by such materials.

**Illustrative guide in science (cause/effect)** The following guide was prepared for ninth-grade general science students described by their teacher as "relatively poor readers." This meant that they usually had problems reading the science text. The teacher often substituted other sources of information for the text, mainly relying on lecture.

This particular lesson was part of a larger unit on ecology, with a particular focus on pollution. The lesson's content objectives were to develop understandings that: (1) carbon monoxide is a major source of air pollution; (2) the environment man creates for himself reflects his priorities and his values. The reading selection presented information and ideas appropriate to these understandings in a cause/effect relationship.

Among other appropriate preliminary activities, the vocabulary-preparation materials presented in Chapter 6 of this text were used with the students. Following the use of that material, the students were given the guide materials and the reading assignment.

Students were randomly selected and grouped. They were encouraged to help one another as they worked through the guide and the reading passage. The teacher read the directions for Part I orally as the students followed along. He then led the students as they applied the directions to the first item. Students proceeded to complete Part I, while the teacher moved from group to group providing assistance, clarifying comments, and giving encouragement as needed.

After students completed Part I in their groups, the teacher discussed with the full class one or two of the items to compare responses across groups. He selected particular items that had caused some problems in the small-group discussions and where differences of opinion were obvious among the participants. Notice, however, he did not go over *all* of the items with them. That would have been redundant, unnecessary, and boring. The students already had completed the material; the only purpose would have been to assure the teacher that the students had covered all of the material. But by his monitoring of the small groups he already knew that.

After discussing the specified items from Part I, he distributed Part II of the guide, read through the directions as the students followed along, led the discussion of the first statement as an example of how to deal with the rest of the items, then asked the students to work together and apply the directions to the rest of the items. As they worked in groups on Part II, he again moved from group to group to provide whatever assistance was needed and to participate in the discussion of the items, being careful that his participation did not inhibit the students from exploring and expressing their own views on the statements. A "colearner" was what the teacher tried to be in this work.

When the group discussions of Part II were completed, the teacher led a full-class discussion on a couple of the statements which seemed most representative of the overall content objectives. Using the items in this fashion allowed him to reinforce the content objectives, to reinforce the organizational patterns, to demonstrate again to students the relevancy of their prior knowledge and experience, and to show that there are many ways to view the same issue.

Now, go through the guide with this background in mind.

# AIR POLLUTION

*Part I*

*Directions*: Here are 12 sets of phrases and numbers. The numbers tell the page, paragraph, and lines where you should look in your text for information. The two phrases on each line separated by a slanted line are possible cause-and-effect relationships. For each set of phrases look in the text at the place indicated and check it if the first phrase causes the second phrase. Work together to make your decisions.

_____ 1. carbon monoxide/more than 51% air pollution (113, 1, 1-3)

_____ 2. automobile engines/80% carbon monoxide emissions (113, 1, 6-7)

_____ 3. incomplete combustion/significant percent of CO emissions (113, 1, 4-7)

_____ 4. carbon monoxide/danger, illness, death (113, 2, 1-3)

_____ 5. one gallon gasoline/three pounds CO (113, 2, 6)

_____ 6. mild CO poisoning/highway accidents (114, 1, 1-2)

_____ 7. faulty exhaust systems/poisoned people (114, 1, 9-11)

_____ 8. CO poisoning/oxygen starvation (114, 2, 1-2)

_____ 9. hemoglobin and CO/strong chemical bond (114, 2, 1-2)

_____ 10. heavy smoking/permanent combination of hemoglobin and CO (115, 0, 4-6)

_____ 11. inhaling CO/trouble with hearing (115, 1, 9-11)

_____ 12. reduction in traffic/obvious remedy (115, 1, 1)

## CARBON MONOXIDE*

(a) **Sources.** Carbon monoxide (CO), a colorless, odorless gas, accounts for more than 51% of the total annual air pollutant emissions in North America. This gas is almost entirely a man-made pollutant. The most significant source is incomplete combustion, during which each carbon atom combines with only one atom of oxygen. Estimates show that automobile engines alone contribute more that 80% of the *global* carbon monoxide emissions. Combustion in industry, power plants, residential heating, and refuse disposal accounts for the remainder (see Fig.). Photochemical reactions (reactions initiated by light) of hydrocarbons in polluted atmospheres also produce tiny amounts of carbon monoxide. Very few natural sources of this gas are known. Under abnormal conditions plants can produce carbon monoxide. Certain marine organisms, such as

*Reprinted by permission of the publisher from William A. Andrews (ed.), *A Guide to the Study of Environmental Pollution*, Englewood Cliffs, N.J.: Prentice-Hall, Inc., pp. 113-15. © 1972 by W. A. Andrews.

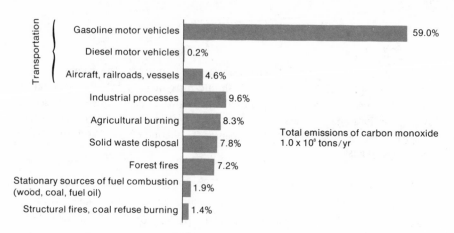

Nationwide sources of carbon monoxide emissions—U.S. 1968. (Data published by U.S. Department of Health, Education, and Welfare.)

jellyfish, can emit gas bubbles containing as much as 80% carbon monoxide. However, these natural contributions are not considered significant.

(b) Effects. Carbon monoxide is extremely dangerous. Just 10 ppm of carbon monoxide in air is sufficient to cause illness. Within 30 minutes, 1,300 ppm is fatal. Many deaths attributed to carbon monoxide have resulted from inhalation of exhaust fumes from a running automobile engine in a closed garage. Approximately 3 pounds of carbon monoxide are released for every gallon of gasoline which is consumed by automobile engines. This means that about 300 pounds of carbon monoxide are released for every 100 cars on the road during an average 15 mile drive. Yet for many years, authorities claimed that carbon monoxide did not present a hazard as long as it was released into the open air. More recent scientific studies contradict this theory with increasing evidence of chronic carbon monoxide poisoning. Although carbon monoxide levels are not high enough to prove fatal, the effect of gradual poisoning may accumulate in the body. They produce mild symptoms such as drowsiness, nausea, or dizziness.

Such mild carbon monoxide poisoning is suspected as the cause of many highway accidents which were formerly blamed on driver fatigue. A one-hour exposure to a carbon monoxide concentration of 120 ppm can significantly impair driving ability. Yet measurements of this gas indicate concentrations as high as 100 ppm in tunnels, parking garages, and the streets of major cities such as New York, Chicago, Detroit, and London, England. Many people complain of headaches after driving to work engulfed in the exhaust produced by heavy traffic. Faulty car exhaust systems are particularly dangerous because carbon monoxide tends to seep up from beneath the floor and poison the occupants. In addition, the smoking of a single cigarette in an unventilated car has been shown to raise the carbon monoxide level sufficiently to affect driver and passengers alike.

The effects of carbon monoxide poisoning are similar to those of oxygen starvation. Hemoglobin in the red blood cells carries oxygen, absorbed from air in the lungs, to the rest of the body cells. Unfortunately, hemoglobin finds carbon monoxide at least 200 times more attractive than oxygen. Carbon monoxide also forms stronger and more efficient chemical bonds to hemoglobin than does oxygen. A complex molecule, carboxyhemoglobin, is formed. This complex is very stable and the important hemoglobin molecules are not released to continue oxygen distribution for several hours. During this time, the body is effectively deprived of its necessary oxygen, just as if many of the red blood cells had been lost. An 8 hour exposure to an atmosphere containing 80 ppm of carbon monoxide reduces the oxygen-carrying capacity of the blood about 15%, or more than would the loss of one pint of blood.

Ordinarily, we have a greater exposure to carbon monoxide during our active daily lives. Traffic jams can produce carbon monoxide levels as high as 400 ppm! Any physical exertion increases both the rate of respiration and the amount of air inhaled each time. Ironically, we breathe in more carbon monoxide just when our individual oxygen requirements are greatest. Obese people and those who suffer from respiratory, chronic heart, or vascular diseases are particularly affected by carbon monoxide. Heavy smokers, who regularly inhale a personal supply of carbon monoxide, may have as much as 5% of their hemoglobin permanently combined with carbon monoxide. It is not surprising to doctors that habitual smokers are among the first to require hospital treatment during severe air pollution episodes. Carbon monoxide concentrations reach the toxic level in their bloodstreams faster than in those of non-smokers.

Recently, tests were completed involving people who worked in offices located within 100 feet of main traffic arteries in New York City. Although office air was filtered through air conditioners, the carbon monoxide level was three times higher than the level which affects mental processes. When blood is unable to supply the brain with sufficient amounts of oxygen, coordination and mental agility suffer. Since the performance of these workers in a normal atmosphere had never been compared, the problem had not been recognized. For example, research volunteers reacted only 60% as accurately to sound after inhaling 50 ppm of carbon monoxide for almost an hour. A driver or pedestrian affected to this extent would certainly be more accident-prone.

The obvious remedy to this growing problem is a great reduction of traffic on city streets. In Tokyo, Japan, congested streets restrict the multitude of cars to the speed of a bicycle. Japanese policemen, directing rush hour traffic, must stop every half hour to breathe from oxygen tanks located at station houses! Any attempted traffic restrictions have swiftly proven successful. Beginning in August, 1970, desperate Tokyo authorities banned automobiles from downtown Tokyo every Sunday. Within one hour of the initial closure, the carbon monoxide level dropped from 10.5 ppm to 2.3 ppm. Delighted Japanese officials have now made the Sunday ban permanent. Surely other cities can learn from this example.

*Part II*

*Directions*: Read each of the following statements and check those you believe to be reasonable. Consider the work you did in Part I of this guide as well as other ideas you have about pollution.

_____ 1. People will risk their lives to have what they want.

_____ 2. What a person wants is not always what he needs.

_____ 3. Good replaces bad more easily than bad replaces good.

_____ 4. What you can't see won't hurt you.

_____ 5. A surplus can cause a shortage.

On Pages 197-200 there is a discussion of the reasoning behind specifying the location in the text where Part I statements might be found. You may want to refer to that discussion at this time.

**Illustrative guide in social studies (comparison/contrast)** The following guide was prepared for eighth-grade students in U.S. History who were "average-to-poor readers," according to their teacher. He said that their attention span was very short and that he usually had to prepare a variety of activities to hold their interest for the entire class period.

This particular lesson was part of a larger unit on the Constitution. The content objectives for this lesson were to develop an understanding that: (1) citizens benefit most when there is a balance of power among institutions, agencies, and forms of government; (2) provisions in the Constitution make possible this balance of power.

The teacher started the lesson by helping students realize how much they already knew about the concept of *power* and by helping them organize that knowledge as a context for the lessson. This activity, which focused on vocabulary development, is described on pages 152-55.

The students were randomly grouped and encouraged to work with one another as they responded to the guide and the reading passage. The teacher went over the directions with the students and together they did the first item in Part I of the guide. As each group finished Part I, they were given Part II and instructed in how to complete the activity. When the small groups had completed both parts, the teacher then led a discussion among the groups on selected items from both parts to further develop understandings consistent with the overall content objectives.

As was true for the preceding science lesson, references to specific locations in the text accompanied each of the items in Part I of the guide. This information was provided to help the students acquire essential information from the text and discern the presence of the organizational pattern in the presentation of that information.

## BALANCE OF POWER

*Part I*

*Directions*: Here are some comparisons that may be contained in your text. Some may be directly stated. Others may be implied. All relate to the powers held by states, by the federal government, and by branches of the federal government.

If you believe the authors made a comparison, place a check on the numbered line. You are given locations in the text to which you should refer. (*This is America's Story*, pp. 228-233)

Be prepared to explain your decisions.

_____ 1. Rule of the People/Rule of Kings (p. 228, col. 1 and 2)

_____ 2. Constitution/Articles of Confederation (p. 228, col. 2)

_____ 3. Central Government/State Governments (p. 229, col. 1)

_____ 4. Powers of the States/Powers of the United States (p. 229, col. 1)

_____ 5. Powers of a State/Powers of States (p. 229, col. 1)

_____ 6. Power to Declare War/Power to Punish Crime (p. 229, col. 1)

_____ 7. Freedom/Government (p. 229, col. 1)

_____ 8. Original Constitution/Freedom/Bill of Rights (p. 229, col. 2; p. 230, col. 1)

_____ 9. The Congress/The President/The Supreme Court (p. 231, col. 1 and 2)

_____ 10. Tyranny/Justice (p. 231, col. 2)

_____ 11. Separation of Powers/*Unity* of Power (p. 231, col. 2)

_____ 12. Independence/Influence (p. 232, col. 1 and 2)

_____ 13. Living Document/Dead Agreements (p. 233, col. 1)

_____ 14. Horse-and-Buggy Age/Jet Age (p. 233, col. 1)

*Part II*

*Directions*: Think about the comparisons you made in Part I. Considering those comparisons and your own ideas about government, decide which of the following statements seem reasonable. Check your choices and be ready to tell why you checked the ones you did.

_____ 1. A person or government cannot *take* power; it must be *given.*

_____ 2. Government involves control; freedom is a matter of who does the controlling.

_____ 3. Freedom increases as the number of people in power increases.

_____ 4. What you don't use, you lose.

_____ 5. With freedom and power, the more you give the more you have.

_____ 6. Balance means equality.

**Illustrative guide in social studies (cause/effect)** The following reading guide illustrates how another history teacher guided his eleventh-grade honor students in the use of the cause/effect organizational pattern as they read a rather complicated selection from their history text. In previous years, the teacher had assumed that such students could read the text with no difficulty— but he always had to lecture on the content because they failed to grasp the significant ideas from their reading.

The teacher was correct in his assumption that the students could read well. They scored well on standardized reading tests; they had no trouble reading at the literal level of comprehension and relatively little at the interpretive. However, they had not been guided sufficiently in the use of the organizational patterns at the interpretive level and, as a consequence, were missing ideas contained in complicated passages. Therefore, the teacher constructed the guide and gave it to students as homework to complete as they read the text. He discussed the cause/effect pattern and told the students they would be applying that structure as they read the selection. The guide was to simulate the experience for them.

Each student completed the guide as homework. In class the next day, students were divided into groups. Their assignment was to compare their responses and, where they had differences, attempt to resolve them. And there were differences.

When the lively discussion was over, the teacher focused his comments only on those items the students were having difficulty resolving. He summarized, then moved on to the next unit. His lecture from previous years was unnecessary. His students had learned the content and apparently they had learned how to apply the cause/effect organizational pattern where it was appropriate to do so.

Now, consider the guide this teacher prepared. The content objective was to develop an understanding of how the interaction between the British and the Americans prior to the Revolutionary War contributed to the eventual state of war.

## THE ROAD TO REVOLUTION

*Directions*: In history it is very difficult to be sure that one event is the direct cause or effect of another. We can, however, by applying common sense to a series of events, at least tentatively conclude that one has helped cause another. In the following two lists, place the letter or number representing a probable *cause* in the blank beside the appropriate *result*. More than one cause may be indicated for a result; one cause may be important to several results. You will quickly notice that a result may in turn become a cause of something else. Dotted lines are guides to time periods. Some items may be irrelevant or false. Look anywhere in the opposite column for causes of actions or policies; they are not necessarily found within the same dotted lines.

| *American Actions or Policies* | *British Actions or Policies* |
|---|---|
| _____  1. American custom of smuggling, 1760s. | _____  a. Writs of Assistance, 1763. |

*American Actions or Policies*                    *British Actions or Policies*

____ 2. Failure of Americans to           ____ b. End of Salutary Neglect.
fully support French and          ____ c. Sugar Act of 1764, with
Indian War.                               duties to be paid in
____ 3. Peace of Paris, 1763.                  gold and silver.
____ 4. High cost to Britian              ____ d. Trials in Admiralty
of administering the                   Courts without
colonies.                              juries.
____ 5. American desire to                ____ e. Proclamation of 1763.
settle the Ohio                   ____ f. Stamp Act, fees to be
Valley.                                paid in gold and silver.
____ 6. Shortage of gold and              ____ g. Stationing of 10,000
silver in the                          British troops in
colonies.                              America.
                                          ____ h. Lord Grenville appointed
                                               Minister of Finance.
____ 7. Americans violated law            ____ i. Fights new war with
in settling west of                    France in Europe.
the Appalachians.                 ____ j. Townshend duties.
____ 8. Boycott of British                ____ k. British governors and
goods, 1865.                           judges to be paid
____ 9. Continued smuggling,                   from British revenue.
1864.                             ____ l. Suspension of colonial
____ 10. Colonial alliance with                legislatures of
Spain.                                 New York and Massachusetts.
____ 11. Formal protests to               ____ m. Repeal of the Stamp Act
Britain by colonial                    and passage of Declaratory
legislatures.                          Act.
____ 12. Cooperation of nine              ____ n. Boycott of American goods.
colonies at Stamp
Act Congress, 1765.
____ 13. Violence and riots,
1765.

The left column lists American actions or policies; the right column lists British actions or policies. Looking at the upper left column, we see that the Americans took certain actions which can be identified as causes; looking at the upper right column, we see that the British reacted (identifiable as effects) to the Americans' actions. But we know from history that the Americans did not quit after the British reacted. They reacted to the British reaction to the Americans' action; thus, the British effects became causes, so one matches the items in the lower left column to the items in the upper right. And reactions continued: the Americans' reactions (effects) to the British reactions (cause and also effect) to the Americans' actions (cause) in turn became causes for subsequent British reaction (effects), and so on through the entire selection. The original guide contains another page.

The teacher inserted items, suited to the students' ability, that were somewhat related but didn't really belong, and the students were to discard them. Also, the students could draw from any item in the opposite column when relating effects to causes. This latitude encouraged more critical and creative thinking, developed greater discrimination in reading and reasoning, and provided greater excitement and probing and value in the group discussions. By selecting carefully the items to be incorporated in the guide and by structuring the guide so that it emphasized the concepts to be learned as well as the organizational pattern to be applied to the expository material, the teacher taught content and reading simultaneously.

The purpose of this guide was to simulate the complex organizational pattern. By manipulating the components of the pattern—assembling it, as it were—students developed competence with the pattern.

Note that there are no references to signal the location of information in the text. Students were all competent readers and were of comparable ability. This being true, it was not necessary to provide such information for them. Also note that the possible differences present among the students in terms of how they applied their ability was provided for in the very nature of the items in the guide. There was sufficient abstraction in the items so that each student could apply, to the extent of his desire, the combination of ability and insight at his command. It also allowed the students to learn from one another, in that many students had insights that others did not have but discovered through the group discussions.

**Illustrative guide in literature (internal organization of the short story)** An English teacher designed the following guide for her students to use as they read a short story. She was teaching them the internal structure of this literary form and gave them the guide to help them develop a feeling for it as they read. After responding individually to the guide, they were to work together in groups to resolve differences.

Note the level of sophistication of this material. It assumes reading skill at the literal and interpretive levels. The purpose is to simulate the organizational pattern of the genre. Students analyze what they read in reference to this structure and identify parts of the story that fit into various aspects of the genre.

Discussion of their work reinforces the simulation and the sensitivity to the internal organization of the short story. There is also a simultaneous appreciation and understanding of the story itself—a perception of the author's message as well as his craft.

## THE QUIET MAN

*Directions*: Using the chart and the information on the chart, write the names of the parts of the plot on the dotted lines. Then read carefully the list of sentences taken from the story. Each sentence fits under a part of the plot on the diagram, but the sentences are not in correct order. Write the sentence numbers on the solid short lines, being sure to put them under the correct part of the plot. Try to put the sentences as close to chronological order as possible.

The *exposition* is the beginning. It explains all that is necessary to understand the following action (setting, mood, main character, point of view, background).

The *complication* is that part that presents the problem or conflict implied in the beginning situation.

The *turning point* or crisis is that part where the story or action takes a decisive turn.

The *climax* is the point of highest emotional intensity, the point of highest suspense.

The *resolution* is where the author unravels the complication and thus provides answers to the main question.

1. One evening before a market day, Ellen spoke to her husband: "Has Big Liam paid you my dowry yet, Shawn?"
2. A woman, loving her husband, may or may not be proud of him, but she will fight like a tiger if anyone, barring herself, belittles him.
3. Then he would smile to himself—a pitying smile—thinking of the poor devils, with dreams of fortune luring them, going out to sweat in Ironville, or to stand in a breadline.
4. Shawn Kelvin came home and found that he was the last of the Kelvins, and that the farm of his forefathers had added its few acres to that ranch of Big Liam O'Grady of Moyvalla.
5. And forthwith, Shawn Kelvin, with one easy sweep, threw the crumpled ball of notes into the heart of the flame.
6. "Mother of God!" she cried. "The trouble I had to make a man of him?"
7. Shawn Kelvin, a blithe young lad of twenty, went to the States to seek his fortune.
8. "It is a great pity that the father of my son is a Kelvin and a coward."
9. Shawn set out to demolish his enemy in the briefest space of time, and it took him five minutes to do it.

10. He realized that he was at the fork of life and a finger pointed un-
    mistakably.
11. A quiet man under middle size, with strong shoulders, and deep-set blue
    eyes below brows darker than his dark hair—that was Shawn Kelvin.
12. But Big Liam O'Grady, for all his resolute promptness, did not win Kathy
    Carey to wife.
13. "Ask me again, Shawneen," he finished . . . .

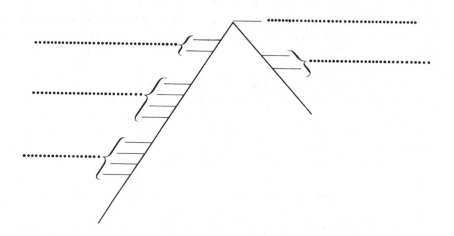

**Variations** The illustrative guides you have examined represent some of
the ways you can guide students' reading of content materials so as to develop
an understanding of both the content and the organizational pattern by which it
is presented. The format for patterns guides can vary according to the imagination of the person creating them and the nature of the textual material which
they are designed to accompany. The basic principle of showing how, rather
than telling or testing, is the critical element in constructing patterns guides.
Using the equivalent of declarative statements, as discussed in Chapter 3 in reference to levels guides, contributes strongly to the "showing how." Further
illustrative materials for organizational patterns are found in Appendix B, should
you wish to study them.

Should students be taught what a pattern is before they are given a guide for
the reading material organized according to that pattern? Some teachers are
inclined to spend quite some time just discussing the organizational pattern itself: the concept of cause/effect; of comparison/contrast. Following that instruction the students are asked to apply the pattern as they now understand it, using
the guide provided for that purpose. Teachers oriented toward the direct teaching of reading are more inclined to provide this preliminary instruction than are
teachers oriented toward the functional teaching of reading.

Developing students' awareness of the organizational pattern and how it functions is the instructional purpose for using a patterns guide. You really don't need to teach the pattern first. Of course, the pattern is introduced as part of the directions for using the guide. If students are totally unfamiliar with the type of relationships inherent in the patterns, then more explanation may be needed. Generally, however, it is sufficient if the teacher discusses the pattern as part of the structure of the total lesson, so that students are aware of the process they are to apply. As discussed earlier with respect to the relationship between patterns and levels, students who have used levels guides already have a sense of relationships which exist in information contained in texts. Therefore, once the teacher provides the label for that relationship, students will make the connection, at least at the awareness level. The patterns guide, then, helps students discern the patterns in what they are required to read.

### External Organization

Thus far you have examined the internal organization of the materials, the patterns of relationships that exist in the presentation of information and ideas in the text. You also should be aware of the external organization of the materials.

External organization is a gross characterization, focusing on format and physical features. Graphic aids appear in most expository texts: tables of contents, indexes, appendixes, chapter headings, divisions and subdivisions shown by distinctive type, maps, charts, pictures, graphs. These contribute to the external (gross) structure of written material. From such aids students can gather clues about the priorities authors place on ideas and information in the material.

Moreover, students learn to identify the nature of the content merely by viewing the external peculiarities (organization) of the material. Formula and problems written in numerical form are seen as having to do with math and/or science. Poetry and drama are revealed by their typographical style; so too is the exposition characteristic of science, history, or economics. "Word problems" in science and math as well as technical materials in distributive education and the crafts are easily identified by their form.

This aspect of external organization, features unique to each subject area, seems so obvious as to be absolutely unnecessary to "teach." Perhaps so, but many understandings appear obvious after they have been understood and have become a part of our set of reflex understandings. They are not obvious to the person struggling to acquire the insight. Sometimes a teacher must run the risk of belaboring the obvious to avoid the risk of assumptive teaching.

Awareness of such clues, of course, prepares students to read "math" when they encounter material with the external organization that triggers that association. The corresponding mind set will occur when they see material in science, literature, and social studies.

External organization related to graphic aids and the structure of the text is less obvious. Jewett (1965), Shepherd (1965), and Summers (1965) give valuable suggestions for helping students derive maximum value from such aids. Their comprehensive comments are of practical benefit and are worth investigating. They point out clearly that competence with these guideposts to external organization is learned. Students who acquire such competence can use their texts with greater efficiency.

Again, we are confronted with the obvious. Is it possible that students read their texts and do not use graphic aids? Unfortunately, unless their value and usefulness is pointed out, students ignore these aids. Many students view maps, charts, graphs, and pictures as filler which reduces the number of words they must cover when reading from page $x$ to page $z$. Unless taught to do so, many do not see these aids as authors' devices to clarify their exposition. And because this is an area where "assumptive teaching" clearly occurs (who can believe that students don't use maps to clarify exposition!), relatively few students receive adequate instruction.

Aiding students is relatively simple and can be a regular part of the curriculum. Early in the school year, teachers can lead students through their texts and resource materials, pointing out special features related to format and graphic aids. Subsequently, as each assignment is given, teachers can point out (or draw from students) the particular graphic aids that are pertinent to the concepts to be acquired from the reading. As necessary—students' response being the determiner—teachers can give specific instruction in how to make proper use of the aids. Such incidental, functional instruction promotes students' competence with the external organization of materials.


## APPLICATION

For practice, now, design a patterns guide for the following reading selection. Since it is taken from a professional journal and is addressed to teachers, you will be preparing a guide for adults. Because the process is the same, this is as good practice as designing guides for children. In some ways it is easier, and therefore good for initial practice because your own level of thinking is similar to that of the adults for whom you are preparing the practice materials.

Use the following procedure: (1) establish a content objective—What overall concept should the reader acquire from the study of this material?; (2) determine the predominant organizational pattern in which the information is presented; (3) design a guide to help the reader apply the pattern and attain the content objective.

When you have completed your own guide, share it with colleagues who have done the same thing. Compare guides and discuss the differences. You then may want to compare yours with the one that appears in Appendix A, page 257.

# WHAT DOES THIS HAVE TO DO WITH READING?*

"If you don't have a loud place for them—a lounge of some sort—the kids will turn you off. You'll never reach them." So said an earnest young man, a paraprofessional deeply involved in a middle school project designed to involve every student and every teacher in a skills training program appropriate to his needs. For the teacher, it was the skill of teaching reading within his subject. For the student, it was the ability to absorb and use the content of his subjects.

So what does the young man's argument have to do with reading? Really, a great deal. He was urging us to do something to eliminate the dichotomy between the students' real world and the "school world." We listened carefully to his ideas.

He did not convince us that blaring record players in a student smoker would open students' minds to the truths preserved in print. He did convince us, however, that more sensitivity to the students' real world would make school programs more productive. A student lounge, we conceded, would be a desirable adjunct to the Learning Center we were planning.

And what about teachers? They, too, have a curriculum quite different from what they display either in their own classrooms or in the courses where they are students. The extent of the dichotomy between the teachers' real world and the school world can be assessed easily by stepping into a faculty lounge and then following the persons you meet there into their classrooms—listening to them carefully in both settings.

We do not argue for the "relevant" curriculum that allows each student to study—or each teacher to teach—whatever suits his fancy. The values of scope and sequence are not entirely specious.

However, we would argue that, as consumers of knowledge, skills, and attitudes, students do have something to say to us about how they learn and whether the curriculum has any relationship to the world as they know it. If we let them talk and if we listen to them, then perhaps they can infuse the school curriculum with the life we have looked for.

Perhaps, also, if we provide teachers with opportunities to talk to one another about the art and science of teaching—over an extended time during the school day—then their real world would illuminate their professional world.

Do you think this has anything to do with reading?

## SUMMARY

Students are successful readers when they can readily accommodate their skills to meet the demands of various content areas and levels of sophistication. Part of those skills is an awareness of levels of comprehension and how to

*Reprinted by permission of the publisher from "What Does This Have to Do With Reading?" by Harold L. Herber, *The Journal of Reading,* International Reading Association, pp. 519-20, May 1971.

function at each. Initially emphasizing the levels gives students the feeling of success. The simplicity of levels avoids burdening them with a multiplicity of skills (of questionable origin).

When secure in their use of levels of comprehension, students are receptive to being shown how to use the organizational patterns peculiar to expository material and/or literary genre. They learn to accommodate the patterns (a more difficult task than accommodating the levels of comprehension) as they move from subject to subject and grade to grade. They become aware that the relationships they perceived in the interpretive and applied levels of comprehension are very much the same as the relationships they perceive when applying the organizational patterns. Then they discover that organizational patterns exist within the levels of comprehension. They were using them successfully before they knew what they were called. This discovery adds to their confidence.

Throughout their experience in learning how to apply the patterns, students are guided by the teacher. The teacher does not assume they already know what she is to teach them. She uses guides to develop their understanding of levels of comprehension and organizational patterns. And because these guides relate to the students' required textbooks, they learn the content of the course while they learn how to read the material.

When there is no guiding structure, the students are abandoned to their own resourcefulness to find a way to discover the content (a feat accomplished by many, but in an unnecessarily inefficient manner). How much better for students to expend energy *using* skills to explore content rather than *discovering* the skills by which the content eventually will be explored. Although we should fear too much structure, we should also fear the lack of it.

*     *     *     *     *     *

## REACTION GUIDE

*Part I*

*Directions*: Listed below are twelve statements. Place a check on the numbered line before each one which states or paraphrases information or ideas presented in this chapter. Be ready to cite evidence to support your decisions.

_____ 1. Patterns constitute the internal organization of the text.

_____ 2. There are four organizational patterns that are characteristic of expository materials.

_____ 3. Each of the four patterns has a set of signal words which reveal the organization of a given reading selection.

_____ 4. Organizational patterns characterize entire works as well as single paragraphs.

_____ 5. The principle that content determines process is particularly important when you decide what organizational pattern to stress with a given reading selection.

_____ 6. There is a logical, interacting relationship between organizational patterns and levels of comprehension.

_____ 7. Prior experience with literal and interpretive levels of comprehension provides an appropriate reference for developing an understanding of how to perceive the explicit and implicit relationships within the patterns.

_____ 8. Patterns are logically imbedded in the levels, particularly the interpretive level.

_____ 9. It is useful to know the organizational pattern inherent in a reading selection before beginning to develop reading guides for levels of comprehension.

_____ 10. External organization of materials is a gross characterization, focusing on format and physical appearance.

_____ 11. When there is no guiding structure, the students are abandoned to their own resourcefulness to find a way to discover the content.

_____ 12. Although we should fear too much structure, we also should fear the lack of it.

### Part II

*Directions*: Listed below are seven statements. Place a check on the numbered line before each one that expresses an idea you believe is supported by information in this chapter. Be ready to cite evidence to support your decisions.

_____ 1. Part I of a patterns guide can use both literal and interpretive levels of comprehension.

_____ 2. Part II of a patterns guide can use both interpretive and applied levels of comprehension.

_____ 3. Students can use a reading or reasoning process without knowing what it is called or being able to define it.

_____ 4. Organizational patterns expand students' repertoire of available tools for deriving meaning from text material.

_____ 5. Organizational patterns expand teachers' alternatives for ways to enhance students' comprehension of text material.

_____ 6. While patterns are imbedded in levels, levels are also imbedded in patterns.

_____ 7. Patterns and levels help students develop a sense of connection in what they read.

*Part III*

*Directions*: Listed below are five statements. Check each one that you can support by a combination of ideas from the text and related personal experiences. Be ready to cite evidence from both sources to support your decisions.

____ 1. There is a fine line between order and chaos.

____ 2. The more options one has for dealing with a problem, the more likely it is that one will solve the problem.

____ 3. As one increases options, one increases the need for making decisions.

____ 4. It is discomforting to change the way one works and/or thinks.

____ 5. Efficiency is closely related to habit.

\* \* \* \* \* \*

## REFERENCES

JEWETT, ARNO. Using book parts. In Harold L. Herber (ed.), *Developing study skills in secondary schools*. Newark, Del.: International Reading Association, 1965.

NILES, OLIVE. School programs: the necessary conditions. In *Reading: process and program*. Urbana, Ill.: National Council of Teachers of English, 1976.

SHEPHERD, DAVID. Using sources of information. In Harold L. Herber (ed.), *Developing study skills in secondary schools*. Newark, Del.: International Reading Association, 1965.

SUMMERS, EDWARD. Utilizing visual aids in reading materials for effective learning. In Harold L. Herber (ed.), *Developing study skills in secondary schools*. Newark, Del.: International Reading Association, 1965.

VACCA, RICHARD. *An investigation of a functional reading strategy in seventh grade social studies*. Unpublished doctoral dissertation, Syracuse University, 1973.

# five

# Reasoning In, Around, and Beyond Reading

---

## VOCABULARY

The following terms are important to an understanding of this chapter. Each is defined in context. Read through the list to identify those for which you have uncertain meanings. Then as you read the chapter, pay particular attention to their definitions. Also, make certain that the meanings attributed to the remaining words by their context in the chapter correspond to the meanings they hold for you.

open reasoning                    content-free
closed reasoning                  reasoning guides
content-bound

The following terms, which have been used in previous chapters, are important to an understanding of this chapter as well. You may wish to review their definitions and the meaning attributed to them in the previous contexts before reading further.

functional teaching               simulation
intrinsic generalization          information source
extrinsic generalization          nonprint media

## IDEA DIRECTION

This chapter is unique in that its content is implicit in most of the other chapters of the book. Reasoning permeates all of our teaching and learning activities—or at least it should. Presumably the power to reason separates man from the lower forms of animals (though occasionally the product of his reasoning seems to make him their equivalent or less). Thus, reasoning processes must be considered in any plan to improve instructional skills and learning opportunities. The chapter should be read with this idea in mind.

## READING DIRECTION

This chapter is organized somewhat differently than those on levels of comprehension and organizational patterns. It starts with an explanation, then an example, in order to establish the focus of the chapter. You will notice other variations, none of which should cause you problems.

---

## TEACHING THE PROCESS OF REASONING:
## AN EXPLANATION

Students' natural ability to reason can be enhanced by instruction. Failure to teach students how to reason can put them at a learning disadvantage. Yet comparatively little attention is given to helping students polish their reasoning skills. Instruction that enhances students' reasoning power and facility serves them well in their pursuit of knowledge and understanding throughout their lives.

Note that the suggestion is that students be taught *how* to think, not *to* think. They already *can* think. And that is what this chapter is about: helping students develop more competence and confidence in the use of their reasoning powers. Since this textbook is about reading, part of the focus is on reasoning in reading. But since this book is also about the content areas and since they include activities other than reading, which also require reasoning, part of the focus is on reasoning around and beyond reading.

Thus, reasoning has several important relationships to reading. Each is discussed below, and two are identified as the focus of this chapter.

### Prereading Activities

Chapter 9 discusses in detail the importance of preparing students for reading tasks in an instructional setting. The better the preparation, the better the students' performance with the reading assignment. Indeed, it is likely that if students were more carefully prepared for their reading assignments in the content areas, many of their "reading problems" would disappear.

Of concern to this chapter is the fact that most of the valuable preparation activities involve students in a variety of reasoning skills. Chapters 7, 8, and 9 present suggestions for such prereading activities. You are invited to study those chapters as appropriate to your interests and needs.

### Reading Activities

If you have read Chapters 3 and 4, you realize that reading involves reasoning. The comprehension process, as described by the levels-of-comprehension construct, engages students' minds in a variety of reasoning. The close analysis of information to discern relationships and develop ideas surely involves reasoning. The synthesis of those ideas with the readers' prior knowledge and experience also involves reasoning.

Discernment and application of the organizational patterns in expository materials involve reasoning. The perception and utilization of the relationships implicit in these patterns cannot be accomplished by an idle intellect.

Use of the suggested methods and materials related to levels of comprehension and organizational patterns will serve your students well by enhancing their natural reasoning abilities. Because those two chapters cover this aspect of reasoning's relationships to reading, it is unnecessary to repeat it here. If you haven't read Chapters 3 and 4, you are invited to study them as appropriate to your interests and needs.

### Postreading Activities

Students not only reason about what they are reading while they are reading it; they also reason about it after reading it. As students progress in learning how to read content materials well, they may need less and less guidance while they read. Instead they may need help in reasoning about what they already have read, learning how to apply a variety of reasoning processes to the content in retrospect. This chapter will present methods and materials for providing such help, will describe the reasoning processes which can be taught in this fashion, and will identify the students for whom such instruction is appropriate.

### Nonprint-Related Activities

Much that is done in content-area classrooms does not require a printed text. To be sure, printed words are involved in photographs, films, and television—but the primary means for acquiring information is auditory, coupled with visual interpretation. Both require reasoning; and students can benefit from instruction in how to respond more thoughtfully to such media. Similarly, some media, such as tapes or records, are exclusively auditory, providing information, ideas, and impressions through spoken words and sound. When students are shown ways to respond to such media, they benefit from the ideas and information and impressions they gain as well as from the reasoning processes they develop. This chapter presents methods and materials for providing this kind of help.

### EXPERIENCING GUIDED REASONING

This first example presents both a prereading and postreading activity that involves reasoning about a poem. The material, prepared for use with adults, will give you a feeling for this kind of guidance in reasoning. Before you look at or read the poem, you might want to engage in the following prereading activity to gain a sense of the complete lesson related to this poem.

With colleagues in your group, list in five minutes as many words as you can which have some bearing on the word *perspective*. Then study your list to develop categories in which you can place your words. Share with other groups both your lists and your categories.

Now, read the poem and then do the activity that immediately follows. Be certain to read the directions and follow them carefully.

### *PERSPECTIVE*

The centipede was happy quite
Until the toad in fun
Said, "Pray, which leg goes after which?"
And worked her mind to such a pitch,
She lay distracted in the ditch
Considering how to run.

*Directions*: Listed below are eight statements, each preceded by a numbered line. Read each one and think about its meaning. Place a check on the line if you find support for the statement in the poem or if you think the statement is a possible extension or application of ideas expressed in the poem. Be ready to discuss your reasons for accepting the statements you did.

_____ 1. Acting without thought is easier than thinking without action.

_____ 2. Coordination is more a mental state than a physical attribute.

_____ 3. Self-assessment is a virtue until it interferes with progress.

_____ 4. Contentment is often equated with unquestioned assumptions.

_____ 5. Yesterday's disrupting confusion is tomorrow's status quo.

_____ 6. Analysis, confusion, and clarification are highly interrelated.

_____ 7. One of life's most devastating experiences is to see yourself as others see you.

_____ 8. Confusion is a relative state, whether mental or physical.

## Analysis

After discussing your responses with your colleagues and sharing the reasons for and evidence of your support for the statements you selected, compare the consensus of your group with the following observations.

All of the statements can be checked, given the criteria in the directions. Statements 1, 2, and 8 represent ideas intrinsically related to the content of the poem. They are, as Joan Nelson (1976) suggests, primarily "content-bound." That is, they are closely tied to information directly stated in the poem.

The poem implies that as long as the centipede was not thinking about the action of her legs, everything proceeded normally and life was easy. But when she began analyzing the action she was distracted to the point of immobility and her thoughts in that mode were painful. This seems to support the first statement.

The evidence just cited seems also to support the second and eighth statements. To outward appearances, her coordination seems to be a physical attribute—indeed, a physical marvel! However, her response to the toad's question seems to suggest that the ultimate control is mental, not physical; even so, the confusion is relative.

Statements 3 through 7 represent ideas more extrinsically related to the content of the poem. They are mostly "content-free" (Nelson, 1976). That is, they are stimulated by the content and thus are related to its ideas, but they extend beyond it. They illustrate ideas in the content, but elaborate upon them.

Statement 3, although obviously related to the poem, has a primary relationship to experiences outside the poem. One thinks of the negative effects of excessive piety for example, where, as one minister put it, "People are so heavenly-minded they are no earthly-good," and nothing can be accomplished.

Statement 4 also is grounded clearly in the poem but can be amply supported by experiences with persons who enjoy the certainty which comes from ignorance.

Statement 5 is more remote. However, it is supported by thoughts of confusion in our society caused by the strange dress and behavior of the younger generation, which became the status quo when taken over by the elders. "Disrupting confusion," while describing the centipede's experience, triggered this association.

Statement 6 reminds one of a reaction cycle set off by reasoning. Analysis of a problem may first bring confusion, but if the thinker is tenacious, clarification comes. We left the centipede at the point of confusion, but we shall hope she reached clarification in time.

Statement 7 needs little explanation. Who has not suffered the objective glimpse of oneself and been astonished at the vision?

## RATIONALE

The need for postreading and nonprint-related reasoning is clear to most teachers. The problem is how to promote this reasoning. How does one teach students how to think, how to reason?

The inclination is to do with reasoning skills what has been done with reading skills: isolate the skills, find materials through which the skills can be taught, and teach the skills directly. But the direct teaching of reasoning skills seems to be as much a failure as the direct teaching of reading skills has been.

The better instructional response seems to be the functional approach, doing with reasoning processes what this book also suggests for reading processes. Purposes of the reader and the content of the text determine the reading process to be applied; the content of the media, whether print or not, and the purposes of the responder determine the reasoning process to be applied. Even as students are guided in applying reading processes in this functional approach, so they can be guided in applying the reasoning processes in a similarly functional approach.

This requires that reasoning be simplified so that it becomes teachable, even as is true for reading. It can seem naive to suggest that so complex a process can be made simple. Perhaps so, but we must remember that our purpose is not to teach our students *about* reasoning; rather, it is to teach them *how to apply* the process effectively. There is much more hope for success in teaching how to reason than in teaching what reasoning is and, happily, our purposes are on the hopeful side. Simplification favors the "how-to" task; it doesn't favor the "what-it-is" task.

Simplifying reasoning to render it more teachable has been an illusive goal and much still remains to be done before attaining it. However, understanding the following chain of events may be helpful to you. At least, it is the basis for this chapter and explains materials you will find later on.

"How to explain how to teach reasoning skills" was the objective. When the literature was searched for discussions of reasoning skills, a pattern began to emerge. Labels for reasoning processes or skills seemed to fall into pairs:

convergent  — divergent
critical    — creative
analytical  — elaborative
intensive   — extensive

deductive     — inductive
interpretive  — inferential
objective     — subjective

To teach each of the pairs or to teach each skill in each pair would be to fall into the trap of "fragmenting" reasoning and would depart from the principles of functional teaching of simplified processes. "Think about how your mind feels" was the thought that came to mind as these pairs were reflected upon. "Are there categories to which these pairs belong?" "Is there some commonality across one element in each of the pairs and another commonality across the other element in each of the pairs?" These questions came to mind as this list was contemplated. And answers also came to mind.

The first answer: When I contemplate all the labels on the left side of each pair, my mind feels closed. I see myself bending over the information source, studying it carefully, fitting together the information and ideas that are there. I feel tied to the content of what I read or see.

Ah, but when I contemplate all the labels to the right in each pair, my mind feels open. I see my head up and thrown back as I experience a flash of insight that, prompted by what I read, carries me out and beyond the confines of the text into new insights, new ideas, new experiences.

The second answer: Why not call the reasoning processes described to the right "open" and those to the left "closed"? Does "closed" suggest limitations, narrowness, "closed-mindedness"? It could, but it doesn't have to. Perhaps it would be better to think of these processes as being "content-bound," intrinsic to the text, intrinsic generalizations that reflect the essence of the information or ideas presented. They have much in common with the literal and interpretive levels of comprehension.

And what of the term "open"? Does that suggest what is happening in the processes described by labels on the right? Yes, because that's how my mind feels. Perhaps it would be better to think of these processes as being "content-free," extrinsic to the text, an extrinsic generalization stimulated by the text but drawing its substance from the world of related experience and its cohesion from a flash of insight, the "intuitive leap" (Bruner, 1965). These processes have much in common with the applied level of comprehension.

The third answer: It seems too neat; too tidy. Are the processes labeled on the right always "open"? Are those on the left always "closed"? Not always. But what are they when they are not open or closed? Depending on the material and the purposes and experiences of the reasoner, one finds that those processes listed on the right would be more "closed" than "open" and those on the left would be more "open" than "closed."

It would be naive to believe that these two categories are mutually exclusive. In the description of any process, the greater the simplification the more uncertainty there is in assigning any part of the process exclusively to any particular category of the description. Overlap among categories increases as the number of categories decreases. For example, there is more possibility for overlap when a process is divided into two categories than when that same process is broken down into fourteen categories.

Thus, simplifying the description of a process results in a loss of preciseness. Those who use the description must have a tolerance for ambiguity, an open-minded flexibility that helps them realize that there are few absolutes in the world. As is clear from this discussion, the description of the reasoning process is not one of those absolutes. But what is lost in preciseness is gained in manageability. The content-area teacher can give more attention to two categories of reasoning, open and closed, than to fourteen, which one would have if each process were to be taught separately.

### Teaching the Process

Manageability—teachability—is the issue. To be taught effectively, the reasoning process needs to become an integrated, natural part of the curriculum; it needs to be taught functionally rather than directly. As is true for the reading process when the skills are separated out and taught directly, the direct teaching of reasoning skills is not as effective as the functional. For example, direct teaching of specific reasoning skills generally failed to produce change in achievement in those reasoning skills as measured by the *Watson Glaser Critical Thinking Appraisal* (WGCTA) (Herber, 1959). On the other hand, guiding students in tasks which involved the application of reasoning skills (functional teaching of reasoning) did produce significant gains in achievement in reasoning skills as measured by the WGCTA (Murphy, 1960). In the first study, special materials were constructed to provide carefully sequenced instruction in specific reasoning skills. The study was an example of the direct teaching of reasoning. In the second study, students were given lists of words with multiple meanings and asked to work in pairs to classify the words under categories. A different word list was classified under a different set of categories during each instructional period in the experiment. As students assigned words to categories and discussed their reasons, they were applying the reasoning implicit in the various subtests of the *WGCTA*: Inference; Interpretation; Deduction; Evaluation of Argument; Recognition of Assumption. Such activity is an example of the functional teaching of reasoning.

A logical extension of this and similar evidence is to create instructional experiences for students in which they apply the reasoning processes we hope for them to develop over time. As discussed in detail in Chapter 8, this involves simulation as we guide their skills development in the content areas. Thus, if it is true that the skills in reasoning can be described by two categories, and if it is true that these skills can be taught functionally, then it is also true that creating learning situations in which students reason about the curriculum content will raise their achievement in applying open and closed reasoning.

Think back to your responses to the statements related to the poem "Perspective." Your response to three of the statements—statements 1, 2, and 8—involved you with more open than closed reasoning. As noted on page 107, these statements are more "content-bound." That is, they focus more on the content of the poem, as the literal and interpretive levels of comprehension do. In thinking about the statements, you are more involved *in* the poem: you're more analytical, more objective, more critical, more intensive as you consider its content. You take the statement as a generalization and deduce its support from the poem, gathering your experiences and converging them on the content as you do so. Thus, through your response to these three statements as they have bearing on the poem, you are involved in closed reasoning, applying the various skills or processes associated with that kind of reasoning.

The remaining statements are more "content-free," as suggested earlier in this chapter. They represent generalizations more extrinsic to the content, ideas which seem to spring from and extend beyond the poem. (In contrast, the other statements—1, 2, and 8—seem surrounded, or held in, by the poem.) In thinking about the content-free statements, you are more elaborative, more subjective, more creative, more extensive as you reach beyond the poem to expressions which synthesize the poem with other ideas and feelings and experiences. Using your knowledge and experience and ideas from the poem, you induce generalizations represented by the statements. Stimulated by the poem your thoughts diverge from it and identify with statements which express that expansive response. Thus, through your response to these five statements as they bear on the poem, you are involved in open reasoning, applying the various skills or processes associated with that kind of reasoning.

Note that the statements were not labeled "open" or "closed." Before you responded to them you probably had given no thought to the category to which they belonged or even that there were such categories. Nevertheless, your mind was engaged in the type of reasoning similar to that described above as you deliberated on the statements. What was true for you also is true for your students: application of the reasoning process is not dependent upon being able to label the skills. Just thinking about the meanings of the statements in reference to the poem engaged your mind in a multiplicity of reasoning skills.

Not knowing which *particular* reasoning skill was involved when you thought about the appropriateness of a given statement did not inhibit your thinking or prevent you from accepting or rejecting the statement or identifying the specific support for your position. Thus, even though you had not been taught the specific skill (if there was one) which was basic to that statement, you were not prevented from responding to the statement. And what is true for you is also true for your students. They can apply reasoning skills which are natural to their intellect without receiving direct instruction ahead of time. We are providing them with experience which helps them exercise their natural propensity for reasoning. Then they are more inclined to use their reasoning powers skillfully instead of letting them wither through lack of use.

### Eligible Students

Good reasoning is not the exclusive domain of the brilliant or the college-bound student. One finds that good reasoning is relative to many factors. One finds it in young children and old adults, required across subject areas and grade levels, among persons with limited as well as seemingly unlimited abilities. The process of reasoning is the same for all persons; it differs only in degree of sophistication, not in kind (Bruner, 1960). And contrary to a logical notion, the degree of sophistication does not necessarily correlate directly with level of basic intelligence. Many students do not have great intelligence but, by virtue of their experience and environment, they do have a great and finely tuned capacity for reasoning.

Unfortunately we often find that students in the lower ability range of a given class are either themselves so resigned to failure or are by their teachers so consigned to failure that little is done to improve their achievement. In either case the student is the loser. Because in teaching we always operate as though our assumptions about students are correct, we have a way of making come true the expectations that spring from our assumptions. Our students would stand to gain if we would err on the side of optimism rather than pessimism and expect more for all rather than less for some.

It is important to believe that *all* our students can benefit from opportunity to enhance their reasoning skills. The suggestions in this text are appropriate for all students. You will have to adjust the sophistication level for their needs, but be optimistic and let them stretch. You'll be pleasantly surprised at how far they can reach.

## ILLUSTRATIVE REASONING GUIDES
## FOR PRINTED MATERIALS

Students need not analyze reasoning processes to learn them. Rather, students apply these processes—capabilities they already possess—in an environment conducive to such behavior and as a consequence they gain confidence. Many skills seem to contribute to the reasoning process just as many ideas contribute to the product, but these skills are enhanced functionally, not taught directly. The environment and structure are the important elements. The environment is embodied in the teachers' attitude; the structure in reasoning guides.

### Teachers' Attitude

Teachers know that students can develop competence in such intellectual activity, if teachers provide the proper classroom environment. It takes secure teachers to allow such activity—ones who are not afraid to say, "I don't know," ones who will accept solutions to problems that differ from their own as long as they are valid, ones who will applaud a flash of insight enthusiastically even while knowing they likely would never have produced the idea. It takes teachers who will allow students to challenge their ideas and present alternatives, and do not always feel that they have to be right; teachers who believe the productive pursuit of an idea is more important than coverage of a prescribed segment of the curriculum in a prescribed period of time; teachers who can pose stimulating, open-ended questions that produce creative reasoning rather than carefully circumscribed, closed questions that require students to guess what is in their minds. These teachers perceive at least part of their role as being to get out of their students' way so that their students can pursue their own ideas within the structure provided and learn from one another, and so that the teachers can learn from the students, too. This is not laissez-faire education, as the reasoning guides will point out, but it is much less restrictive than the "I lecture —you listen, I ask— you answer" kind of instruction.

### Reasoning Guides as Simulators

Reasoning guides are simulators (see Chapter 8) of the open and closed reasoning processes. They are contrived situations within which students respond to ideas. The statements that make up the guides are sufficiently broad to simulate open reasoning and yet sufficiently related to the information source to simulate closed reasoning as well. But, at the same time, the guides are such that students are not locked into a prescribed line of reasoning. The guides provide a suitable context within which students learn a new kind of behavior—pursuit of their own ideas rather than just the author's or the teachers'.

As indicated above, these reasoning guides are as appropriate for students of limited ability as for the very able. They assume that students have some means of accessibility to the information and ideas about which they are to reason, either through printed materials or other media. For all ability levels, the guides remain the same in principle and structure; they differ in the type of statements placed in them. The statements should be related to the students' background of experience and understanding and appropriate to their intellectual range; they should be sufficiently open-ended so every student can stretch to the maximum and should be coupled with the opportunity for discussion that lets students share the benefits of their own productive reasoning and learn from one another (see Chapter 8). The statements should also be coupled with the teachers' own contributions, which will be as open to analysis, acceptance, modification, and rejection as the students'. For immutable laws and principles, the person with the knowledge can assume the authoritative role—this most often is the teacher. But for pursuit of the product of reasoning, who is to say that a student's view is any less valid than a teacher's or that the idea of the most brilliant student is more valid than that of the least brilliant student?

Below are several illustrative reasoning guides, developed for use in different subject areas for students of varying ability levels. Some seem to give more emphasis to open reasoning, being content-free; some give more emphasis to closed reasoning, being content-bound. The differences spring from a combination of variables: the teacher's purpose, the nature of the material, the students' needs. But in no case was the guide designed to emphasize one type of reasoning over the other. As repeated over and over in this text, content determines process. The reasoning guides were developed to reflect the content objective. Whether the statements in the guide reflected one or the other or a combination of the types of reasoning was not the primary concern. Over time, students encounter both types of reasoning and the component subskills of each in quantities sufficient to increase their reasoning achievement.

**Reasoning guides for literature** A teacher of eleventh-grade honors English felt that her students were not deriving the potential benefit from exploring Thoreau's ideas as expresses in *Walden*. Her procedure had been to have the students read the work. Then she would present a lecture that explored Thoreau's ideas and related them to our society as well as his. In other words, she assigned the reading and then explained to students what it meant to them. After exploring the use of reasoning guides, she concluded that she would design a guide to help students discover for themselves what, if anything, Thoreau had to say to them.

She gave them this reasoning guide as homework, to be completed either as or after they read the work. She applied the various elements of the Instructional Framework, described in Chapter 9. Although the students were proficient in reading, they needed assistance to creatively pursue their own ideas when studying basic works in the curriculum.

The students brought the completed guide to class. They were assigned to groups and their task was to compare their responses. Where they discovered differences, they were to pursue them and see if they could or should be resolved. Where the responses were the same, they were to determine if their reasons were the same or different.

The teacher said this was one of her most exciting lessons. Students discussion of their responses proved very fruitful. Students explored the relevancy of Thoreau's ideas to their own society and developed some new insights on how literature in general, and this work in particular, comments on contemporary affairs even though the author may have lived centuries before.

Note the format of the guide. The teacher listed significant quotes from the work, then gave students specific directions as to what they were to do with the quotes and with the statements that followed. She created open-ended reaction situations that were designed to link Thoreau's ideas with students' experiences. Her hope was that students would see relationships between the two and the thought thus stimulated would be pursued to a fruitful conclusion.

Such a guide places side by side an author's ideas and a student's experience with the hope that by synthesizing these two elements the student will develop new insight and understanding. Such a guide combines both open and closed reasoning as students analyze the author's ideas and then their own.

### ADVENTURES IN AMERICAN LITERATURE
### THOREAU: WALDEN

*Directions*: Below are some sentences from *Walden*:

A. "I went to the woods because I wished to live deliberately, to front only the essential facts of life, and see if I could not learn what it had to teach, and not, when I came to die, discover that I had not lived."
B. "Our life is frittered away by detail." "Simplify, simplify."
C. "It [the nation] lives too fast."
D. "What news!" "How much more important to know what that is which was never old."
E. "When we are unhurried and wise, we perceive that only great and worthy things have any permanent and absolute existence, that petty fears and petty pleasures are but the shadow of the reality."
F. "Time is but the stream I go a-fishing in."

*Part I*

Consider the following statements. Do you think Thoreau would have approved of them? In Column A answer *yes* or *no*.

*Part II*

In Column B write the letter indicating the quotation of Thoreau which you considered in deciding your answer.

*Part III*

For Number 10, write an original statement which you think Thoreau would have liked. This should be based on E.

A     B

\_\_\_\_ \_\_\_\_ 1. I have to stay up to listen to the eleven o'clock news.

\_\_\_\_ \_\_\_\_ 2. I am going to give these extra hats to my cousin.

\_\_\_\_ \_\_\_\_ 3. I have to attend three meetings today.

\_\_\_\_ \_\_\_\_ 4. I'd rather take the side roads than the thruway.

\_\_\_\_ \_\_\_\_ 5. I have all the time in the world to watch the sunset.

\_\_\_\_ \_\_\_\_ 6. I'm collecting pictures of my favorite actor. I now have seventy-nine pictures.

___ ___ 7. The president of the company spent Monday in New York, Tuesday in Chicago, and Wednesday in San Francisco.

___ ___ 8. I'm going to budget some time for myself each day so that I'll have a little time to think.

___ ___ 9. My life will be ruined if I'm not elected to this club.

<u>yes</u>  <u>E</u> 10. _____

_____

_____


An English teacher wanted his twelfth-grade students to develop an understanding that time is the true test of human experience, the measure of emotion, the commentator on the human condition. He used the interaction between a poem by Emily Dickinson and a reasoning guide related to that poem as both stimulus and vehicle for pursuing his objective. Note that the directions and order of response to the guide and poem make the reasoning required by the statements in the guide first content-free *(open)* and then content-bound *(closed)*.

### DICKINSON: "FINAL HARVEST"

*Directions*: Read the following set of statements. Place a check on the numbered line for each one you find acceptable. Be ready to share reasons for your decisions.

Next, read the poem by Emily Dickinson which follows the statements. Then go back over each statement and decide if Dickinson would agree with you. Circle the number of each statement you believe she would accept. Discuss in your groups the possible reasons for the similarity and difference between your view and Dickinson's.

____ 1. Time is the eternal healer; all our wounds will eventually abate.

____ 2. Strife develops the firmest resolve in people; they will endure in spite of it.

____ 3. Love for one can never be unrequited, if love for another is found.

____ 4. The poet and artist have moments of deepest insight after periods of loneliness and despair.

____ 5. When there's a will, there's a way.

____ 6. Man, like the oak, must weather the storm to gain whatever benefits it may offer.

____ 7. Ills which are conjured up by our minds and disappear after a while are not the real causes of human anguish.

____ 8. Time is the cross mankind must bear.

## From FINAL HARVEST

They say that "Time assuages"—
Time never did assuage—
An actual suffering strengthens
As Sinews do, with age—

Time is a Test of Trouble—
But not a Remedy—
If such it prove, it prove too
There was no Malady—

**Reasoning guide for history** A seventh-grade honors class was studying Alexander Hamilton's contribution to the solvency of the new nation after the Revolutionary War. From past experience, the teacher knew that students would have no difficulty reading the text or memorizing the plans and the purpose of each plan, as expressed by Hamilton and interpreted by the author of the text. The teacher was concerned about assimilation, about awareness of the significance of the plans for the new nation, about their contemporary relevance, and about their importance to the students themselves. He prepared the following guide.

### STORY OF THE AMERICAN NATION

*Directions*: Alexander Hamilton developed five plans to solve the financial problems of the new nation. See if you can identify the plans by which the problems, listed below, might be solved. Write the letter of the plan on the line before the statement of the problem which it solves. More than one plan might be used to solve one problem.

*Plans*

A. The national government must pay its war debts in full.

B. The national government must take over war debts of the states.

C. The national government must raise money with an import tax and a tax on whiskey.

D. The national government must issue coins and paper money for all the nation.

E. The national government must establish a bank to help deal with money problems.

*Problems*

_____ 1. A nation with poor credit finds it difficult to borrow money.

_____ 2. It is difficult to carry on trade when there is not a standard currency.

_____ 3. It is necessary to be able to borrow money in order to expand the economy.

_____ 4. The government requires income in order to operate properly.

_____ 5. If people are to have a voice in the government, they must support it in every way.

_____ 6. Any organization is only as strong as its weakest part.

_____ 7. Money must "work" to expand and grow even as people need to work to grow and prosper.

_____ 8. Businesses in one country need protection from competition in other countries.

_____ 9. People must have confidence in their government before they can support it fully.

_____ 10. If private citizens join the government in business it could be helpful to both parties.

Note the format of the guide. The teacher listed interpretations of Hamilton's plans rather than their names. He identified several situations which were relevant both to Hamilton and the students. Students were to judge how the problems could be solved by combining solutions (Hamilton's plans) into various sets. Thus, as they explored the relevancy of Hamilton's thinking to contemporary problems, students were involved in both open and closed reasoning.

After being prepared for the activity as described in the discussion of the Instructional Framework in Chapter 9, students were assigned the reading selection from their text and the reasoning guide as homework. The next day they were divided into groups and their assignment was to compare responses and explore the validity of the differences. Students learned a great deal from one another. They were excited by being freed to pursue their own insights and those of their classmates. The teacher was available as a resource and was careful to play the role of only an arbiter not the authority. Good reasoning was evidenced everywhere. Students knew, consequently, not only _what_ Hamilton's plans were, but _how_ they worked and the essence of their value.

**Reasoning guides for math** Here are two reasoning guides for math. The first, developed for fourth-grade students, guides students' reasoning about mathematical operations as they pertain to number sentences. The statements in the guide promote more _closed_ than _open_ reasoning.

## INCHES, FEET, AND YARDS*

_Directions_: Below are six number sentences. Place a check on the line before each one you can use to find the number of inches in one yard.

*Reprinted by permission from _GO, Reading in the Content Areas_, by Harold L. Herber, Book 4, p. 100 (1973), © 1973, 1974, by Scholastic Magazines, Inc.

_____ a. 12 + 1 = ?                    _____ d. 3 x 12 = ?
_____ b. 12 x 3 = ?                    _____ e. 12 + 3 = ?
_____ c. 12 + 12 + 12 = ?              _____ f. 3 x 1 = ?

Now place a check on the line before each statement which gives a reason for your choices.

_____ 1. You must change both units of measurement to inches.
_____ 2. You can multiply the number of inches in one foot by the number of feet in one yard to change both units of measurement to inches.
_____ 3. You must change both units of measurement to yards.
_____ 4. You can add the number of inches in one foot as many times as there are feet in one yard to change both units of measurement to inches.
_____ 5. You can multiply the number of feet in one yard by the number of inches in one foot to change both units of measurement to inches.

The second guide was developed for fifth-grade students. It guides students' reasoning in practical considerations about differences in mathematical figures. The statements in the guide are closed in that they are content-bound, but open in that they require imaginative conceptualization of the spatial relationship between the two figures.

### WHAT'S YOUR THINKING?*

An outdoor skating pond is _circular._ It has a _diameter_ of 50 feet. The indoor skating rink is _rectangular._ It is 50 feet wide and 100 feet long. Two boys skate at the same rate of speed. Check the statements below which you think are true.

_____ 1. The pond and the indoor rink are the same size.
_____ 2. It will take longer for a boy to skate around the indoor rink than around the pond.
_____ 3. It will take longer to skate across the pond than to skate across the indoor rink.
_____ 4. It will take twice as long to skate the length of the indoor rink as across the pond.
_____ 5. One boy has more room to skate in than the other.

**Reasoning guide for science** This guide was developed for sixth-grade students. It guides their reasoning about a reading selection related to the study of migration. The text presents factual information about the migration of various animals and discusses some of the theories that attempt to explain migration. The statements in the guide represent conclusions that could possibly be drawn from the information. Students analyze the statements in light of the information to judge the validity of the conclusions, then determine if the conclusion is based on fact or theory. Both decisions require careful reasoning of the closed variety. Some, however, require more open reasoning (items 5 and 9, for example).

## THINK ABOUT IT *

*Directions*: You are often asked to *draw conclusions* from information you read or discover in science. The reading selection "On the Move" gives both facts and theories. You can use them to draw conclusions.

Think about each statement below. Decide if it could be a *conclusion* you might draw from what you have read in "On the Move." If it is, check under A. Then decide if it is based on fact or theory or both. Write *F* (fact), *Th* (theory), or *Both* on the line under B.

A    B
___  ___  1. Everything that flies south is not always a bird.
___  ___  2. When a bird is hungry, it may fly south.
___  ___  3. Scientists do not know much about why animals migrate.
___  ___  4. Creatures migrate twice a year.
___  ___  5. You can know that something will always happen even if you do not know why it happens.
___  ___  6. Some living creatures know about the seasons.
___  ___  7. If you do something that somebody tells you to do, you do not do it by instinct.
___  ___  8. A person can draw conclusions from facts or theories.
___  ___  9. If scientists use their instincts, their conclusions will not be correct.

### ILLUSTRATIVE REASONING GUIDES FOR
### NONPRINT MATERIALS

All that has been stated about reasoning guides for printed materials is also true for reasoning guides for nonprint materials. One obviously must allow for the different mode of presentation—the different medium—but that is of minor consequence.

*Reprinted by permission from *GO, Reading in the Content Areas,* by Harold L. Herber, Book 6, p. 147, (1974) © 1973, 1974, by Scholastic Magazines, Inc.

Both open and closed reasoning are found in response to nonprint media, whether still or motion pictures, whether audio or video taped. Because the information that stimulates the reasoning comes in a form different than print, students have to make some accommodations. Where the medium is strictly audio or fleetingly visual and audio (as are motion pictures or television), one does not have ready access to the information for applying the closed type of reasoning. If such media are to be used instructionally and reasoning skills also are to be enhanced, it is important that purposes be clearly established for the particular tape or film or record being used. Such purposes, set with students ahead of time, help them attend to detail as they listen to and view the message. They can either depend on memory, jot down key words, or take more formal notes as they are exposed to the message, then use those sources as they respond to the reasoning guides.

A very effective method is to have students react to the statements in the reasoning guide *before* they listen to or view the message. This is discussed in detail in Chapter 7 in relation to printed sources, but it is equally applicable here. The reasoning guide is much the same as those previously presented in this chapter, being comprised of a set of statements. Assuming the teacher has applied appropriate techniques to prepare students for the activity (see Chapters 6 and 9), students are able to react to the statements according to their own experience. They decide what they think or how they feel about each of the statements. This engages them in open reasoning, with the stimulus and basis being the previous and preliminary study related to the content objective. They then listen to the tape or record or view the film with this purpose: "Decide whether or not the persons creating the message would agree with you on these statements."

This defines for students their purpose for viewing or listening, gives them a catalyst for gathering information from the medium, and provides a basis for the closed reasoning which examines the content closely. Both types of reasoning are further enhanced when students work together in small groups to discuss the statements and resolve differences they have and cite supporting evidence from the instructional source as well as from their experiences and other sources. In this entire process the students are applying the desired reasoning skills and developing a feeling for that reasoning process as applied to such media.

Pictures provide another source of information and ideas in most curriculum areas and serve to enhance students' reasoning processes as well as their acquisition of the content objective. The following example from social studies illustrates the opportunity.

Study the picture of the New York harbor scene. It is part of a unit of study, the content objective of which is to develop an understanding of why and how large urban areas are important to the United States' economy, government, and society in general. Two types of reasoning guides can be used with this picture. The first is comprised of a list of single words or phrases. The second is made up of a list of declarative statements. The teacher's inclination or the students' interests and capabilities would determine whether one or the

**New York Harbor** (*Courtesy of The Port Authority of New York and New Jersey*)

other, or even a combination of the two, would be used. Both the word list and the set of statements could be adjusted to meet the needs of students according to their levels of sophistication.

### Alternative Reasoning Guide Number One

*Directions:* Listed below are fifteen words. Each may have something to do with the picture of the New York harbor. If you think that a word has some relationship either to details in the picture or to the picture as a whole, place a check on the numbered line. Be ready to give reasons to support your decisions.

| | | |
|---|---|---|
| ____ 1. Transportation | ____ 6. Culture | ____ 11. Congestion |
| ____ 2. Pollution | ____ 7. Immigration | ____ 12. Resources |
| ____ 3. Finance | ____ 8. Customs | ____ 13. Risk |
| ____ 4. Economy | ____ 9. Emigration | ____ 14. Opportunity |
| ____ 5. Trade | ____ 10. Business | ____ 15. Labor |

## Alternative Reasoning Guide Number Two

*Directions*: Listed below are eight statements. Each may have something to do with the picture of the New York harbor. If you think that a statement does have some relationship either to details in the picture or to the picture as a whole, place a check on the numbered line. Be ready to give reasons to support your decisions.

_____ 1. International trade is made possible by good seaports.

_____ 2. A good harbor provides shelter from storms as well as a place for normal docking.

_____ 3. In transportation, embarking is as important as debarking.

_____ 4. The economy of an area is determined by its natural resources.

_____ 5. Communication occurs in many ways.

_____ 6. Gains in transportation and communication bring losses in pollution control.

_____ 7. Commerical centers always are also large population centers.

_____ 8. In large urban areas, things are built more for the convenience of businesses than people.

As you can observe by examining the statements in reference to the picture of New York harbor, they cover a range of sophistication and abstraction. Some relate more specifically to the picture than others; these involve more closed reasoning. The others call for more open reasoning. Depending on your purposes and the experience and capabilities of your students, you would adjust the level of abstraction and sophistication of the statements. But as indicated earlier in this chapter, remember that students often can do more than we think they can. Helping them stretch their minds is exciting to them and to us when they find their ideas both accepted and respected. Materials such as these help in that stretching and that excitement.

The word lists serve a similar function to that of the statements. Levels of sophistication and abstraction are covered by these words. Obviously the students must at least know the definitions of the words if they are to become involved in the reasoning process. The teacher who is constructing the materials can use words that students already know, or students can be given a set of definitions ahead of time, or students can pool their knowledge within their group, and use the dictionary to find definitions of words unknown by group members. Whatever the source of the definitions, they are basic to the activity. As is apparent, some words are clearly related to the picture, representing or closely related to objects or activities observed in the picture. These would involve students more in closed reasoning. Other words are symbolically related to objects or activities in the picture. Perceiving the relationship between those words and the picture involves students more in open reasoning.

Whether using statements or word lists or other approaches which guide rather than test, students are developing a feeling for the application of their reasoning powers to specific problems and situations. As they pertain to such nonprint media, this involves students in reasoning beyond reading in the truest sense.

### REASONING GUIDES AND
### THE APPLIED LEVEL OF COMPREHENSION

Teachers frequently ask, "What's the difference between a reasoning guide and a guide for the applied level of comprehension?" The answer: "There's no difference in their design and often none in their appearance; there is considerable difference in their use and assumptions."

A reasoning guide can be thought of as an applied level guide standing alone. Recall that the applied level is built upon the literal and interpretive levels and students progress through the three levels while reading a given information source. By the time students respond to the applied level guide, they have reacted to the essential information in the passage (literal level) and have begun to perceive the author's meaning by examining the relationships which exist in all of that information (interpretive level). *Then* the students deal with the applied level guide, reacting to broad statements which can be supported from ideas in the text and from experiences and ideas gained in other settings. Therefore, the sequence through the levels is important.

As noted earlier in this chapter, as students become less dependent on guidance *while* they read their texts, they will need instead guidance in postreading reasoning activities—reasoning about what they have read. In a sense it is as though the students have developed reasonable independence in the literal and interpretive levels of comprehension, but still need guidance at the applied level. The reasoning guide provides it.

Experience suggests that students need not have been guided in the use of levels of comprehension before they can be guided in the use of reasoning skills, even though that sequence seems more logical and is more often used. When the statements in the reasoning guide are sufficiently open, students can connect their own knowledge and experience to what they are seeing or hearing or doing at the moment. Even so-called slow students make connections which astonish their teachers and please themselves.

Remember that the reasoning guides also can be applied to nonprint media. This assures the involvement of those students who have difficulty acquiring information at the literal level from a printed source because of some basic reading problems. As indicated earlier, experience demonstrates that once students have acquired the information related to the content objective, they

can participate in reasoning about it in both an open and closed fashion. Therefore, reasoning guides serve students at all stages of development in their reading achievement and gives the teacher another option with which to teach both
course content and related learning processes.


## DEVELOPING A REASONING GUIDE

There are several logical steps one can follow in developing a reasoning
guide:

1. Establish your content objectives. Decide what information and ideas you
   want your students to acquire from studying this particular part of your
   curriculum.
2. Identify the sources which contain the information and the base for the
   ideas you want your students to encounter.
3. Decide whether the students need to be guided in response to the source
   *as* they read it (requiring a level or pattern guide) or *after* they read it
   (requiring a reasoning guide).
4. If they need a reasoning guide rather than a levels or patterns guide, reflect on the relationship between the content objectives and the ideas
   presented in the source the students will read.
5. As the relationships come to mind, write them out in declarative
   statements.
6. Decide what format to use in presenting the statements to the students as
   a reasoning guide: Should it be a list to which they react, such as those on
   pages 107, 116; or should it be a combination with information or interpretations of information from the source where students must relate the
   two in some way, such as those on page 115; or should it be some other
   design of your own choosing?
7. Write directions appropriate to the format, task, and purpose; edit the
   statements to suit the format and distribute both to the students.
8. Have the students work in groups to either (a) do the entire guide together, or (b) do the guide separately, then discuss responses and evidence
   together. The first option involves in-class activity. The second can be
   homework or in-class activity.
9. Move from group to group as students are involved in their discussions so
   that you can get a sense of the understandings they are developing about
   the content objectives and a sense of their facility with the reasoning
   process being stimulated by the activity.
10. Don't ruin the lesson by going over every item again in a full-class discus-
    sion. The students will have developed the understandings you want in
    their group discussions; if not, you will have clarified these understandings
    in their groups. There is nothing to be gained by going over *all* the items
    again. Pick out one or two items which caused problems in all the groups

and/or which are most important to the overall content objectives. Lead a full-class discussion of those items for clarification purposes. This full-class discussion of selected items gives students in each group an opportunity to demonstrate to those in the other groups what they have learned and how well they have applied the reasoning processes. This discussion also gives you opportunity to acknowledge the quality of the reasoning which took place in the small-group discussions as well as in the full-class exchange.

## Application

Have some fun. Here is a poem by Anonymous. Develop a reasoning guide for it that could be used by colleagues in your school. Compare yours with others in your group, and then with the one in Appendix A, page 258.

### DILEMMA

A bit beyond perception's reach
I sometimes think I see
That Life is two locked boxes, each
Containing the other's key.

## SUMMARY

The curriculum in all content areas involves students in the application of reasoning skills. Reasoning power, while natural to the human being, can be enhanced by instruction which helps students to refine the skills and extend the effectiveness of their application.

Such reasoning is related to, but not limited to, reading. It occurs during prereading, reading, and postreading activities. Moreover, it occurs apart from the reading act, as students respond to nonprint media.

Thus, guiding students' reasoning so as to enhance its power and effectiveness can be done simultaneously with teaching the course content, regardless of the media used. And such guidance helps all students across all ability and achievement levels. For some students more time is needed for preparatory activity; for others, less. But by adjusting the reasoning guides to the needs of students, more are better served than when it is assumed that the reasoning process is the exclusive domain of the brilliant students.

\*     \*     \*     \*     \*     \*

## REACTION GUIDE

*Directions*: Listed below are ideas which are stated or implied in the chapter. They are followed by statements which reflect practices, attitudes, and beliefs frequently observed among students and teachers. In column A place a check if you agree with the statement. Place a check in column B before each statement with which you believe the author of the book would agree. In column C enter the numbers representing ideas that you believe support your response. Be prepared to disucss your responses with your colleagues particularly focusing on your points of disagreement with the author's ideas.

### Ideas

1. For immutable laws and principles, the teacher can assume an authoritative role; for pursuit of open reasoning, who is to say that a student's view is any less valid than the teacher's?
2. Reasoning guides provide a suitable environment within which students learn a new kind of behavior—pursuit of their own ideas rather than the teacher's.
3. In most schools there are many students who read too well for their own good.
4. The teacher's challenge is to aid students' application of reasoning in, around, and beyond the reading process.
5. Creative reasoning generates new ideas from an analysis of old ideas.
6. Creative reasoning presumes some grounding in the fundamental disciplines related to the ideas being manipulated.
7. One does not enhance the reasoning process by analyzing it; rather, one exercises it in any environment conducive to such behavior and gains confidence in the process as a result.
8. Students can develop competence in open and closed reasoning if teachers provide the proper classroom environment.
9. Reasoning guides can be simulators of both open and closed reasoning.
10. Reasoning applies to any medium.

### Statements

A   B   C

___ ___ ___   1. My students are very creative. They don't need to read the texts.

___ ___ ___   2. Students won't develop insight into this concept unless I tell it to them.

———  ———  ———  3. Why worry about this class? No one in it scores below the 94th percentile on the standardized reading test we use in the district!

———  ———  ———  4. Related to the reading act, one reasons before, during, and after.

———  ———  ———  5. Unless students already possess ideas, they can't create new ones.

———  ———  ———  6. "Psyching out" the teacher to ensure an *A* may produce closed reasoning but rarely open.

———  ———  ———  7. One cannot make something from nothing.

———  ———  ———  8. Functional exercise of open and closed reasoning requires a conducive environment.

———  ———  ———  9. Squelched students and insecure teachers are highly correlated.

———  ———  ——— 10. Students should have the right to be wrong.


\*    \*    \*    \*    \*    \*


## REFERENCES

BRUNER, JEROME. The act of discovery. In *On Knowing*. New York: Atheneum, 1965.

BRUNER, JEROME. *The process of education*. Cambridge, Mass.: Harvard University Press, 1960.

HERBER, HAROLD L. *An inquiry into the effect of instruction in critical thinking upon students in grades 10, 11, and 12*. Unpublished doctoral dissertation, Boston University, 1959.

MURPHY, MARY. *Vocabulary development by classification of multiple meaning words*. Unpublished master's thesis, Boston University, 1960.

NELSON, JOAN. *Pillow talk*. Homer, N.Y.: TRICA Consultants, Inc., 1976.

# six

# Vocabulary Development

---

## VOCABULARY

The following terms are important to an understanding of this chapter. Each is defined in context. Read through the list to identify those for which you have uncertain meanings. Then as you read the chapter, pay particular attention to their definitions. Also make certain that the meanings attributed to the remaining words by their context in the chapter correspond to the meanings they hold for you.

vocabulary-acquisition skills
context
structure
structural analysis
dictionary
definition
meaning
technical vocabulary
reinforcement
structured overview
graphic organizer

word recognition
criteria for selection
key concepts
relative value
students' background
facilitation of independence
presentation of vocabulary
teaching of vocabulary
semantic clues
syntactic clues

## IDEA DIRECTION

Communication in any subject area depends on facility with the language of that subject. This chapter presents ways to develop that facility. Distinctions are made between presenting and teaching new words. A means for enhancing concept development, while at the same time developing vocabulary-acquisition skills through the study of specially selected technical vocabulary, is discussed and illustrated. A distinction is made between "definitions" and "meanings" of words; vehicles for the reinforcement of both are described and illustrated. Consider how these suggestions relate to prereading, reading, and post-reading activity.

## READING DIRECTION

The chapter deals with selecting, teaching, and reinforcing the technical vocabulary in a subject area. You will want to pay particular attention to these three dimensions of vocabulary development as you read through the chapter. You will want to recall specific problems from Chapter 2 and see how these suggestions relate to them. You will also want to recall the discussion of levels of comprehension in Chapter 3 and reasoning in Chapter 5 since the contents of both have bearing on this chapter.

## BACKGROUND

Any discussion of vocabulary development in content areas must take into account several factors: need; time constraints; method; materials. This chapter will deal with each of these, giving primary emphasis to the last two.

Need for vocabulary development seems clearly evident. Basic concepts in any subject are communicated by words to which students must attribute special definitions and meanings. If students hold limited meanings for the words, they also will hold limited understandings of the concepts, hence limited understandings of the subject.

You know, in fact, that students *do* have problems with technical vocabulary—words with special meanings in the various subjects. Their problems generally arise because they lack the related experiences and understandings from which the meanings for the technical vocabulary are derived in those disciplines. This is not news to any content-area teacher who has struggled with the problem of teaching students how to communicate in the special language of a discipline. The need is clear; the obstacles are surmountable.

Time constraints clearly influence curricular and instructional decisions. The school year, hence the curriculum, is divided into approximately 180 days. The allotted one hour per day does not give content-area teachers much time to teach their students all that the curriculum requires. Most teachers do give attention to the technical vocabulary of their subjects; but because of the limited time, that attention often is superficial. Willingness to help students is not the problem; time is.

It is not possible for a teacher to teach to students all of the new words they will encounter in a given subject. Time does not permit it: to teach one word adequately can take from two to five minutes. One unit of study might contain fifteen, twenty, or thirty words which students should know. Teaching thirty words at three minutes each would consume one and a half hours. This is a large proportion of the total instructional time to devote to thirty words in one unit—and so, you know, it is not done.

But the need remains. The answer lies in methods and materials which integrate instruction in vocabulary-acquisition skills with instruction in the content of the subject so that: (1) teachers provide students with access to many words by carefully teaching just a few; (2) students make better use of what they already know about concepts being studied and the words which represent those concepts; (3) students become more actively involved in defining and developing meanings for the technical vocabulary.

Methods and materials interact to produce the desired results. This chapter focuses on these two factors. You may find it useful to consider the rationale on which the methods and materials are based. Or you may prefer to study the materials and related commentary on pages 150-68 first, then return to study the rationale.

## RATIONALE

### Vocabulary Development
### and Reading Instruction

Persons oriented toward the direct rather than the functional teaching of reading make a clear distinction between "vocabulary-development" and "word-recognition" skills.

With the latter emphasis, students are taught phonemic information to develop an operational understanding of the relationships between the symbols which make up words and the sounds which those symbols represent singly and in combinations. Though there is general agreement that students need to develop this understanding, there is considerable debate on how best to do it. The objective is for students to be able to pronounce strings of words encountered in printed materials. Most teachers of reading would extend the objective beyond mere pronunciation of the words. They also want students to be able to attribute meanings to the words they pronounce singly and in combination so as to derive from the strings of words the messages they convey.

Vocabulary-development skills are those which allow persons to expand their own vocabularies independently. These skills focus on both the acquisition and expansion of word definitions and word meanings: use of word parts (roots, prefixes, suffixes); use of the dictionary; use of context.

Content-area teachers and reading teachers agree on this need for vocabulary development and for word recognition. They differ only in focus or emphasis. Very often reading teachers emphasize the word-recognition skills more than vocabulary-development skills because of the nature of their jobs. On the other hand, content-area teachers are more concerned with vocabulary development than with word recognition because of the nature of *their* jobs. The focus of each group is reasonable, given their prime responsibilities. The reading teachers' responsibility usually is to help nonreaders or very poor readers learn to read, and the basic skills related to sounds and symbols often are lacking. The content teachers' responsibility usually is to help students learn the meanings of words so that they will develop an understanding of the subject. Problems arise when attempts are made to impose the reading teachers' principal focus on content-area teachers. Such attempts are impractical, unnecessary, and futile.

By the time most students enter fourth grade and begin more formal study of various content areas, they have acquired the basic word-recognition skills which allow them to pronounce most words they encounter in print. The relative ease with which this is done will vary from child to child. But given time to study the words encountered and to pick up clues from the context, most students will be able to utter a reasonable facsimile of the words. If they have sufficient experiential background and understanding (and recollection) of related concepts to connect with the words, some meaning will be attributed to the words. If they have neither experience nor concept background to bring to the words, pronunciation will be all they have and of minimal help.

For the specialized vocabulary of a content area, the vast majority of students experience the meaning problem much more than the pronunciation problem. That is, they need more help in building the related concepts and experience needed to attribute meanings to the words than they do in learning word-recognition skills that enable them to pronounce the words.

This clearly establishes the content-area teachers' priorities in vocabulary development: primary emphasis on definitions and meaning; secondary emphasis on pronunciation. You, or perhaps some of your colleagues, may take strong exception to this view. You—or they—may have experienced students who lack the ability to pronounce new words they encounter in their textbooks. "They can't read," is a familiar refrain.

Probably what should be said is, "They don't read" or "They won't read." Follow such students around and observe their activities before and after school and between classes. You will observe that they *can* read what they want to read. Pronunciation is not the problem that their behavior in class suggests it is.

If you complain that your students cannot read, beware that you don't buy into some program which focuses on phonics in the content areas. If you do you'll shortly realize you shouldn't have! You will not be addressing the real problem.

## Vocabulary Development in Content Areas

Vocabulary development is "the ability of the child to sort out his experiences and concepts in relation to words and phrases in the context of what he is reading" (Goodman, 1970). This is the appropriate definition of vocabulary development in the content areas. It establishes a clear perspective on the balance between concept and skills development.

From the perspective of this definition of vocabulary development, several specific problems can be listed that you will undoubtedly recognize and which this chapter will address. All have to do with what happens when students are confronted with a new word or phrase (in printed form) as they study a specific unit of the curriculum in a specific subject (Goodman, 1970, pp. 25-26).

1. The reader encounters a printed form he does not recognize for a word in his oral vocabulary. This is the simplest vocabulary problem since he has experiences and concepts to relate to his oral vocabulary.

2. The reader encounters a printed form which is not familiar and not in his oral vocabulary. But the concept is a known one. He has other language forms to express it. In this case the problem is to associate new language with old.

3. The reader encounters a printed form which is unfamiliar, has no oral counterpart for him, and represents a concept which is new to him. He may, in fact, lack relevant experience on which to base such a concept. This is the case in which vocabulary must follow conceptual development. Otherwise, we have a fourth possibility.

4. A written form is familiar and may even have an oral equivalent, but the reader has no meaning for it. Within narrow limits he may even use it to answer test questions correctly without understanding what he is reading.

5. The final possibility exists as readers become proficient. They may encounter printed forms and come to attach concepts to them without ever encountering them in oral speech. One does not have to be able to pronounce a word to understand it.

*Problem 1* points out that when there is a gap between the vocabularies for oral communication and written communication students' reading performance is limited. They may have the word "pneumonia" in their oral-communication vocabulary but not in their written. When they can connect the sound of the word with its appearance (configuration, spelling, letter sequence), they also connect with the written word the experiences and understandings associated with the oral word. How to help students make that connection is part of the purpose for the methods and materials discussed in this chapter.

*Problem 2* is a variation on problem 1. The written word is not familiar. Let's say the word is *conundrum*, and it is not in the students' oral-communication vocabulary. But let's say that they have ample vocabulary to express the same concept. Let's say that they encounter the word in the context of a discussion of the mysterious so-called Legionaires' Disease that struck after the Legionaire's Philadelphia Convention in 1976. The doctors were baffled by the problem and could only guess at possible answers. They had never before encountered such a *conundrum.* You might decide that a *conundrum* is either a mysterious disease or a baffling, intricate problem. Further refinements in the discussion would lead you to induce the latter rather than the former. Your prior experience with or awareness of seemingly unsolvable problems would connect with the new word and it would become part of both your oral and written vocabularies.

*Problem 3* is the major one for content-area teachers. Many of the words and phrases essential to an understanding of the subject are not part of the students' vocabularies for either oral or written communication. Sometimes students will have engaged in the study of related concepts at previous grade levels or in previous units and the teacher can draw on those experiences to help them attribute meanings to the words or phrases. This would be a more sophisticated application of problem 2. But when they delve into new concepts, students do not have the experiential or conceptual background to draw upon. Here, as indicated in the statement of the problem, is where time must be spent building an experiential and conceptual base that enables students to connect meanings to the words and phrases.

*Problem 4* should not occur if problem 3 is adequately handled. This problem, however, is often created by methods which are viewed as useful only because they are habitual. The memorization of lists of words and their definitions, followed by a quiz, is one of the more notable ones. Without experiential or conceptual background to associate with the word, the definition is devoid of meaning that enlightens. The words are sterile, rarely to be used, soon to be lost after the course requirements are passed.

*Problem 5* is a problem only as it hampers oral communication related to the concepts being encountered through the reading. In most subjects, the teacher wants students to develop competence in such communication. Every effort is made to have students hear as well as see the important words for the unit of study under consideration. But, as noted on page 138 under the discussion of selecting words for emphasis, the teacher must make choices according to some criteria, and such choices do mean that some words are omitted. They may well become the type identified in problem 5.

As is clear from the recitation of these problems, students have more than one kind of vocabulary. Actually, they have four: speaking and writing, which are the expressive vocabularies; listening and reading, which are the receptive vocabularies. Speaking and listening vocabularies, obviously, are applied in oral communication; writing and reading, in written communication. Although not startlingly new, taking this obvious information into account when dealing with the problem of vocabulary development in content areas is very important.

The relative size of these vocabularies is also important. Vocabularies for oral communication generally are larger than those for written communication, simply because a person engages more in oral communication than written and will use or recognize in conversation words he or she would not use in writing or might not recognize in reading.

Another way of looking at relative size of vocabularies is to apply the general principle that it is easier to recognize a word than it is to produce it. Based on that principle, one can conclude that usually a person's listening vocabulary is greater than the speaking vocabulary. How often have you heard someone using a word in conversation which you know but do not use because it does not come readily to mind when you speak? The principle is operating.

Similarly, have you not frequently encountered words in print that you yourself would not use in your own writing because they do not come readily to mind? The principle is operating and you can conclude that your reading vocabulary generally is greater than your writing vocabulary.

### Pronunciations, Definitions, and Meanings

We have already established that pronunciation is not the primary problem for most students reading content-area materials. Most have sufficient word-recognition skill to determine the correct pronunciation of a word, being aided as necessary by the context in which it is used and by coaching of the teacher or fellow students. Of greater concern are the definitions and the meanings of words.

Dictionaries, glossaries, or lexicons provide ample evidence that words in isolation can have definitions. But these alone are like having form without substance, a body without life. Being able to define a word does not guarantee that one knows what the word means. True, the definition is a start. But until the word is connected with other words, with related experience, it does not develop its own character, its meaning for the user.

One can draw a parallel between definitions of words and the literal level of comprehension. At this comprehension level the reader determines the information, determines what the author says. The definition of a word gives information about the word; it identifies what the word says. Definitions are essential for the student to fully communicate in the language of the various subjects. But definitions must not be considered ends in themselves. There is more.

Words take on meaning when placed in the context of other words and when considered in light of prior experience and related concepts. There is a parallel between meanings of words and both the interpretive and applied levels of comprehension. At these two levels of comprehension, readers first connect information together, perceiving relationships which convey the author's ideas. Then they connect those ideas with their previous ideas and experiences to enlarge both. Meanings of words are derived from their use and that use involves relating them to other words, ideas, and experiences.

### Word Meanings

The ultimate purpose in presenting and teaching the technical vocabulary of a subject is to help students develop meanings for those words and an understanding of the content of the discipline they represent. In descending order of difficulty, the four areas of responsibility for developing word meanings in the content areas are:

**New words for new concepts** Students' experiences can provide a basis for understanding and assimilating new concepts in any subject. Words which stand for those concepts can be presented in such a way that the association between the concepts and their labeling words is clear. This is the most time-consuming aspect of vocabulary development. It is also the aspect most clearly associated with instruction in the content of the discipline. When content teachers teach this kind of vocabulary they truly feel that they are teaching their subjects.

Because content teachers can most comfortably devote significant chunks of time to them, it is with these words that the functional teaching of vocabulary-acquisition skills seems most reasonable. And, while this aspect of vocabulary development seems most difficult to accomplish, it also seems to be the most rewarding. Suggestions for instruction in this aspect of vocabulary development are on pages 142-47.

**Old words for new concepts** Whether this or the next aspect of vocabulary development is more difficult instructionally is debatable. Old labels for new ideas may be more or less or just as difficult to handle as new labels for old ideas. In synectics terminology (Gordon, 1973), the former involves "making the strange familiar" and the latter involves "making the familiar strange." It really doesn't matter as long as there is a realization that both aspects must be handled. To some teachers it may seem more difficult to help students enlarge their vocabulary relative to ideas they have held for some time. To other teachers it may seem more difficult to help students to conceptualize a new idea and then see how words used to describe familiar ideas can also describe the new idea.

It probably takes more time to build the experiential base necessary for the acquisition of a new concept than it does to show how a new label belongs to an old concept. The former is the task for the teacher in this aspect of vocabulary development. Explanation, experimentations, illustrations, anything which helps students develop a feel for the new idea is appropriate. The object is to help students connect the new idea with ideas and experiences which they have on the same subject.

The timing for connecting the old word with the new idea is a matter of debate. Some teachers prefer to develop the idea first and then apply the label. Others prefer to use the label as they develop the idea. Usually it depends more on the concept and the subject area than on the teachers' preference. Some concepts cannot be discussed without using the label; others can. In any case, either as or after the concept is developed, the old word is associated with the concept and the students' vocabulary is enlarged. It is interesting to point out to students that their vocabularies can be enlarged in ways other than just by adding new words. Learning multiple meanings for a single word also enlarges one's vocabulary.

**New words for old concepts** It probably takes less time to attach new labels to an old idea than old labels to new ideas. If the concepts are already in students' minds, one needs only review them and recall where they fit in the subject under consideration. Then the new words can be introduced and related background experience reviewed to demonstrate their connection with the old concept. The instructional focus is on creating the need and opportunity for students to use a new word with sufficient frequency that the word's connection with the old concept is fixed in their minds. If the objective is to have the word become part of the students' expressive vocabulary, they must have more frequent need and opportunity to use the new word than if the objective is to have the word become part of the students' receptive vocabulary only. This is because of that previously mentioned principle that it is easier to recognize a word than to produce it. The words which you use most frequently in speaking and writing are the words which you use most frequently. To have words readily available, they must be used often enough to be automatically called to mind when the context warrants their use.

**Old words for old concepts** This aspect of vocabulary development is probably the easiest because it involves only a review of what already has been learned. Review can be boring or fun; it can be perfunctory or purposeful. Suggestions in this chapter and in Chapter 10 accent the positive.

## Word Definitions

The purposes served by definitions and meanings in the process of vocabulary development will vary with teaching and learning styles, with the objective of the lesson, and with the concept being developed. Some teachers prefer to teach inductively; thus, definitions would be induced from observing the use of words in the information source and subsequently confirmed by reference to the dictionary or glossary. Other teachers prefer to teach deductively; thus, definitions would be presented prior to observing the words used in the information source. In the first instance, definitions initiate the study of the words; in the second, definitions confirm the study of the words. There is merit to each, and using both gives variety.

The relationship between the definitions and the meanings of words is interesting to contemplate. In a sense the ultimate beginning has to be definitional. Meaning can be derived only when words surrounding the target word are known, even as comprehension can occur only when the information-bearing words are known. Thus, before information sources heavily saturated with technical words new to the students can be assigned, definitions will have to be presented if much comprehension is to occur. Once the new words have been assimilated by the reader and associated with experiences and known concepts, they can serve as the context for the development of meanings for other words. Happily, most texts designated for a given grade include sufficient old words to provide this context. Students thus are not totally dependent upon definitions.

### SELECTION FOR EMPHASIS

We have already established that as we teach the curriculum in our subjects, we will have to present to our students both old and new words related to both old and new concepts. But a basic concern which underlies our instruction is having sufficient time to accomplish all of the objectives for our curriculum. Vocabulary development is only one among many objectives. We know that it takes longer to teach new words and new concepts than it does to review old ones. This fact helps us make decisions on the distribution of available time for instructional purposes.

Four specific criteria can be used to separate the words which should be carefully taught from those which—though important—should be handled in other ways. These criteria are useful because each segment of the curriculum contains more words which students need to learn initially or to review than you have time to handle in a direct teaching situation. As indicated earlier in this chapter, although the words are important and should be taught, not all of them can be; you must omit some from direct instruction. The criteria will help you make those decisions.

### Key Concepts

Most curricula are divided into manageable segments, each to be taught in an allotted time. These segments are never equal in importance; the time you assign to each indicates the relative value you place on each.

Each segment is made up of concepts which also vary in importance. Again, the time you assign to each indicates the relative value you place on it. Those you decide to emphasize most, the ones most crucial to your content objectives, are the "key concepts" of the segment. You will feel that each should be taught or reviewed, but you will have difficulty setting aside a sufficient amount of time to do so.

### Relative Value

The first criterion will give you a lengthy list, but all the words will not be equally important. As pointed out in the previous section, there is a relative value among the concepts which comprise the curriculum. There is also a relative value among words which comprise a given concept and their contribution to the concept. Assuming that you do not have time to teach all the words, you set priorities among them, determining which should be taught without fail. Applying this criterion of relative value, you narrow the list; but still it is too long. It must be narrowed further because it still contains more words than you have time to teach directly. The third criterion helps you do this.

### Students' Background

Your list will now contain words your students may already know because of their backgrounds. They bring a surprising amount of knowledge and experience to the study of concepts in your curriculum, and tapping into both makes your teaching more manageable.

To determine which words your students do know, you can be so formal as to administer a pretest or so informal as to make subjective judgments of their knowledge based on prior instruction they have had. Both are valid; both are used, the latter more often than the former in all probability.

There are certain dangers in the subjective approach. One world history teacher, for example, made the judgment that his students would know the word *famine*. Alerted to the danger of teacher assumptions through an in-service course, he decided to check his judgment. He found that twenty percent of his college-bound students and over fifty percent of his "general" students could not connect a definition with it. Since they were in the process of studying about India, those who did not know the word probably missed an important insight into the problems of that continent.

In any event, one can narrow the list for direct teaching by determining which words the students already know. Those can be set aside for inclusion in review and reinforcement activities. They can serve as contexts for deriving meanings of the unknown words.

The list is rapidly becoming more manageable, but it is still too long. Students' ability and achievement have bearing on their background and what they bring to the study of new concepts. Ability and achievement also have bearing on the students' need for instruction in vocabulary acquisition skills and, thus, a close connection to the final criterion.

### Facilitation of Independence

Durrell (1966) uses the term *word power* when he discusses the development of students' vocabulary skills. He suggests by this term the need for students to be able to analyze new words independently, to be able to add to their reading vocabulary without aid from teachers or fellow students. When students have this power, their reading can be a pleasure; it can be a major source for learning; and the textbooks in their courses will no longer be monuments to frustration.

Applying the criteria discussed above will produce a refined list of words important to the study of the segment of the curriculum under consideration. No doubt, a high percentage of these words will appear in the textbook assignment related to the study of this concept. Some may not but, since you undoubtedly teach students more than just what is in the textbook, you will have no problem with these additional words. The concepts to be learned are the determining factor, not the textbook.

The text does have an important part to play. It is an important information source. A text may be any printed source which students read to obtain information about the concept under consideration.

Reading competence is necessary for the development of understandings through the use of the textbook. It is to facilitate the reading of the text that vocabulary development is stressed. It is to assure independence in this reading that vocabulary-acquisition skills are taught through words from the list constructed by applying the preceding criteria.

This final criterion is applied in two steps. First, the reading selection is examined to see if it contains the words on your list. Teaching those which appear both in the text and on your list will facilitate students' reading of the text. The remaining words on your list still will need emphasis, according to the previous three criteria. Altogether, there will be more words than you have time to teach.

Second, you shift the focus of your criteria from content to process. At this stage, *all* of the words on your list *should* be taught. All represent important concepts. There is not enough time to teach them all, but there is no content-related reason to choose some over others for emphasis. Therefore, a different kind of criterion is now applied: a skills-oriented criterion. This criterion asks the question: "Which of the words now remaining on the list (all of which I *should* teach to students if I had the time) will give me opportunity to stress skills which will add to my students' *word power*?" Those are the words which are finally chosen for careful teaching, stressing the skills as noted on pages 142-47.

Your knowledge of your students' ability and their reading achievement will help you determine which words to select for this skills-oriented emphasis. The skills which can be taught with these words will depend on their use in the text as well as the nature of the words themselves. With all these factors in mind, the words which will be taught are finally identified.

Even after applying this fourth criterion, you still will have too many words which must be taught and too little time to teach them. These can be presented to the students in list form, or written on the board. Merely pronouncing the words for the students as they read the list will help them recall the word the next time they see it. Giving them a brief definition along with the pronunciation does not take too long and, although this does little to develop independence in vocabulary-acquisition skills, it does at least give them a feel for the vocabulary. Subsequent reinforcement materials and experiences will build on this first encounter and help students develop understanding of the word in light of the content objective.

### Relationships Among the Criteria

Using these criteria, the teacher limits to realistic possibilities the total number of words to be taught. These words will develop understanding of the major concepts of the unit and will be appropriate to the needs and potential of the students. Students will learn the important language of the subject.

Some teachers become concerned about all the words they eliminate when applying the criteria. What happens to students who don't know words that are in the sources to be read but are not selected for emphasis? Will they not be stumbling blocks to successful reading? Should they not be taught—or should we not find material on an easier level for these students?

Students need not know every word in material they are reading to understand what is being said. If they have an understanding of the most important words, they usually piece together a sufficient understanding of unknown words through context clues to keep going. In addition, if grouping is used *within* content classes, there is opportunity for students to receive help from one another in reference to unknown words. If no member of the group knows a given word, the teacher can be consulted. Students learn well from one another, and a system or arrangement of this sort takes advantage of the fact.

Applying the criteria to a segment of the curriculum is not as time-consuming as the foregoing explanation may lead you to think. Once accustomed to the conscious application of the criteria, you will find that the first three are applied almost simultaneously. You will *not* need to develop a list from the first criterion and then refine it by the second criterion to produce a second list, refining it further by the third criterion to produce a third list. Simultaneous application of the criteria winnows the words and produces one list of the words most essential to your particular students. *Then* the fourth criterion is applied and the words are selected for careful teaching.

This final criterion may take longer to apply than the others, particularly if you are not used to thinking about the kind of skills which are implicit in the technical vocabulary you use. But again, once you become comfortable with the entire procedure and familiar with the skills, you will find that relatively little time has been added to your lesson preparation.

One other point must be mentioned. Most content-area teachers who are successful in communicating to students the content objectives of their courses already know a lot about vocabulary development. You may be saying, "So, what else is new?"

Sometimes the problem is not what we don't know but what we do know. Both knowledge about vocabulary development and the application of that knowledge may have to be raised to a more conscious level to realize its maximum potential benefit. Thinking through the criteria as they are applied builds a list which is more productive for students *now* in *your* class. Thinking through the instructional presentation of selected words is more beneficial for students *now* in *your* class. Reviewing and rethinking sharpens our minds, our objectives, and our knowledge.

## PRESENTATION AND INSTRUCTION

There is a difference between presenting and teaching a word. Teaching does involve presenting, but presenting does not necessarily involve teaching.

### Presentation of Vocabulary

Words students already know in printed form can be presented to them through review procedures which remind them of previous learnings and of where they fit in the new content being studied. A brief presentation, oral or visual, is sufficient to remind students of the meanings of the words and their probable application in the current unit of study.

A variation of the above suggestion can be applied when students have a word in their oral but not in their visual vocabularies (problem 1, page 133). The purpose of the presentation is to aid students in making the connection. An example of this from a science lesson appears on page 152. Words from the list which were in the students' oral vocabulary were pronounced as the students followed along, encountering their visual form. A major purpose of the presentation was to point out to students words they already knew and what the visual form for them looked like. A sight vocabulary is readily built that way. A careful teaching of each word is not required because students already have a sense of its meaning.

All of the words on the list produced by the first three criteria for selection of vocabulary can be *presented* to the students, usually as a list, perhaps written on the board, or on an overhead projector transparency, or on a multilithed sheet. As students follow along, the teacher pronounces each word and notes the definition if provided. That is the total presentation. Anything more would be teaching.

## Teaching Technical Vocabulary

One obvious purpose for teaching the technical vocabulary in a content area is to help students learn the definitions and meanings. A second, less obvious, purpose is to help students learn the skills needed to acquire definitions and meanings independently. Both purposes are served through those few words identified by the fourth criterion for selecting words for instructional emphasis. The second purpose *is* the fourth criterion, with the skills being the focus of concern.

The skills which help students develop independence in acquiring new vocabulary are: (1) use of context; (2) use of structure; (3) use of dictionary, glossary, or similar reference. These skills constitute the fourth criterion for selection of words for instructional emphasis.

**Use of context** Definitions of words can be induced by using a variety of context clues. Some clues are syntactic; some are semantic. As the reader detects the influence of both types of clues on a given word in a sentence, he or she can infer at least a definition for that word, often a meaning.

Semantic clues come from the way a word is used in a sentence or at least with a sufficient combination of words to allow an inference as to its possible meaning. Hook (1965) identifies seven such clues:

1. The experience clue, which enables the students to draw on their own experience; e.g., their experience with crows enables them to define *raucously* in "A pair of crows called raucously."
2. The comparison or contrast clue, as in the example of *tractable* as in "The children were more tractable than she had anticipated; in fact, only Joel was at all stubborn."
3. The synonym clue, in which the sentence contains a near-synonym.
4. The summary clue: "He was completely *disheveled*. His hair was mussed, his shirttail was out . . ."
5. The association clue: "He was out of it in an instant with the *agility* of a pickpocket."
6. The reflection of a mood or situation clue, as with the word *melancholy* in the first sentence of *The Fall of the House of Usher*.
7. The previous contact clue: students' knowledge of the Emancipation Proclamation should help them to understand *emancipate*.

Some authors provide semantic clues which do not require the reader to induce meanings. Rather, by expanding the context, the author presents a statement of meaning (Robinson, 1975). The author may use the device of marginal notations or may use footnotes. The author may place the definition in parentheses immediately following the word or may place it in apposition to the word, setting it off by commas. The author may present a formal definition of the word in the same sentence in which it appears or place it in a sentence immediately before or after its use. These clues are signaled by many devices and the reader is well served by a teacher who points these out: use of italics for the word being defined or for the definition, whether in parentheses or in apposition; use of parentheses and commas; signal words such as *that is* or *or* or *is* . . .

You may decide to teach words from your list because they provide opportunity to emphasize some of these semantic (context) clues. They can be taught directly by calling students' attention to the use of the word in context and to the various signals which the author provides for them to use to derive meanings. Spending a few moments acquainting students with such information pays rich dividends by increasing their knowledge of the subject as well as their development of independence in the use of basic resources in the subject. This is true not only with respect to teaching semantic (context) clues but also syntactic (context) clues.

Syntactic clues concern the placement of the word in a sentence, the form in which the word is presented, and the signal words attached to it. The position of a word frequently indicates whether it is a noun or a verb, an adjective or an adverb. It is useful for students to develop a sense of whether a word represents something which is doing the acting or is being acted upon; whether it represents the action that is taking place; whether it qualifies in some way the thing which is acting or being acted upon; or whether it qualifies the action being acted upon; or whether it qualifies the action taking place. Though none of these clues convey meaning in themselves, their presence contributes to meaning and awareness of their function enhances the probability of use.

The so-called inflectional endings for words provide syntactical clues that can contribute to meanings. For example, the presence of *ed* at the end of a word usually signals that it is a verb; *ion* at the end of a word indicates *the act of* and is the noun form of a word which often appears as a verb (*create* becomes *creation,* the act of creating). As such clues appear with the words you choose to teach, you can call them to the students' attention and point out how they contribute ultimately to the meaning of the word. Doing so consistently, as appropriate to the words being emphasized, helps students develop independence in vocabulary acquisition and precludes the need for isolated drill through direct instruction in inflected endings.

Signal words, or markers, provide syntactic clues to the meanings of words with which they are associated. Capitalizing the first letter of a word which is not the first word in a sentence suggests that the word is a proper noun. When an article (*a* or *the*) precedes a word, that word usually is a noun. Words such as *will* or *have* or *has* or *had* often signal that the next word in the sentence is a verb. A prepositional phrase often is used to qualify the meaning of the word it modifies, so awareness of the signals for such phrases is useful (for example, *of, by, for*). Similarly, clauses are often used to explain or qualify or elaborate; when they are used in a sentence with the target word, it is useful if students are aware of the signals so that their potential can be realized (*since, because, if, when, that,* etc.)

**The structure of words** Through structural analysis students examine a word to determine if there are clearly recognizable parts that give clues to its definition: prefixes, roots, suffixes. Definitions of many technical words can be derived in this way.

Structural analysis is taught functionally. The specific word parts to be taught are dictated by the word selected from the list for this kind of emphasis, not the reverse. Further, the word parts—hence, the definition of the word—are taught inductively. You draw from students what they already know, adding new information whenever needed and appropriate. For example, one might teach the word *prestidigitator* in the following manner:

"Take a look at this word on the board. Are there any parts of that word that seem familiar to you? *Digit?* OK; what does that suggest? *Finger or number?* Yes. And what else do you see? *Or?* Which suggests . . . ? *One who has or one who does?* Usually that's the case. And is there anything else you see? *Pre?* Yes, suggesting . . . ? *Before?* Usually so. But now we have a couple of things hanging here: *at* which appears just before the *or*; and the *sti* which immediately follows the *pre*. What do we do about those items? Is it possible that we have separated them from something else to which they belong? What about the *at?* . . . That's right: sometimes *ator* suggests one who has or one who does something, just as *or* does without the *at*. We're getting there; what about the *sti? 'Maybe it should go with the pre?'* That's a good hypothesis because sometimes root words are used as prefixes for other root words and *presti* could very well be one of those cases. True, *pre* usually does suggest *before* but that knowledge may have led us astray in this case. Let's test it out: what does *presti* suggest to you? Does it give you a feeling, a sense of something? *'Quick or fast . . . presto/chango?'* Makes sense, doesn't it? Any other ideas? No? Well, let's try to put it all together.

"We have: numbers or fingers; quick or fast; one who has or does. When you put all of that together, what definition can you come up with for the word *prestidigitator?*

*"An accountant; someone who works quickly with numbers?" "How about a computer operator; someone who has nimble fingers and can work quickly with numbers?" "How about a magician; someone who has fast fingers or hands?"*

"These all seem to be reasonable guesses, don't you think?" How are we going to determine which is appropriate?"

*"See how it's used in the sentence." "How about the dictionary; you can find the definition there." "I did and it says that a prestidigitator is a magician."*

Notice that you draw from students what they already know about word parts, and you will be pleasantly surprised as to how much they do know. When they run out of information you can add it, and they are receptive because they have a need to know and because they have provided most of the information themselves, or at least as much as they had to give. Word parts which are new to them are explained, related to the word being taught. Problems with contemporary changes in meaning are explained so that students do not attribute "old" meanings of root words to "new" words. Roots being used as prefixes, or other problems, are identified as appropriate to the words being taught.

Word parts are not taught for their own sake. You do not spend time in isolated drill on roots, prefixes, or suffixes. The word being taught was selected for emphasis, first, because it is important to the concept being developed and, secondly, because it provides opportunity to teach the value of structural analysis. As the word is taught, its structure is analyzed and a definition is derived. This is confirmed either by the dictionary or glossary or by reference to the context in which the word is used. When this is done consistently, students develop an appreciation for and familiarity with word parts and move closer to independence in the acquisition of new words.

Burmeister (1974) and Deighton (1959) present useful information about word parts. This information can help you better judge which words to select from your list for this kind of emphasis. Be cautious, however. Don't use the information to produce isolated drills on structural analysis.

**Use of dictionary, glossary** The dictionary is one of the most obvious tools for acquiring vocabulary independently. Unfortunately, too often the student is exposed to the dictionary as a tool through series of rather meaningless drills which force him to work with words in isolation, words that may have little currency or urgency or appropriateness.

The dictionary becomes more relevant to students when it is used to substantiate or refute definitions developed through use of context or structure. If students apply structural analysis to a word but are uncertain whether the definition they attribute to the word is correct in that particular instance, they confirm their findings by referring to the dictionary. The same is true when using context clues. If they have a general idea of the meaning of a word from context clues, they may want to determine more precisely what the word means in this instance by consulting the options listed in the dictionary.

Of course, students will come upon words for which their skill in the use of context and structure does them no good. In such cases, the dictionary is the obvious tool.

It is important that students view the dictionary as such a tool, not as the means for series of torturous drills. Most skilled adults use the dictionary functionally—to confirm hunches where there is uncertainty, to find definitions when no other tool provides them. Recognizing this practicality in our own use of the dictionary, we should teach students how to use it in the same manner.

Rather than having isolated drill on the locational skills related to the dictionary (such as use of guide words or alphabetizing), point out these skills to students as they use the dictionary to confirm hunches, to settle differences among themselves, and so on. Rather than having isolated drill on the use of the pronunciation key, use it to confirm hunches about pronunciation of words. Rather than having isolated drill on origins of words, use derivations when confirming hunches and analyses related to structure.

As are the other tools for independent acquisition of vocabulary, the use of the dictionary is taught functionally, never just for its own sake.

## Combining Old and New Words

The presentation of familiar words and the teaching of new words usually are combined in a given instructional effort. Familiar words are used to develop contexts for the new words so that students can assimilate them. A useful means for such a combination are "graphic organizers."

The purpose of a graphic organizer is to help students develop a sense of the structure of concepts being studied. They can perceive the relationships which exist among the words representing the ideas which form the concept. A graphic organizer also serves as a vehicle for presenting familiar words and teaching new words.

When used prior to reading a related passage in the information source, graphic organizers have been called "structured overviews," a term coined by Barron and Earle (1969). Words to be placed in the structured overview are drawn from the word list developed by applying the criteria for selection of words for emphasis. Earle suggests the following procedure for the development and use of the structured overview. A structured overview for a lesson on Balance of Power is presented and analyzed as an illustration in Appendix A and on pages 152-55.

1. Take the list of words . . . selected [for emphasis in this instructional unit] and arrange and rearrange them, add to them, and delete from them until you have a diagram which shows the relationships which exist among ideas in the unit, as well as their relationship to the semester's [or year's] work and to . . . [the subject area] itself.

2. On the first day of the new learning unit, write the diagram so constructed on the board. *While you are doing this,* explain why you arranged the terms as you did. Encourage the students to contribute as much information as they can. Between the students and yourself, the reasons for the diagrammatic arrangement should be verbalized.

3. Throughout the unit, as it seems appropriate and comfortable, refer back to the diagram. Sketch portions of it on the board. The major objective here is to aid the students in their attempts to organize the information in meaningful ways.*

*Richard A. Earle, *The Use of Vocabulary as a Structured Overview in Seventh Grade Mathematics.* Unpublished doctoral dissertation, Syracuse University, 1970, pp. 39-40.

Clearly, this procedure is a useful mix of old and new words, involving both presentation and teaching. Though not indicated by Earle in this procedure, teaching of new words can be included as one develops the structured overview with students. With the familiar words providing a meaning reference, a new word is taught with emphasis on whichever skill seems most appropriate to that word: context, structure, dictionary.

The structured overview is motivational for students in that they contribute to it out of their own knowledge, if the teacher organizes its development in that way. It is instructive with respect to the concepts being developed under the content objective in that it gives students a sense of the organization of the material, information, and ideas which make up the overall objective. It provides a framework into which new information can be placed as students derive it from their texts and other sources. Thus, it not only organizes what students already know and what they are to learn, it also organizes the new information and ideas as they are learned.

Graphic organizers can be used following the reading of the assigned passage for reinforcement and review. Barron suggests the following procedures for this postreading use.

1. Analyze the vocabulary of the reading/learning task and list all the terms you feel are necessary for the students to understand.

2. Arrange (rearrange) the list of words into a schema or diagram which depicts key relationships among the terms.

3. Add to the schema terms you believe are understood by the students to clarify relationships between the learning task and the course (or discipline) as a whole.

4. Type each of the words included in your structured overview on a ditto master.

5. Following the students' reading of the passage or the material to be learned, introduce the idea behind the structured overview to the class with an example at the blackboard.

6. Place the students in groups of two or three and distribute the list of terms and a packet of $3'' \times 5''$ index cards to each group.

7. As the students work, circulate about the room to provide assistance.

8. Terminate the activity and provide feedback.*

Using such procedures, Barron found that students' understanding of the concepts was enhanced significantly. His findings were similar to those of Walker (1975), who applied a variation of this approach to the use of graphic organizers with students in grades five and seven. Having students work in groups to arrange key words into a display which represented the concepts being studied seemed to make a significant difference in their understandings of the concepts.

*Richard F. Barron, "Research for Classroom Teachers: Recent Developments on the Use of the Structured Overview as an Advance Organizer," In Harold L. Herber and James D. Riley (Eds.), *Research in Reading in Content Areas: Fourth Year Report.* Syracuse, New York: Syracuse University Reading and Language Arts Center, 1978.

Words used in postreading organizers are, of course, mainly words familiar to the students—either because of exposure to them during the reading or because of experience with them prior to the initiation of the lesson. In either case, students explore the relationships among the words to develop some representation of the connections among the essential information and ideas.

Several examples of structured overviews are provided on pages 155-58 and in Appendix B. Remember that these structured overviews, in the form displayed on those pages, represent the arrangement as conceptualized by the teacher who prepared the lesson. The structured overview produced with the students will resemble the one prepared by the teacher; its format might differ and the placement of words within the structured overview might differ somewhat from the teachers' notes. This is to be expected if the structured overview is to be developed by drawing from students' knowledge. As long as the teacher has thought through the arrangement of words ahead of time, the exact order and placement may vary without problems emerging. Form is not the issue; substance is, and that is demonstrated by a clear portrayal of the implicit relationships among key words, no matter what the format.

The postreading graphic organizers are subject to the same variability. Students will see things differently than teachers and from one another. It is good, as Barron suggests, for the teacher to have thought through his or her own arrangement of the words for purposes of comparison, clarification, and confirmation.


## REINFORCEMENT

Traditionally, vocabulary development takes the following form: students are given lists of words; they look up the definitions in the dictionary and use each word in a sentence; they memorize these definitions for a subsequent quiz; they are quizzed on the words periodically to determine whether or not they can recall and use definitions as they were memorized.

This is a rather meaningless ritual. The exposure to vocabulary has little apparent relevancy to the students' needs; the ritual does little to reinforce an understanding of the ideas represented by the words; the definitions selected and memorized by the students frequently are not correct for the context in which the words are being studied.

The evidence indicates that words must be used many times in many situations before they are sufficiently well assimilated into our vocabulary to be readily available. Merely having students memorize definitions is not sufficient, nor is having words written on the board and discussing them with students before they read. Students develop vocabulary when they use words in situations which have meaning, in conversations and animated discussion not only with the teacher but with fellow students. Thus, words become part of the speaking vocabulary of students as well as part of their listening and reading vocabularies.

Experience and experimentation have shown that when students are provided meaningful contexts for the exploration and reinforcement of vocabulary, greater retention occurs (Barron, 1971; Earle, 1970; Walker, 1975).

There are many ways to facilitate this reinforcing use of vocabulary. As students participate in the construction of the structured overview, they are reinforcing their familiar vocabulary and creating a context for a discussion of the new. The structured overview is reviewed periodically as the study of the unit progresses, and this provides reinforcement of the words which were new when the structured overview was created.

Guides for levels of comprehension, patterns of organization, and reasoning facilitate the reinforcement of new and familiar vocabulary. To discuss their responses to statements in the guides, students must use the vocabulary that expresses the ideas. This reinforces the vocabulary presented and taught prior to the use of the guides.

There is a third way to facilitate the reinforcement of vocabulary. It is through use of exercise materials that guide students in the use of both old and new words. Depending on the purpose, timing, and design of the materials, they facilitate reinforcement of definitions and/or meanings.

Materials used to guide the reinforcement of new or old vocabulary can be focused either on definitions or meanings or both. Any exercise which reinforces the definition of a word without requiring a simultaneous consideration of the meaning of any other word can be called a "definitional" exercise. Any exercise which requires the meaning of a word to be considered in reference to the definitions or meanings of other words and/or to the experiential and conceptual backgrounds of the students can be called a "meaning" exercise.

Matching exercises, crossword puzzles, acrostics, and bubblegrams are examples of reinforcement materials for word definitions. Categorizing, analogies, and identifying meanings of words in the context of a sentence are examples of reinforcement materials for word meanings.

### ILLUSTRATIVE MATERIALS

A variety of materials used in the presentation, teaching, and reinforcement of vocabulary in various subject areas appears on the following pages. These materials are drawn from different units of study in different subject areas and at different grade levels. In no case is a full set of materials presented for a given unit of study. Rather, parts are drawn from a variety of units to allow a broader range of illustration.

Ideally one would prepare and use the following materials for each unit of instruction: the content objective; the list of words to be presented and taught; an indication of how familiar words on the list will be presented; an indication of how new words on the list will be taught; reinforcement materials for word definitions; reinforcement materials for word meanings.

Realistically, however, you would not have time to use all of the materials since there are other things you and your students must do. But, *if* all of the materials were available in a resource unit, having been developed either by your-self or by other teachers through some curriculum-development project, you would select only those items which would be most useful to your current students. Another year, you might select different ones. If all these materials were not already prepared for a given unit, you would be selective in which ones you did produce for your students, focusing on their needs and your objectives. For the next unit of instruction you might produce a different set of materials— or none at all, because you just had no time to do so. In any case, involved teachers, over time, can prepare excellent materials for use with their students: designing them selectively and carefully; keeping, revising, and adding to them from year to year as students' needs dictate.

### New Words/Old Ideas

The following procedure was used in a ninth-grade science lesson. Its purpose was to help students connect written and oral expressions of words when the oral was familiar to them and written was new.

The science lesson was the one for which the illustrative guide for organi-zational patterns were presented on pages 87-90. The content objective for the lesson was to develop an understanding that: (1) carbon monoxide is a major source of air pollution; (2) the environment man creates for himself reflects his priorities and his values. The students were of average ability but were relatively poor readers. Even so, the teacher felt that most of the key words were in the students' oral vocabulary and could be presented to them in a way that would trigger an association with the visual form of the words and their prior knowl-edge of the ideas they represent.

The teacher distributed the following work sheet to the students and asked them to keep the page face down on the desk. He then read the directions orally while the students listened. He asked them to turn the page face up, cover the right-hand column, and look at the words in the left-hand column as he read each one aloud. He shared his opinion with the students that the words in the list were probably ones which they had heard before, even if they had not seen them before. He then asked them to cover the left-hand column and look at the words in the right-hand column as he read the words from that list. He shared his belief that they probably knew these words at least in their written form. After presenting to the students the words from both lists in this manner, he asked them to form groups of five students each so they could work together on the task outlined in the directions.

This exercise guided students in: (1) connecting a word in their oral vocabulary with its written form; (2) connecting a newly learned technical word (in its written form) and the students' experiential and conceptual base for that word.

With this experience as a background for reading the assignment in the text, during which they used the guide for organizational patterns that appears on pages 87-90, they seemed to have little difficulty with the words as they appeared in the text.

## AIR POLLUTION

*Directions:* Here are fourteen pairs of words. If you believe the two words have a similar meaning, write the letter *S* on the line between them. If you think the words have opposite meanings, write *O* on the line.

1. pollution   \_\_\_\_   clean
2. pollutant   \_\_\_\_   dirt
3. emissions   \_\_\_\_   escape
4. significant   \_\_\_\_   unimportant
5. incomplete   \_\_\_\_   finished
6. combustion   \_\_\_\_   burn
7. faulty   \_\_\_\_   wrong
8. exhaust   \_\_\_\_   to let out
9. poison   \_\_\_\_   harmful
10. starvation   \_\_\_\_   being filled full
11. combination   \_\_\_\_   joining together
12. permanent   \_\_\_\_   lasting
13. reduction   \_\_\_\_   make larger
14. remedy   \_\_\_\_   cure

### Structured Overview

As noted in the discussion of the structured overview earlier in this chapter, its purpose is to present familiar words and to teach new words for the unit (or lesson) in such a way as to: (1) demonstrate the relationships among the words which form the overall concept; (2) provide a framework into which new ideas and information can be fitted; (3) develop a context from familiar words which will help clarify definitions and meanings of new words; (4) provide an opportunity to teach or reinforce specific vocabulary-acquisition skills implicit in the words themselves as appropriate to the students' needs.

The following structured overview was developed with these purposes in mind. It was part of an American history lesson prepared for eighth-grade students who were average-to-poor readers. The lesson itself was part of a unit on the Constitution. The content objective for the lesson was to develop an understanding that: (1) citizens benefit most when there is a balance of power among institutions, agencies, and forms of government; (2) provisions in the Constitution make possible this balance of power. This lesson is the one for which the illustrative guide for organizational patterns was discussed on pages 90-91. The structured overview was used to prepare students for that reading assignment.

The actual structured overview is shown in Appendix A, page 258, in the form in which it appeared after being developed with the students. You will find it helpful to follow through the explanation before you refer to the finished product. If you write down the words as they are mentioned, you will be developing the structured overview with me, then you can confirm its appearance by reference to the finished form. A reminder: you build the structured overview *with* students; you do not present it to them as a finished product.

The teacher began by writing the word *power* on the board and asking students what words—or ideas—came to their minds as they saw that word. Students began giving him words: *strength, energy, electric, atomic,* etc. Some were synonyms; others were adjectives. One student said *political,* which was a word the teacher had hoped someone would mention. He listed all of their words on the board, including *political,* and when they ran out of words, he rewrote *political* directly under the word *power* and drew a line connecting the two. As he did so he complimented the students on the extensiveness of their list, observing that they already had a good sense of range of meanings for the word and applications of the ideas it represented. He also said he was selecting just one of their words, *political,* because it most closely described the kind of power they would be considering in this lesson. Obviously the teacher did not want just to casually discard all of their other suggestions or imply by his actions that the students' contribution of words was merely an exercise in trying to guess what he had in mind—thus, the compliment (genuine) and the explanation of why he was focusing on only the one (necessary).

He wrote the word *balance* directly under the word *political* and told the students that this was a key word in the lesson because they were going to be studying about "balance of political power," what it is, and what makes it possible. He asked the students for their ideas about what *balance* might mean. They responded from their prior knowledge and experience, demonstrating that they had a good sense of the variety of uses of the word: *equal, to stand up straight, teeter-totter, gravity, equality, checkbook, scale,* etc. The teacher used this moment to emphasize the skill of structural analysis as applied to this familiar word for two purposes: (1) to sharpen the students' focus on the meaning of the word; (2) to teach or reinforce their knowledge of the function of word parts and their contribution to the definitions of words. Therefore, he wrote *bilanx* on the board saying that the word balance comes from the word *bilanx.* He asked if anyone had a definition for *bilanx* and no one did. Then he asked if any part of the word was at all familiar. In chorus the students said that *bi* means *two.* He said that he thought so too and then said, "Given what you seem to know about the idea of balance, what would you guess that a *lanx* might be?"

Again the students displayed an interesting background of ideas and information and an ability to hypothesize. *Sides, weights, forces, objects, coins* were words they suggested, among others. The teacher then said, "Let me draw you a picture that may help," and he drew the following:

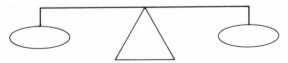

The students were able to identify the drawing as a representation of a scale or a balance. Pointing to the two receptacles on either side of the fulcrum, he asked what they were and students said, "Weights, dishes, pans." He wrote the word *plate* on the board next to the *two* for *bi*. He reviewed by saying that bilanx or balance means *two plates* and the word itself probably sprang from the manner in which people once determined the weights of objects.

In teaching the word *balance* the teacher was demonstrating to students that they already knew a lot, that this knowledge had a place in lessons they studied in school, and that this knowledge was both accepted by the teacher and respected by him. All of this, as you can imagine, is highly motivational for students and encourages them to stay with the teacher and the lesson. Also, because they have contributed so much to the lesson, they feel more central to the lesson—that they are studying a part of themselves rather than some unrelated piece of history.

The teacher then pointed out that the word *balance* was used not in the sense of weighing objects but in the sense of weighing power, of determining equality in political power. He then drew a line from the word *balance* at a forty-five degree angle down to the left and wrote the words *levels of government*. In an exchange with the teacher, the students identified *local, state,* and *federal* as the levels, which he wrote under the words *levels of government* and connected the two sets of words with lines.

He drew a sketch of a scale under the words *state* and *federal* and said, "The authors of the text talk about how it is possible for there to be a balance of political power between state and federal governments through a process called 'division of powers.'" As he said this, he wrote the word *division* in the left-hand tray of the scale, the word *of* on the fulcrum, and the word *powers* on the right-hand tray.

The teacher drew a second line from the word *balance*, this time at a 45 degree angle down to the right and wrote the words *branches of government*. The students identified the branches of government as being the *legislative, executive, and judicial*. The teacher wrote these words under the words *branches of government* and connected the two sets with lines. Under the words *legislative, executive,* and *judicial* the teacher drew another sketch of a scale and said, "The authors of the text talk about how it is possible for there to be a balance of political power among the branches of government through a process called *checks and balances*." As he said this he wrote the word *checks* in the left-hand tray of the scale, the word *and* on the fulcrum, and the word *balances* on the right-hand tray.

He said to the students, "We'll be studying about *checks and balances* and *division of power* and how they are supposed to create balances of political power. But before we do, let me ask you this question: What have we been studying that makes possible these two processes which are supposed to create the balance of political power?"

And the students came back, in chorus, "The Constitution!" whereupon the teacher drew a cricle around all of the words he had connected with lines and labeled it with the word *Constitution*.

He proceeded to place students into groups and to give them a purpose for reading the assignment that related to the structured overview, then he distributed the guide for organizational patterns, which was discussed on pages 90-91.

That shows a structured overview for a lesson and how it was developed with students. You can compare the one you designed as you read through the description with the one the teacher developed with the students, which appears in Appendix A. The structured overview which the teacher had prepared ahead of time, and had in his notes, was very similar to the one produced with the students. But notice that he did not just duplicate his and give it to the students in finished form. The value of the structured overview is in the students' participation in its construction. *Together,* students and teacher organize what they already know, identify what they have to learn, and see how it all fits together. With this kind of preparation, the students already have a sense of the concept to be learned, they have a purpose for listening or reading or viewing (depending on the medium used), and they have a feeling of involvement.

Other illustrative structured overviews are presented on the following pages. These are taken from teachers' notes and represent what they planned out ahead of time for development with their students. They presented the structured overviews in a manner similar to what was described for "balance of political power."

**Science** The teacher established the following content objective for seventh-grade students: To develop an understanding of why satellites stay in orbit. He selected eight words for an introductory lesson which dealt with the question, "Why Satellites Stay Up."

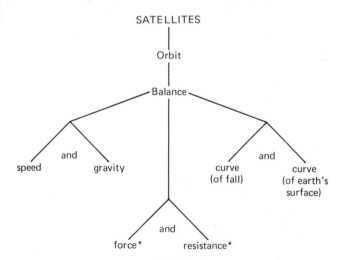

**FIGURE 6-1  Structured overview of why satellites stay up**

*On teacher's original but not used in lesson. Students' background not sufficient to draw inferences about this relationship.

**Home Economics** The teacher established the following content objective for the lesson in which this structured overview was used: To develop an understanding that careful planning for housing expenditures helps families and individuals meet obligations and derive maximum satisfaction from money available for those purposes. Students enrolled in this class were from grades ten through twelve.

The teacher selected sixteen words or phrases for presentation and teaching. She designed the structured overview shown in Fig. 6-2. As she developed the concept with the students, through the structured overview, she used *Housing Costs* as the overall idea.

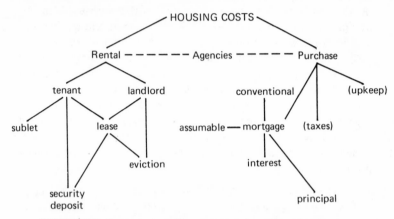

FIGURE 6-2  Structured overview of housing costs, by Patricia Horton

**Mathematics** The teacher established the following content objective for ninth-grade students: To introduce set theory and develop an understanding of the relationship between that theory and what they had learned in math during the previous two years.

She selected eleven words for presentation and teaching. The key word for the development of the structured overview, shown in Fig. 6-3, was *Groups*.

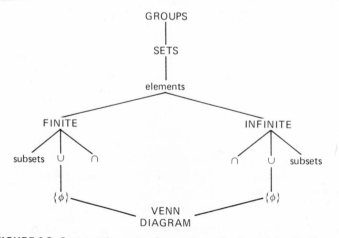

FIGURE 6-3  Structured overview for set theory, by Gwendolyn McKinnon

**Literature** An English teacher developed the variation of a structured overview shown in Fig. 6-4 as students studied "Thanksgiving Hunter." Her content objective was to help them develop an understanding of mental conflict which comes from setting priority between esteem of others and esteem of self.

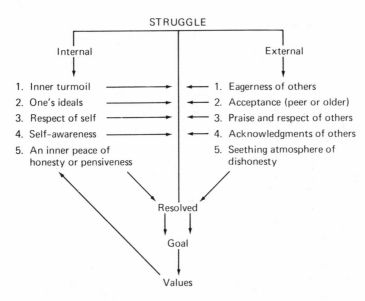

FIGURE 6-4 Structured overview for "Thanksgiving Hunter," developed by Agnes Jeanette Willhite

**History** A teacher of Black History developed the structured overview shown in Fig. 6-5 for her entire course. As she dealt with various concepts within the course, she added to the structured overview, constantly reviewing previously presented information so it served as the context in which newly presented information could derive meaning.

## Reinforcement of Definitions

On the following pages appear a variety of exercises that have been used by teachers in various subjects and at various grade levels to reinforce students' knowledge of the definitions of words. In a two-year study of vocabulary development in biology, Barron (1971) found that the "matching" and the so-called "word-puzzle" exercises were the most productive. The other types are given to provide a variety of formats, with the assumption that such variety is beneficial for motivation and attention. Additional examples are included on pages 159-63.

Teachers often have students work on these exercises in small groups. Sometimes the students in a group do the entire exercise together. Sometimes they do the exercise separately, then compare their responses, discussing and

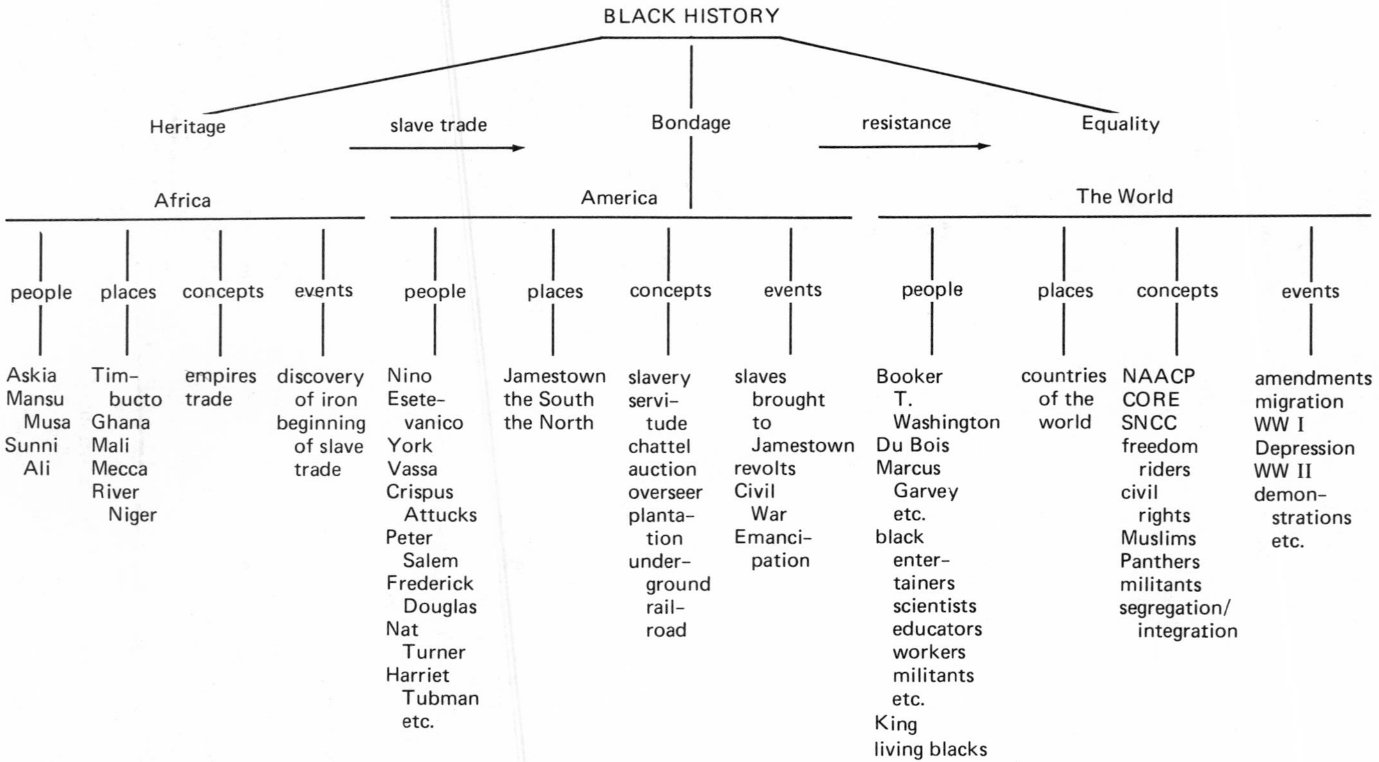

FIGURE 6-5 Structured overview for a Black History course, by Norma Blackman

The chart reads:

**BLACK HISTORY**

Heritage — slave trade — Bondage — resistance — Equality

**Africa**

- **people**
  - Askia
  - Mansu Musa
  - Sunni Ali
- **places**
  - Timbucto
  - Ghana
  - Mali
  - Mecca
  - River Niger
- **concepts**
  - empires
  - trade
- **events**
  - discovery of iron
  - beginning of slave trade

**America**

- **people**
  - Nino Esetevanico
  - York
  - Vassa
  - Crispus Attucks
  - Peter Salem
  - Frederick Douglas
  - Nat Turner
  - Harriet Tubman
  - etc.
- **places**
  - Jamestown
  - the South
  - the North
- **concepts**
  - slavery
  - servitude
  - chattel
  - auction
  - overseer
  - plantation
  - underground railroad
- **events**
  - slaves brought to Jamestown
  - revolts
  - Civil War
  - Emancipation

**The World**

- **people**
  - Booker T. Washington
  - Du Bois
  - Marcus Garvey
  - etc.
  - black entertainers
  - scientists
  - educators
  - workers
  - militants
  - etc.
  - King
  - living blacks
- **places**
  - countries of the world
- **concepts**
  - NAACP
  - CORE
  - SNCC
  - freedom riders
  - civil rights
  - Muslims
  - Panthers
  - militants
  - segregation/integration
- **events**
  - amendments
  - migration
  - WW I
  - Depression
  - WW II
  - demonstrations
  - etc.

trying to resolve their differences. Sometimes the students work out the exercise in groups and then compare responses among groups, seeking to identify and resolve differences.

How you use such exercises will depend on your students' achievement levels and the extent to which they can function independently. You know that discussion enhances reinforcement and that having students work in small groups multiplies the opportunity for each student to participate in the discussion in contrast to the more traditional teacher-led "discussion," which often amounts to much more teacher talk than student talk.

These exercises can be used both before and after students read the assignment in the information source. Logically, it makes sense to have definitions reinforced before reading the material so that meanings can be developed during the reading. But using such exercises after reading also is useful on occasion.

**Matching** This exercise requires only the recall of the definition attributed to each word. Without reference to a context or interrelationships among words in the list, meanings are not involved.

### MUSICAL TERMS*

*Directions:* Match the definition with the term it belongs with. Do this by writing the correct number in the blank to the left of each definition:

1. Recitative

_____ A. A large, long dramatic musical work, nonreligious, with scenery, costumes, and dancing.

2. Chorus

_____ B. A group of singers using mainly polyphonic texture during Baroque.

3. Opera

_____ C. A word from the Italian meaning "sing," a work composed explicitly for a church service.

4. Oratorio

_____ D. A large-scale religious vocal work with no costumes or scenery; usually not performed during a religious service.

5. Cantata

_____ E. A performer par excellence (equal to the best).

6. Aria

_____ F. Savior

7. Virtuoso

_____ G. Famous composer

8. Messiah

_____ H. A sung line imitating speech with few repetitions of text and often abrupt changes of emotional intensity.

9. Baroque

_____ I. A highly melodic section of an oratorio, opera, or cantata dwelling on a single emotion; text repeated often.

10. Handel

_____ J. Period of music history.

*Janet Correll

**Word puzzle** This exercise provides definitions of words as the basic clues. The number of letters in each word is indicated, along with a variety of other clues: placement on the lines of some letters that make up the spelling of the words. The crossword puzzle is similar in purpose. These exercises reinforce definitions of words through such aided recall.

## CHINESE PUZZLE*

*Directions:* Look at the definitions below. Think of a word that has the same number of letters as the number of spaces provided and has the given letters in the same position. Write the word on the line.

1. followers of Chairman Mao
2. last great dynasty
3. customs that have been handed down
4. a sudden and violent change of government
5. an agreement between two or more nations
6. a group of rulers from one family
7. an official order

**Modified word puzzle** This exercise is similar in purpose and function to the word puzzle in the previous exercise. It also sensitizes students to syllabication. Variations could highlight prefixes, roots, and suffixes.

## GET READY TO READ**

Follow these directions:

1. Give a three-syllable word that means a person who comes to make his home in a new country.

   I _ / _ _ / _ _ _ _ _

*James Hepfner
**John Sobolewski

2. Give a one-syllable word that means a division of society based upon wealth, rank, and profession.

C _ _ _ _

3. Give a three-syllable word that means a hostile attitude directed toward a group or an individual.

P _ _ / _ _ / _ _ _ _

4. Give a one-syllable word for the leader of the Jets.

R _ _ _

5. Give a two-word, five-syllable name for a group of immigrants.

P _ / _ _ / _ _    R _ / _ _ _ _

6. Give a three-syllable word for the leader of the Sharks.

B _ _ / _ _ _ / _ _

7. Give a two-word, four-syllable term that means the freedom to develop your own business, and to work the way that you wish.

F _ _ _    E _ / _ _ _ / _ _ _ _ _

8. Give a three-syllable word that means to be faithful to a person, group of persons, or an idea.

L _ _ / _ _ / _ _

9. Give a one-syllable word for the man who owns the shop.

D _ _

10. Give a three-syllable word for Bernardo's girlfriend.

A / _ _ / _ _

11. Give a one-syllable word for a group of persons.

G _ _ _

**Word building**   This exercise reinforces definitions of words. Students use definitions of word parts to call to mind words to which they have been exposed. The exercise enhances structural analysis skills as well.

*Directions:* Below are listed prefixes, suffixes, and root words and their meanings. You are to use these word parts and "assemble" science words. To assemble each word, place each word part and its meaning in the correct column, and the meaning of the assembled word in its column. Some word parts may be used more than once. One is done for you. Refer to a dictionary to see if your assembled word is listed and if spelling changes are necessary.

| Prefixes | Roots | Suffixes |
|---|---|---|
| alti-: height | atom: small particle | -ize: to make |
| anti-: against | meter: measure | -er: one who |
| centri-: center | biotics: pertaining | -ation: the act of |
| chrono-: time |    to life | -or: the state |
| con-: with, together | toxin: living or dead | -con: the act of |
|    with |    organisms pro- | -y: to make |
| ex-: from, out of |    ducing poison | |
| tele-: distance | fuge: to flee | |
| micro-: very small | dense: thick, thickly | |
| |    set | |
| | plode: drive | |
| | graph: write | |
| | vision: see | |
| | scope: to see | |

| Prefix and Meaning | Root and Meaning | Suffix and Meaning | Assembled Word and Meaning |
|---|---|---|---|
| alti-: height | meter: measure | | altimeter, to measure height |

**Following directions** This is a transitional exercise, bridging the purposes for exercises which reinforce definitions and meanings. By perceiving the relationship among the key words, students may generalize the name of the category to which the words belong (reinforcement of meaning). On the other hand, they may follow the directions and unscramble the name or the category (more a reinforcement of definition).

*Directions:* Under each blank line listed below, you will find several words listed. You are to identify the category to which these words belong and write its name on the blank provided.

To help identify the category, you may find all of the letters in the word by following simple directions. You will notice single numbers (15, for example) and/or double numbers (4-3, for example) under each set of words. To the left of each single or double number is a blank.

A single number refers to a letter in the alphabet (15, for example, refers to the letter *O*); a double number refers to the letter in the list (4-3, for example, refers to the fourth letter in the third word from the left). You are to find each letter so identified, then unscramble all the letters and spell the name of the category you are seeking.

1. _____
    algebra     arithmetic     geometry
 ____ 1-1; ____ 3-2; ____ 10-2; ____ 8-2; ____ 5-2; ____ 4-3; ____ 2-3; ____ 1-2;
 ____ 6-2; ____ 19; ____ 6-3.

2. _____
    isosceles     right     scalene
 ____ 1-1; ____ 3-2; ____ 3-3; ____ 5-2; ____ 6-3; ____ 5-3; ____ 7-1; ____ 1-2.

3. _____
    integer   denominate   cardinal   ordinal
 ____ 21; ____ 7-1; ____ 5-2; ____ 2-2; ____ 2; ____ 19; ____ 3-2.

4. _____
   diameter   radius   curve   circumference
 ____ 12; ____ 1-2; ____ 12-4; ____ 2-4; ____ 5-1; ____ 1-3; ____ 6-2.

5. _____
   coefficient    deviation    formula
 ____ 2; ____ 5-2; ____ 3-1; ____ 7-3; ____ 3-3; ____ 6-3; ____ 7.

## Reinforcement of Meanings

On the following pages appear a variety of exercises which have been used by teachers in various subjects and at various grade levels to reinforce students' knowledge of the meanings of words. In his study related to vocabulary development in biology, Barron (1971) found that the categorizing exercise was the most productive. Again, no such evidence is available for other subjects or grade levels. The other types are given to provide a variety of formats with the assumption that such variety will be beneficial for motivation and attention.

These exercises are used by students in small groups, as suggested for reinforcement of definitions. There obviously is much more need for and stimulus for discussion with these exercises than with the definitional type. As students discuss their differences and attempt to at least understand them, even if they cannot resolve them, they learn a great deal from one another. Teachers report that so-called slow students do very well on these exercises, even when in groups with so-called fast students. The experiences of the former are often such that they have developed insights beyond the understanding of the latter, and therefore can contribute importantly to the discussions.

These exercises can be used both before and after students read the assignment in the information source. Logically, it makes sense to have meanings reinforced after reading the material, because more context is available for that purpose. The exercises serve very well as vehicles for review. Completing and discussing such exercises prior to reading also is useful on occasion.

**Categorizing (1)** Words take on meaning as they are related to other words and to associated experiences. Meanings of the words in this exercise are reinforced as students consider each in reference to all three categories and subsequently verify their decisions through discussion.

## GEOGRAPHY*

*Directions:* Below is a list of words from your social studies unit, followed by the names of three categories. Write each word under as many categories as you can. Be ready to explain why you placed the words as you did. Some of the words may connect with more than one category. The first one has been done for you.

| | | |
|---|---|---|
| latitude | longitude | cordillera |
| tropics | meridians | commonwealth |
| roughlands | landforms | flatlands |
| basin | altitude | highlands |
| lowlands | source | tributaries |
| petroleum | nitrate | humus |
| semi-arid | rapids | resources |
| mineral | coke | |

| *Water* | *Land* | *Resources* |
|---|---|---|
| latitude | latitude | |

**Categorizing (2)** This exercise is at a higher level of abstraction than the previous one. Evolving the names of categories is a more abstract exercise than classifying words under given categories. Meanings of the words in each set are reinforced through a study of the associations among them. Experiences and knowledge from other contexts are drawn upon in order to generalize a name for the relationships among the words in a set—and this reinforces meaning.

## CHORUS–CHOIR–CHORALE**

*Directions:* In sets 1 through 6 below, three of the four words are related; in sets 7 and 8, four of the five words are related. Cross out the one word which does not fit with the others in the set. On the line at the top of the set, write the word or phrase that explains the relationship which exists among the remaining words.

*Jacqueline Manier
**Janet Correll

1. vocal group
   chorus
   vocal ensemble
   orchestra

2. melodic
   aria
   ABA
   rondo

3. recitative
   polyphonic
   chordal accompaniment
   speech-like

4. Handel
   Debussy
   Bach
   Baroque

5. Cantata #140
   Messiah
   Opera
   Palestrina

6. virtuoso
   beginner
   performer
   soloist

7. madrigal
   recitative
   aria
   opera
   chorus

8. oratorio
   lute
   chorus
   aria
   recitative

**Categorizing (3)** This exercise is at a still higher level of abstraction than the previous two. Perceiving possible sets of related words out of one longer list and then evolving a name to generalize the relationship, is more abstract than when the words already are placed in sets.

## BODY SYSTEMS*

*Directions:* Listed below are several words from the unit you have been studying. They can be grouped under three broad categories. Look for relationships among the words and identify the three categories, writing their names below in the spaces provided. Be ready to identify the words you would place under each of the categories.

stomach
skin
connective

nerve
digestive
pancreas

*Ena Stein

| | |
|---|---|
| endocrine | muscle |
| respiratory | bone |
| spleen | cartilage |
| medulla | blood |
| small intestine | secretory |
| esophagus | cells |
| epiglottis | nasal passage |
| appendix | gastric juice |

_____          _____          _____

**Categorizing (4)** This exercise is a variation on the categorizing (2) exercise. The difference is that there are at least two categories among the words within each set. Words for each category in the set must be separated out and the category named. This is more sophisticated but basically it still reinforces meanings through connections among words and associated experiences.

*Directions:* Four sets of words appear below, with five words in each set. Circle two words in each set so that the remaining three will also have something in common other than not being selected. In the space provided, write the term which describes the relationship among or between words in each group.

Is there more than one set of combinations for each main set of words? If so, write them down.

1. host          guest          visitor          employer          company

    GROUP ONE:_____

    GROUP TWO:_____

2. game          quarry          prey          sport          chase

    GROUP ONE:_____

    GROUP TWO:_____

3. plot          author          play          theme          story

    GROUP ONE:_____

    GROUP TWO:_____

4. wealth          values          culture          ideals          education

    GROUP ONE:_____

    GROUP TWO:_____

**Analogies** This is perhaps the most difficult of the exercises for reinforcing meaning. It requires students to perceive concepts in new, specific, and perhaps unusual relationships. But the exercise reinforces meanings because it forces consideration of relationships among words.

## CHINA *

*Directions:* Complete the following analogies, using the words from the following list.

| | |
|---|---|
| revolution | tradition |
| treaty | mandate |
| rebellion | dynasty |

1. *Goodwill* is to *peace* as _____ is to *change.*
2. *Integrate* is to *mix* as _____ is to *customs.*
3. *Writing* is to *corresponding* as a _____ is to an *order.*
4. *Rage* is to *anger* as _____ is to *insurrection.*
5. *Terminal* is to *depot* as a _____ is to an *agreement.*

**Associations** This exercise is a variation on categorizing exercises (3) and (4). The values derived are similar.

*Directions:* Place an *X* on the blank to the left of each word in the third column that creates a sensible relationship when combined with the other words in the set. Be ready to identify the relationship you see among the words.

| 1. acute | adjacent | _____ complementary |
|---|---|---|
| | | _____ supplementary |
| | | _____ vertical |
| | | _____ equal |
| 2. obtuse | adjacent | _____ complementary |
| | | _____ supplementary |
| | | _____ equal |
| | | _____ corresponding |
| 3. interior | supplementary | _____ exterior |
| | | _____ adjacent |
| | | _____ right |
| | | _____ triangle |
| | | _____ alternate |

*James Hepfner

4. vertical            central              ____ equal
                                            ____ obtuse
                                            ____ acute
                                            ____ supplementary
                                            ____ complementary
5. corresponding       complementary        ____ acute
                                            ____ obtuse
                                            ____ equal

**Shades of meaning** This exercise reinforces word meanings by having students draw on previous knowledge and experience to speculate on possible synonymous relationships between a key term and a set of words.

*Directions:* Examine the words listed below each phrase. Before those that are closely synonymous with the given personality trait put an *S*. Before those characteristics that are likely to accompany the given one, put a plus sign. If the characteristic *could* accompany the given one but probably would not, put a check. If the trait is definitely incongruous, put a minus sign.

| I. | II. | III. |
|---|---|---|
| a *strait-laced* person | a *sedate* person | a *volatile* person |
| ____ 1. tolerant | ____ 1. loquacious | ____ 1. steadfast |
| ____ 2. conservative | ____ 2. talkative | ____ 2. stolid |
| ____ 3. compliant | ____ 3. conservative | ____ 3. sensitive |
| ____ 4. sedate | ____ 4. cautious | ____ 4. constant |
| ____ 5. garrulous | ____ 5. cynical | ____ 5. cautious |
| ____ 6. indulgent | ____ 6. grave | ____ 6. phlegmatic |
| ____ 7. amorous | ____ 7. aggressive | ____ 7. emotional |
| ____ 8. fastidious | ____ 8. shrewish | ____ 8. consistent |
| ____ 9. reticent | ____ 9. fervid | ____ 9. listless |
| ____ 10. suave | ____ 10. persistent | ____ 10. garrulous |
| ____ 11. voluptuous | ____ 11. contentious | ____ 11. pertinacious |
| ____ 12. fluent | ____ 12. stubborn | ____ 12. flightly |
| ____ 13. frivolous | ____ 13. glib | ____ 13. aggressive |
| ____ 14. whimsical | ____ 14. fluent | ____ 14. colorless |
| ____ 15. melancholy | ____ 15. strait-laced | ____ 15. conventional |

### APPLICATION

To practice (and have a basis for comparison with your colleagues) on the various phases of vocabulary development, the following word lists are provided. The first is from a fifth-grade social studies lesson; the second, from a tenth-grade general science lesson.

The words one could use to teach context, structure, and dictionary are already noted by asterisks: *, **, ***, respectively. The concept being stressed also is identified.

For each set of words, design a structured overview as well as exercises to reinforce both definitions and meanings of the words. Compare them with your colleagues' and then with those given in Appendix A, pages 159-64. These exercises were written by classroom teachers and are reproduced as they were designed.

### Fifth-grade social studies*

*Concept:* World exploration came from desires for adventure, economic gain, and the spread of religion.

*Word list:*

| | | |
|---|---|---|
| *nation | **fur trader | **adventure |
| *stockade | **trading post | **wealth |
| *colony | **storehouse | ***print |
| *voyage | **settlement | ***press |
| *continent | **printing press | |
| *missionary | | |
| *religion | | |
| *explore | | |

### Tenth-grade general science**

*Concept:* All motion is caused by force, but not all force produces motion.

*Word list:*

| | |
|---|---|
| *motion | **centripetal |
| *force | **centrifugal |
| *matter | *action |
| *energy | **reaction |
| *gravity | *equal |
| *weight | **opposite |
| *mass | *attraction |
| *speed | **cohesion |
| **equilibrium | **adhesion |
| *friction | *molecules |
| **resistance | **oppose |
| *center of gravity | |

*Michael Landers
**Greta Afton

## SUMMARY

The language of a subject is its technical vocabulary. Until a student has facility with that language he cannot communicate ideas essential to the subject.

Functional development of the technical vocabulary has several advantages: vocabulary-acquisition skills are developed in a context relevant to teachers' desires and their students' needs; students develop understanding of and competence with skills that enable them to add to their vocabulary independently; as skills are developed, so is an understanding of basic concepts represented by the words to which the skills are applied.

Vocabulary development can be a continuation of the principle of teaching skills and course content simultaneously.

\*   \*   \*   \*   \*   \*

## REACTION GUIDE

*Part I*

*Directions:* Below is a list of words and phrases. According to the meaning you give each item, place it under one or more of the categories which follow. Discuss your responses with colleagues to compare and resolve differences. You may need to create additional categories in order to include all of the words.

| | |
|---|---|
| vocabulary acquisition skills | graphic organizer |
| context | word recognition |
| structure | criteria |
| structural analysis | key concepts |
| dictionary | relative value |
| definition | students' background |
| meaning | facilitation of independence |
| technical vocabulary | presentation of vocabulary |
| reinforcement | teaching of vocabulary |
| structured overview | semantic clues |
| time constraints | syntactic clues |
| pronunciation | experience |
| concept development | new words |
| old words | new concepts |
| old concepts | reading vocabulary |
| speaking vocabulary | listening vocabulary |

*SELECTION*          *TEACHING*          *REINFORCEMENT*

*Directions:* Place a check before each of the following statements that you find reasonable, given your understanding of the content of the chapter as well as the context of your own experience. Discuss your responses with your colleagues, citing evidence to support your decisions.

_____ 1. A student should not be allowed in a course unless he or she has an understanding of the basic vocabulary of the subject.

_____ 2. Language development is the responsibility of all teachers.

_____ 3. Words selected determine skills to be taught by a content teacher.

_____ 4. Skills selected determine words to be taught by a content teacher.

_____ 5. Subject area word lists are as valid as subject area skills lists.

_____ 6. Independence in vocabulary improvement is relative: to students' competence; sophistication of material; grade level; etc.

_____ 7. One can teach content without teaching the technical vocabulary, but not the reverse.

_____ 8. More words are caught than taught, usually, in content-area classes.

_____ 9. Independent development of vocabulary increases with a student's command of the various vocabulary-acquisition skills.

_____ 10. Knowledge of how to deal with vocabulary is basic to successful reading comprehension.

_____ 11. As a teacher you cannot hope to teach students all the words they will encounter for which they carry no meanings.

_____ 12. In order of practical value to students, means for ascertaining appropriate meanings of words are: dictionary; context; structure.

_____ 13. The probability of emphasis on vocabulary being beneficial to students is enhanced if the words selected for teaching are selected according to some objective criteria.

_____ 14. One cannot reinforce a concept one has not acquired.

_____ 15. Situations—and materials—can be contrived to promote discussion of the meanings of words and, thus, help students to incorporate those words into their readily-available-for-use vocabulary.

_____ 16. *Atrophy* applies to vocabulary as well as to limbs.

_____ 17. Knowledge of the structure of the curriculum is basic to criteria for selecting vocabulary for instructional emphasis.

_____ 18. Students already know enough words about any topic to serve as the basis on which to build a study of that topic.

\* \* \* \* \* \*

## REFERENCES

BARRON, RICHARD. Research for classroom teachers: recent developments on the use of the structured overview as an advance organizer. In Harold L. Herber and James D. Riley (eds.), *Research in reading in the content areas: fourth year report.* Syracuse, N.Y.: Syracuse University Reading and Language Arts Center, 1978. (Monograph)

BARRON, RICHARD. *The use of an iterative research process to improve a method of vocabulary instruction in tenth grade biology.* Unpublished doctoral dissertation, Syracuse University, 1971.

BARRON, RICHARD, The use of vocabulary as an advance organizer. In Harold L. Herber and Peter L. Sanders (Eds.), *Research in reading in the content areas: First year report.* Syracuse, N.Y.: Syracuse University Reading and Language Arts Center, 1969. (Monograph)

BURMEISTER, LOU F. *Reading strategies for secondary school teachers.* Reading, Mass.: Addison-Wesley, 1974.

DEIGHTON, LEE. *Vocabulary development in the classroom.* New York: Columbia University Press, 1959.

DURRELL, DONALD D. *Improving reading instruction.* New York: Harcourt Brace Jovanovich, 1966.

EARLE, RICHARD. The use of the structured overview in mathematics classes. In Harold L. Herber and Peter L. Sanders (Eds.), *Research in reading in the content areas: First year report.* Syracuse, N.Y.: Syracuse University Reading and Language Arts Center, 1969. (Monograph)

EARLE, RICHARD. *The use of vocabulary as a structured overview in seventh grade mathematics.* Unpublished doctoral dissertation, Syracuse University, 1970.

GOODMAN, KENNETH. Behind the eye: What happens to reading. In *Reading process and program.* Urbana, Ill.: National Council of Teachers of English, 1970, 25-26.

GORDON, W. J. J. *The metaphorical way of learning and knowing.* Cambridge, Mass.: Porpoise Books, 1973.

HOOK, J. N. *The teaching of high school English.* New York: Ronald Press, 1965.

ROBINSON, H. ALAN. *Teaching reading and study strategies: The content areas.* Boston: Allyn & Bacon, 1975.

WALKER, NORA. *An investigation into the effects of graphic organizers on the learning of social studies readers in the middle grades.* Unpublished doctoral dissertation, Syracuse University, 1975.

# seven

# Prediction as Motivation and an Aid to Comprehension

## VOCABULARY

The following terms are important to an understanding of this chapter. Each is defined in context. Read through the list to identify those for which you have uncertain meanings. Then as you read the chapter, pay particular attention to their definitions. Also, make certain that the meanings attributed to the remaining words by their context in the chapter correspond to the meanings they hold for you.

prediction                    motivation                    interest

Each of the following terms has been defined previously in this book. If you are not reading the chapters in sequence, you may need to examine the vocabulary lists for the chapters which precede this one for definitions of words for which you have uncertain meanings.

emotional investment          simulation
intellectual investment       curriculum
content objective             concept
information source            grouping

## IDEA DIRECTION

In Chapter 2 of this book several instructional problems were identified and solutions were suggested. So far, the book has addressed these problems by elaborating on their solutions. The purpose of this chapter is to refine the focus on the problems and show how the use of prediction brings together many of the solutions already suggested. The result gives you another option in your instruction, providing variety as well as depth.

## READING DIRECTION

This chapter requires considerable flexibility in your reading. You will have to connect suggested procedures from previous chapters with suggestions in this chapter, requiring a synthesis of information and ideas. Then, as you take part in a lesson taught with the teacher *en abstentia,* you will have read carefully for detail in order to follow the directions exactly. Finally, you will have to read imaginatively, trying to picture the lesson and the class which is described at the end of the chapter.

---

## BACKGROUND

Three concerns about students and one about teachers motivate this chapter—indeed, this book. First, there is a constant concern about students whose *interests* in learning do not seem to correspond with school requirements. It is often believed that such students have no interest in learning. Although this attitude often is attributed to students who seem to respond poorly to instruction, rarely are they actually disinterested in learning per se.

One need only to follow students so labeled through a typical day to discover that they are very interested in learning. When they are involved in the "nook-and-cranny curriculum" they are highly interested students and they learn well. (Hogan, 1971). They teach well, too.

We need to be cautious in so classifying students. The lack of interest in learning which we observe exists with respect to the school requirements. Our task is to somehow capture that general interest in learning and bring it to bear on the school curriculum as well as on the nook-and-cranny curriculum.

A second concern is for those students whose *motivations* for learning do not correspond with the schools' expectations. One hears the same argument about students' motivations that one hears about their interests—that they don't have them. They lack motivation for learning even as they lack interest in learning. But the error is the same, even as the argument is the same.

Students *are* motivated to learn; but they may not be motivated toward what the school expects of them. They act on their motivations and, since the motivations do not correspond to school expectations, such actions are viewed with alarm, as worthy of disciplinary action.

Some would use these problems of interest and motivation to bolster their claim that the school curriculum is irrelevant to the students. They use these problems as the basis for abandoning the current curriculum, substituting "something" more relevant. "Let the students choose their own curriculum, or study whatever they wish in a specific curriculum area," is the proposed solution.

Such is *not* the position taken in this book. There are other ways to go, for reasons discussed in the next section. There is ample evidence to demonstrate that the current curriculum can be made relevant if students can be shown how it fits with what they already know and how they can use what they learn. Students, like their parents, are increasingly pragmatic and want to know how what they learn will work, how it will be helpful to them, how it fits with what they already know.

A third concern is for students whose facility in the comprehension of basic resources used in school does not correspond with the requirements. All of the previous chapters have dealt with this kind of student, and suggestions have been made as to how to help them. That they exist there can be no doubt. Whether there are as many as is claimed in most schools can be seriously doubted.

There is a considerable difference between a student who doesn't read because he cannot read and a student who doesn't read because he won't read. Most so-called "can't" readers really are "won't" readers. Most have more skills than they ever let on to their teachers. Fader's (1971) description of Wentworth and his self-imposed schizophrenia is a classic example of such a student. When there is a proper mix of interest, motivation, curriculum, and instruction, it is amazing how quickly such students "learn" how to read.

*Finally,* there is the problem of teachers feeling inadequate and frustrated as they try to deal with students who have these problems. It is extremely difficult to meet day after day with students and seem not to be able to help them at all, or to a very limited degree. It makes teachers question if they have chosen the right profession. One hopes to avoid the naive optimism of seeing solutions in anything that comes along as well as the desperate pessimism which sees no hope in any suggestion.

The use of prediction as motivation has helped teachers and students in all sorts of instructional settings, across the whole range of subject areas and grade levels. These suggestions are given in the hope that they, or variations on them, will prove to be as helpful to you.

## EXPERIENCING THE USE
## OF PREDICTION

First, you need to develop a feeling for the process being recommended. It is a little more difficult to do for prediction than for the methods suggested in other chapters of this book.

In this lesson you must move through the material step by step and not look ahead to the next step until you have completed the preceding one. If I were able to teach the lesson in person, I would present the steps one at a time, as was done in the original lesson.

You should join two or three other people for this activity and work in a group. The entire lesson deals with the concept of *protest*.

First, discuss among yourselves your ideas of what the word *protest* means to you.

Second, examine the word structurally. Is there a familiar prefix?_____. Right; *pro,* which suggests what?_____. Yes, *for.* And what about the root word, *test*? Given what you already know about the word *protest,* what would you guess the *test* might stand for? Make a list among yourselves; recall other words which have the same root (*testimony,* for example).

*Test* comes from *testare,* which means "to witness." When you are pro-testing, you are witnessing for something, are you not?

Coupling this idea of protest with your own ideas and experiences related to the word, you are ready for the next task. In 90 seconds, write as many words as you can which, in your mind, represent TYPES OF PROTEST. When you finish, compare your list with other groups' lists. Turn to the footnote on page 178 for the next set of directions.

Before reading the rest of the directions, be certain that you are ready to time yourself so that you can start immediately. Also, it is more efficient if one person writes the words for the group while everyone contributes, including the writer. If you have enough people to form more than one group, set up a competition among groups to see which creates the longer list.

When you have completed work with the word lists, proceed to the next task, described below.

*Directions I:* You have searched your mind and shared with others your impressions and ideas related to the concept of *protest.* Using these discussions as a context, consider the meaning of each of the following statements. If you personally agree with a statement, place a check on the numbered line. When you have reacted to all of the statements, compare your responses to those of other members of the group. Where you have differences, discuss the reasons for those differences so that you understand the positions taken by those who differ with you. Where you have the same responses, discuss them to see if your agreements are based on similar or different reasons.

_____ 1. You can't have what you don't work for.

_____ 2. Violence solves problems.

_____ 3. People working together have more power than people working separately.

_____ 4. People have no right to protest.

_____ 5. Protests bring results.

_____ 6. Leaders do listen.

_____ 7. Protests can be peaceful and violent at the same time.

_____ 8. People have the right to live comfortably.

Now examine the next set of directions related to this set of statements. Work out the suggested activity _before_ you read the selection which relates to this lesson, starting on page 264, Appendix A.

_Directions II:_ This lesson, as you know well by now, deals with the concept of _protest._ You have drawn on your knowledge and experience to produce and discuss a list of words related to the concept. You also have reacted to a set of statements which express ideas, values, opinions related to the concept. Soon you will read a passage in which the authors report on an historical event in which a new kind of protest was invented and applied. It brought about new benefits for workers in the United States.

With only that very brief description of what you will be reading about, and before you know the details of this historical event, please make some predictions. Based on just the little information you have about the reading selection, predict whether or not the authors will agree with you as to the acceptance or rejection of the eight statements given above. If you predict that the authors will agree with you on a statement, circle the number of that statement. If you predict they will not agree with you, then leave the number of the statement untouched.

Discuss your predictions with others in your group and as you compare them, explore the reasons for differences you might have.

Now it is time for you to refer to the reading selection. Read through the following set of directions before you read the passage.

_Directions III:_ After you have discussed your predictions, work with others in your group to check your accuracy. Working together, read through the passage and decide whether or not the authors do agree with you on each of the statements. Place an asterisk beside the numbers of statements which the authors apparently would support. This, of course, will tell you whether or not your predictions about the authors were accurate. Be ready to cite evidence from the text to support your arguments as to the position the authors seem to take on each of the statements.

When you have completed the final step in the preceding directions, this lesson is over. If I were actually with you, teaching the lesson in person, we could have a general class discussion on the significance of the development of the unions and how that form of protest relates to other forms which you identified in your word lists and subsequent discussions. You may want to do that for yourselves. Meanwhile, we must continue on and discuss some of the rationale for this kind of lesson as well as the effectiveness of this particular lesson when used with history students.

## RATIONALE

The lesson you just experienced demonstrates how the use of prediction can make operational three instructional principles and how they, in turn, address the concerns presented at the beginning of this chapter. This section first discusses these principles and then shows how prediction activates them in a practical way.

### Instructional Principles

Three instructional principles are operating in this lesson and others like it. When put into practice, these principles provide a practical response to the needs of students identified earlier. They can be applied to any subject at any grade level with results that are exciting both to students and teachers.

1. Students' interest is aroused when you treat the curriculum in a way that lets them discover that much of their prior knowledge and experience is relevant to each new topic.

"So, what else is new," you might be saying. But wait a minute before you write it off as just another truism in education. This principle obviously has reference to the process of review, and *review* is an activity which has been pressed upon you since the moment you became interested in teaching. However, this principle is making a different kind of point and suggests a different purpose.

As teachers we choreograph for ourselves an instructional ballet we call a lesson plan. Review is, naturally, a part of that ballet. But, unless students actively draw on their prior knowledge and experience and relate them to the new concept under consideration, review is of little help. Continuing the process in spite of its lack of effect turns it into a meaningless ritual.

*In 90 seconds, write as many words as you can which, in your mind, represent RESULTS OF PROTEST. When you finish, compare your list with other groups' lists.
Turn to the footnote on page 188 for the next set of directions.

There really is very little which we have students study in our subjects for which they do not already have some prior knowledge and experience, if we treat the concepts or topics or units broadly enough. For example, this lesson on protest was traditionally taught as a lesson on the development of unions and unionism. Students in this school would have had little experience or knowledge to bring to the lesson had the initial focus been directly on that specific topic. However, changing to the broader concept of "protest"—around which the students had considerable knowledge and experience—gave them an opportunity to see how much they already knew about the topic.

The device of having students produce lists of related words is a useful way to guide their review. It helps them become instantly aware of how much they know, individually and collectively, about the topic. They discover quickly that there are no right or no wrong answers, that their ideas and contributions are accepted and respected both by the teacher and by their fellow students. Until students reach the point in the lesson where they must read the passage and judge whether their predictions are accurate, the entire lesson is based on their own knowledge, experience, and opinion. This captivates their interest much more than the more traditional, perfunctory review.

You occasionally will be surprised at the content of students' responses. Since you are tapping into their real world through such a procedure, you have to expect almost anything. When the lesson on *protest* was taught to the eleventh graders in the newly integrated school, the teacher was rather surprised at the words read off by the young man speaking for the group with the longest list of words. (It is useful to have a contest among the groups, with the group having the longest list being declared the winner. True, this rewards quantity alone, but let the students then judge the quality as they listen to the words and compare them with their own. Perhaps, then, you also can have a quality winner.)

The list the young man read was made up of words that the group associated with "types of protest." The teacher was anticipating traditional social studies words such as *strike, embargo, boycott.* Instead, the young man read off the following words: *boy, whitey, honkey, redneck, nigger, etc.* The anticipated social studies words did not appear on his list.

The teacher said that he wasn't clear as to how the group was connecting their words to the word *protest,* since the task was to list words which represented "types of protest." The young man said, "well, we thought we should list words which cause people to protest." They had amended the assignment to fit the topic to their needs and interests, their prior experience and knowledge. The teacher did not protest the variation, since it did fit into the overall concept. The students' interest in the topic was obvious at that point, and they had demonstrated clearly that they had much to offer to the lesson. Also, in drawing on other groups for words not already reported, more traditional words representing types of protest did emerge.

That same group had the longest list of words representing "results of protest." Again, their words were different from those anticipated by the teacher: *death, jail, hanging, beating, lynching, firebombing.* Nearly all of the words were negative. As other groups reported, some positive words also emerged—as a whole, the class developed a negative and a positive list.

In response to both lists, students were demonstrating clearly that they had much knowledge and experience to bring to the lesson. The review was not perfunctory; the students' interest was captivated; they had made both an intellectual and emotional commitment to the lesson.

2. Motivation for staying with the lesson seems assured when the students' prior knowledge and experience becomes the basic "stuff" of the lesson, creating a student-centered lesson in which each has invested intellectually and emotionally.

The students' own word lists became the stuff of the lesson right from the beginning. They invested themselves: their ideas, their feelings. And, as anyone is, students are careful to follow through to see what happens to their investments. As a result they are well motivated.

Since they did not create the statements to which they reacted, you might say that there was a shift away from student-centeredness. That would be true if their task was to decide whether the statements were right or wrong. However, they were asked to indicate whether or not *they* agreed with the statements. There was both an intellectual and emotional investment in this topic since students were drawing on their own knowledge and experience, not on some unknown writer's.

First establishing their own opinion with respect to the statements and then predicting whether the authors might agree *with them* placed the students at the center of the lesson. Their ideas, their experiences, their knowledge, their feelings were the criteria. "Does the author agree with you?" was the question, not the reverse. This is a perfect example of a student-centered lesson, part of a student-centered curriculum. Students are the reference point, with what they subsequently study being a commentary on or a comparison with what they know, or are, or feel. "Does the author agree with you?" is a marvelous question to ask of students. It is much more appealing than, "Do you agree with the author?" The former places the student at the center of things; the latter places the author there. The former is much more motivational than the latter.

Note that the content objective was not lost. Students learned about the development of the unions as a form of protest. But they were able to relate it directly to themselves and were more likely to assimilate it into their experiential and conceptual bases. Clearly, we can have a student-centered curriculum without abandoning what we have found valuable for students, what we believe they should know and experience. The difference is in how we use students' prior knowledge and experience and where we place the students relative to what it is they are to study.

3. Students' comprehension will increase when you show them how to relate information and ideas in the resource materials to their own knowledge and experience.

Students' predictions about the authors' agreement with their own views on the eight statements accomplished two objectives: (1) the process kept the students at the center of things, requiring that the authors' ideas be judged by the students and not the reverse; (2) it established a clear purpose and motivation for reading the assigned passage.

Comprehension and reasoning were enhanced functionally. Students were required to cite evidence from the passage to support their predictions. Thus, they had to locate information pertinent to each statement, interpret the information in light of the statement, and then judge whether their predictions were accurate. The experience clearly demonstrated to students both the process of connecting information from a text to their own ideas and experiences and the process of judging whether that information produces the same opinion or the same idea as their own.

The teacher did not have to take time out to teach students those comprehension skills, even though the students were supposed to be rather poor readers. (Clearly there were "won't" readers in that class rather than "can't" readers.) The statements provided the stimulus; students citing evidence from the text experienced a simulation of the comprehension/reasoning processes the teacher hoped the students would ultimately be able to apply independently.

## Definition of Prediction

Prediction can be defined as an intellectual or emotional extension of one's knowledge and experience into the unknown, under the constraints of specific conditions or actions. Prediction, as defined, is applied instructionally through five specific steps. Each was illustrated in the lesson you experienced. However, each is sufficiently general that it could take many other forms besides the one you experienced. As you apply your own skills and imagination to the entire process, you will come up with your own variations.

1. For the content of the lesson you are to teach, identify the broad-ranging concept which will serve as the focal point for the lesson, the point to which students can connect their own experience and knowledge.

Remember the principle that there is little to be studied in our subjects for which students do not already have some prior knowledge and experience if we deal with a subject broadly enough. In this lesson, you will recall, the teacher used the concept of *protest* rather than the topic of *unions* or *unionism.*

2. Help students connect their prior knowledge and experience to the concept through some organizational scheme or format.

In the lesson you experienced, the scheme was producing lists of words which were related to the concept of the lesson: *protest.* You, from your own knowledge and experience related to the concept, produced basic information for the lesson and were prepared to continue pursuit of the concept because of the investments you had made.

The statements also served as an organizational scheme for helping you connect with the concept. You made decisions about each statement, drawing on your own experience and knowledge to determine its acceptability.

3. Establish conditions or actions for the prediction, into which the knowl-edge and experience is extended.

Recall that in the lesson you experienced, after you had reacted to the statements yourself, you were asked to predict whether the authors of the article you were about to read would agree with your opinions. Conditions for that prediction were established. You were given a brief description of the content of the article:

> Soon you will read a passage in which the authors report on an historical event in which a new kind of protest was invented and applied which brought about new benefits for workers in the United States.

In order to make your predictions, you had to extend your knowledge and experience about protest into this set of conditions and make a decision: As the definition of prediction indicates, it involves the "extension of one's knowledge and experience into the unknown under the constraints of specific conditions."

4. Simulate the prediction. Extending your knowledge and experience into the conditions established by the description of the article, you predicted the probable position taken by the authors on each of the statements. The predictive process retained its student-centeredness by asking you to predict if the authors would agree with your own positions on the statements. In effect, you were saying, "Given these conditions, this is the way my knowledge and experience apply. The authors may agree with me on these things and disagree on these other things."

5. Simulate comprehension. You were finally asked to read the article and determine whether your predictions were accurate. Did the authors agree with you as you thought they might? Did they disagree according to your predictions? What was the evidence by which you determined their position on the statements, hence their agreement or disagreement with you? Information in the article provided the reality within the established condition. Given that reality, you were able to make judgments about the accuracy of your predictions. And making these judgments required you to apply comprehension skills. But you didn't have to apply the skills independently. The process was simulated for you by means of the statements. It will be useful for you to reflect on discussions in previous chap-

ters concerning the use of declarative statements for purposes of simulating comprehension as well as the more detailed discussion of simulation in the chapter which follows this one.

The sample lesson was developed by this sequence. So was the following illustrative lesson, as you will see.

## AN ILLUSTRATIVE LESSON

Here are materials from another social studies lesson which utilized the process of prediction but in a slightly different way. The purpose for using a second lesson from the same subject area is to demonstrate that variation in format and approach is possible within a subject area when applying these principles. They are equally applicable across subject areas.

The lesson was taught to ninth-grade students in world history. The curriculum was topical rather than chronological. At the time of the lesson, the teacher was engaged in the study of the Renaissance.

The students' regular teacher had virtually abandoned any use of printed materials with these students because they were "so deficient in reading." This class was selected for a demonstration lesson to show the integration of instruction in reading with instruction in world history.

The regular teacher was asked what the students were to be studying and what reading assignment would be related to it. The teacher said, "They can't read, so I don't give them assignments."

The demonstration teacher asked, "Well, if they could read, what reading assignment would you give them for this topic?"

The teacher said, "The Declaration of Independence."

Swell! Have you ever tried to teach a demonstration lesson to poor readers using the Declaration of Independence? It's quite a challenge.

The first step was to apply the first instructional principle mentioned earlier: Identify a concept broad enough for students to connect prior knowledge and experience but specific enough eventually to connect with the part of the curriculum being studied. "Freedom" was the concept chosen for the focus of the lesson.

The day for the demonstration lesson arrived; forty teachers and the class of thirty students moved to a double classroom. After appropriate preliminary activities to help the students relax with the new teacher, the lesson was started. No mention was made of the Declaration of Independence.

The first activity involved the students in producing a word list. They were divided randomly into groups of five students and were invited to take part in a contest (as were the observing teachers). The object was for each group to produce a list of words related to a specific topic within a designated time. The group with the greatest number of words on the list would be declared the winner. The topic would be announced just before they received the signal to start writing.

When they were ready, the demonstration teacher said, "In two minutes I would like you to write as many words as you can which you connect in some way with the word . . . FREEDOM. Go!"

Two minutes later, the teacher said, "Stop! Count the number of words you have on your list."

The winning group was identified and the recorder was asked to read the list to the other groups. Before he started, the teacher said, "Now, we have three reasons for listening to this list: (1) to see if the winning list contains duplications; if it does, another group might be declared the winner; (2) to see if your group's list has words that the winning group doesn't have; (3) to see if the winning group's list has words that your group doesn't have. OK? Now, let's hear the winning list."

These are the words which were read from the winning list: *nature, free, hiking, outdoors, camping, poems, boyfriend, bird, animals, happy, loose, carefree, exciting, anything, family, boring, a lot, no homework, wing, solitude, teachers, no one, sky, airplane, smoking, sex, girlfriend, relationship, life, babies, waterfall, fish.*

(After the lesson was over, one of the observing teachers said to the demonstration teacher: "You know, as I looked at my list while listening to the winning list, I never felt so old! I saw *Constitution, Bill of Rights, Declaration of Independence,* as I heard *fish, babies, sky.*")

Each group shared with the other groups all words from its list not mentioned by the others. At the conclusion of that sharing, the teacher indicated that he had some words he wanted to share from his list. He wrote these on the board:

| | |
|---|---|
| equal | individuals |
| separation | organize |
| decision | protect |
| obvious | independence |

He took a few moments to teach *independence* and *protect,* emphasizing structural analysis. He merely presented the rest of the words on his list and made one or two comments about each to identify its definition. He pointed out that the words on his list, along with many on the students' lists, would be appearing in the reading selection related to this lesson.

The teacher asked the students to make a decision about each word on their lists: "Does the word represent a cause or a result of freedom? If it relates to a cause, write *C* before the word; if result, write *R*."

Students discovered quickly that most words could be connected with both causes and results, depending on how you used the words and what point in history you connected with them. They shared that insight through discussion in and among the groups.

The teacher then moved to the prediction phase of the lesson. He said to the students:

"You obviously have done a lot of thinking about the idea of freedom and have both the knowledge and experience to use during your discussions. I would like you now to put yourselves in the place of some people who were having problems with their freedom.

"Suppose you were part of a large group of people and you found that, along with yourself, the freedoms of several others in this large group were being limited. You and these other people made up a rather clearly identifiable group.

"Suppose, also, that you and the others in that smaller group decided that you should pull away from the larger group, become free from them. But you also believed that you should explain to the larger group why you were doing what you were doing.

"What do you think you might say in that explanation? Let's test out some ideas. I'm going to pass out to you a sheet of paper on which are written several statements. You follow along as I read them to you and you decide whether or not you think you might make such a statement if you were intending to break away from that larger group and you wanted to explain why you were doing so. If you think you might make a statement, place a check on the numbered line: if you think you would not make a statement, leave the line blank."

The teacher then distributed the following sheet to the students, asking them to keep it face down until all had received one. Then he asked them to follow along as he read each item. As he completed the reading of each item he asked the students, "Would *you* say this if you were in their place? If so, put a check on the numbered line."

### *WOULD YOU SAY THIS?*

\_\_\_\_ 1. Sometimes certain people are better off being separated from one another than being together.

\_\_\_\_ 2. When one group of people separates from another, both groups are then equal in the eyes of all other groups.

\_\_\_\_ 3. If one group decides to leave another group, it should give the reasons for its decision.

\_\_\_\_ 4. Reasons for groups being separate and equal are really very obvious. Here are some of them:

    \_\_\_\_ a. All individuals and groups are equal.

    \_\_\_\_ b. These individuals all have the right to live, to be free, and to enjoy life.

    \_\_\_\_ c. These rights are made possible when a group organizes itself and puts people in charge of protecting these rights for the group.

_____ d. When the people in charge of a group do not protect these rights, the group has the right to put new people in charge and to tell them how things should be run.

_____ 5. A group should separate from other groups or change people in charge of itself only for the most serious reasons.

_____ 6. However, when it seems necessary to take action, a group should do so even though it seems strange for them to do so.

Students responded individually on each item. The teacher then asked the students to compare their responses and try to resolve their differences by sharing the reasons for the responses they gave. There were many differences and the students engaged in good discussion. Still no mention was made of the Declaration of Independence.

The period ended and the lesson was carried over to the next day. Students were introduced to the Declaration of Independence and asked to work together in groups to determine if its writers agreed with them and actually had statements similar to those on their work sheet. They were asked to cite evidence from the document to support their decisions.

Finally, to focus their ideas on some general principles basic to the curriculum, students were asked to indicate their own support of each of the following statements as well as the hypothesized support of the writers of the Declaration of Independence.

### FREEDOM II

*Directions:* Here are five statements. Think about them in light of the statements you reacted to in the first part of this lesson and also in light of the work you did with words related to "Freedom." Check the statements you believe to be reasonable and prepare your mind to discuss your reasons for your choices.

_____ 1. Belief is as much a part of freedom or slavery as is action.

_____ 2. You may get freedom without working for it but you can't keep it that way.

_____ 3. Separation of people brings equality among them.

_____ 4. Independence occurs more in a person's mind than in his daily living.

_____ 5. Freedom is more a state of mind than condition of body.

This lesson was based on the instructional principles and the five-step procedure outlined in the section of this chapter on Rationale. It engaged students in hypothesizing or predicting in a slightly different way than the lesson on Protest, but it was effective nonetheless. There are as many variations as our imaginations allow. The purposes remain the same.

The use of prediction is recommended to you as are all other suggestions in this book. Try it with your students; adapt it to suit your needs and your style; modify it as necessary; retain the principles and the general procedures; variations in format are inconsequential.


## SUMMARY

Prediction is an effective way to reach and teach students who are having trouble developing and maintaining interest in school and in dealing with the information sources they are required to use. It is helpful because it builds on what students are, what they have, and what they know. It is effective because: (1) the process shows students *how* to function; and (2) the process places students in the center of things, showing them where they fit and just how important they are. Talk about motivation!


\*     \*     \*     \*     \*     \*


## REACTION GUIDE

*Part I*

*Directions:* Listed below are twelve sets of words or phrases. Each represents a possible contrast as presented in the chapter. Check each one you can support with evidence and be ready to discuss your decisions.

\_\_\_\_\_  1. students' interests/schools' requirements
\_\_\_\_\_  2. students' motivations/schools' expectations
\_\_\_\_\_  3. students' achievement/schools' demands
\_\_\_\_\_  4. won't read/can't read
\_\_\_\_\_  5. current relevance/current irrelevance
\_\_\_\_\_  6. naive optimism/desperate pessimism
\_\_\_\_\_  7. principles/practices
\_\_\_\_\_  8. practical problems/practical solutions
\_\_\_\_\_  9. broad treatment/narrow focus
\_\_\_\_\_ 10. student-centered/curriculum-centered
\_\_\_\_\_ 11. investment/withdrawal
\_\_\_\_\_ 12. prediction/confirmation

*Part II*

*Directions:* Check each of the following statements which you can support with evidence drawn from the book as well as from other sources. Be ready to support your decisions in discussions with your colleagues.

\_\_\_\_ 1. Relevance involves more than curriculum; it involves attitude as well.

\_\_\_\_ 2. The unknown is a great equalizer.

\_\_\_\_ 3. Centeredness serves ego needs.

\_\_\_\_ 4. Relevance relates to self.

\_\_\_\_ 5. A teacher-centered curriculum cannot serve student-centered needs.

\_\_\_\_ 6. If you want to capture someone's attention, make that person feel important.

\_\_\_\_ 7. Most people want neither something for nothing nor nothing for something.

\_\_\_\_ 8. Time restrictions make the relevant irrelevant.

\* \* \* \* \* \*

## REFERENCES

FADER, DANIEL. *The naked children.* New York: Macmillan, 1971.

HOGAN, ROBERT. "You'll like it. It's Caneloni" *Phi Delta Kappan*, 52, April (1971), 468-70.

*Select *one* word from your "Types" list to connect with *one* word from your "Results" list to form a *concrete* relationship. Share your pairing with other groups. Select *one* word from your "Types" list to connect with *one* word from your "Results" list to form an *abstract* relationship. Share your pairings with other groups. Return to page 176 to cont'nue the lesson.

Checklist referred to on page 249:

## REASONING

____  1. Open

____  2. Closed

____  3. Inductive

____  4. Deductive

____  5. Interpretive

____  6. Inferential

____  7. Convergent

____  8. Divergent

____  9. Extensive

____ 10. Intensive

____ 11. Critical

____ 12. Creative

____ 13. Analytical

____ 14. Elaborative

____ 15. Content bound

____ 16. Content free

____ 17. Objective

____ 18. Subjective

____ 19. Functional

____ 20. Direct

____ 21. Guide

# eight

# Simulating, Guiding, and Grouping

## VOCABULARY

The following terms are important to your understanding of this chapter. Each is defined in context. Read through the list to identify those for which you have uncertain meanings. Then as you read the chapter, pay particular attention to their definitions. Also, make certain that the meanings attributed to the remaining words by their context in the chapter correspond to the meanings they hold for you.

| | |
|---|---|
| simulation | multiplier effect |
| questioning | work group |
| guiding | training group |
| grouping | work-training group |
| student involvement | group roles |
| learning environment | group-member skills |
| individualization | group-leader roles |
| | leadership styles |

The following terms have been defined previously in this book. If you are not reading the chapters in sequence, you may need to examine the vocabulary lists for the chapters which precede this one for definitions of words for which you hold uncertain meanings.

| | |
|---|---|
| assumptive teaching | organizational patterns |
| curriculum | open reasoning |
| levels of comprehension | closed reasoning |
| independence | |

## IDEA DIRECTION

This chapter identifies three critical factors that support and make possible the successful application of the ideas and procedures outlined in the preceding chapters. The guides and reinforcement materials simulate for students the processes appropriate to the related reading tasks. Guiding students' responses so that they learn the processes being simulated is accomplished through guides: for levels, patterns, reasoning, and vocabulary reinforcement and extension. Grouping is the classroom organizational format which promotes the interaction among students and facilitates the simulating and the guiding. Each of these factors is discussed in detail. You will want to review ideas and suggestions from each of the preceding chapters and apply them as you read this chapter.

## READING DIRECTION

Since this chapter relates to the preceding chapters, you will have to refer back to specific sections to refresh your memory on specific ideas. Don't rely solely on recall, even if yours is unusually powerful.

---

## SIMULATING AND GUIDING

Education is replete with examples of assumptive teaching. That is, a teacher often behaves as though the persons being taught already know what is being taught. Failure to prepare students adequately for the learning task is assumptive teaching, the assumption being that students already have organized the background information they need in order to develop an understanding of what is to be learned.

Failure to show students how to identify, analyze, and synthesize ideas in the required information source is an example of assumptive teaching. The assumptions are that students already know enough about the subject to be able to discern the important information and that they know how to process the information for concept development. Giving students a reading assignment without instructing them in *how* to read it is assumptive unless they already are skilled readers and are reading familiar material. The assumption is that they already have the reading and reasoning skills which allow them to cope with new material on a higher level of sophistication than they have handled before. Such assumptions make teaching nothing more than a combination of assigning and telling. Effective teaching, in contrast, is a combination of guiding and showing.

Central to the guiding and showing is the process of simulating. For our purposes, simulation can be defined as

> an artificial representation of a real experience; a contrived series of activities which, when taken together, approximate the experience or the process that ultimately is to be applied independently (Herber & Nelson, 1975).

In astronautics, simulation provided the astronauts with an artificial environment that approximated what they would experience during space flight. Scientists and engineers were so accurate in their approximations that when the astronauts actually did fly in space it seemed to them as though they had been there hundreds of times before. Their bodies and minds, conditioned by the simulation, *had* been there before.

Driver education serves as another example of the values of simulation. The simulator creates the environment and the conditions that approximate what drivers will experience behind the wheels of their own cars in traffic. Without risk to themselves, other drivers, or pedestrians, drivers-in-training can develop their skills in handling an automobile. They can develop confidence in their own competence and move out into real traffic secure in the belief that they can handle almost any situation.

In astronautics and in driver education, the objectives are established and the desired independent behavior, which follows instruction in the simulator, can be described clearly. All of the instruction through the simulator is focused on those objectives and that ultimate behavior. Why shouldn't teaching, speaking generally, do the same? Why shouldn't reading instruction, speaking specifically, do the same? Why shouldn't reading instruction in content areas, speaking precisely, do the same?

Teachers often teach as though students already had attained the independence which is the goal of formal education. This attitude is demonstrated in many ways, not least of which is the lament about students' inadequate background of knowledge and skills, and the fervent wish that they were better educated so that "I could really teach them my subject." But even as they recognize the students' needs implicit in their laments and wishes, the teachers will proceed to teach the students as though they really did have that background and skills. This is not a conscious act of maliciousness, of course. It comes from having no instructional alternatives which acknowledge that students *have not* attained independence, that they must be helped to develop the background, that they must be shown how to function.

If our curriculum really is cumulative, if it really represents steadily increasing levels of sophistication, then students are never truly independent until they have learned what we have to teach them. *Then* they are independent with respect to what we taught them, but not with respect to the *next* level of sophistication. The next level of teachers can be no more assumptive than we were, if the curriculum is cumulative in its substance and its demands.

Simulation is showing how; it is the response we need for the challenge. Simulation has been an integral part of everything discussed in the preceding chapters.

## Simulating Levels of Comprehension

Helping students read with better comprehension is probably the goal of every teacher who gives reading assignments in an information source. The almost automatic response to that objective is to provide students with questions which will guide their reading and help them develop those comprehension skills. One observes this among reading teachers as well as among content-area teachers.

But questions are assumptive. To be able to answer questions, one must be able to apply the reading skill or skills implicit in the relationship between the questions and the content. But test the logic of this: the questions are asked to help the readers because they need help in comprehending the reading selection, presumably because they don't have the necessary skills. If students already are able to identify the significant information, to perceive the relationships in that information so as to formulate related ideas, or to synthesize those ideas with prior knowledge and experience, they already would have the skills which the teacher intended to teach when he or she asked the question. If the students cannot do all this because they lack the skill, then no amount of asking—at whatever rate or frequency—will teach them how to apply the unknown skill.

This scenario obviously assumes that the teacher's purpose is to develop students' reading skills as well as their understanding of the course content. That assumption is not always valid, as you know. Often the questions are asked only as a matter of form, as the traditional way to make certain students have read the assignment. The teacher gives little thought to the skills students must have to answer the questions adequately. That use of questions, that way of dealing with reading assignments, is even more assumptive than the other.

You will remember that the guides for the levels of comprehension in Chapter 3 were made up of declarative statements rather than questions. The reason for this is basic to attempts to simulate comprehension.

A person who can read independently at the literal level of comprehension can sort through all of the information presented in the reading selection and distinguish the important from the unimportant. This is accomplished by establishing some purpose or objective for the reading, which becomes the criterion for judging the significance and relevance of the information. A reasonably skilled, independent reader can be guided at this level of comprehension by questions which are either self-imposed or teacher-imposed because he or she has the skills necessary for responding to the questions. The questions reinforce the skill the reader already possesses.

For students who do not have sufficient skill for independent responses to questions at the literal level, declarative statements are provided. These statements represent information which might be in the text. Students determine if it actually is included. The students accomplish two purposes as they decide if each statement reflects "what the author says": (1) they develop a sense of accuracy in sorting through information to determine what is actually presented; (2) they develop a sense of the relative importance among all the information presented by the author.

Some statements do present information found in the text; some don't; some shade the information so that it is not exact and must be corrected to be fully acceptable. This process develops students' sense of accuracy and discernment.

The teacher prepares the statements for the students with the content objective in mind, identifying information essential to accomplishing that objective. Before students begin their reading, the teacher helps them establish a purpose that reflects the content objective. Thus, as students compare the statements with the author's information, that purpose serves as a criterion for judging the relative importance of information in a text.

This is a simulation of the literal level of comprehension. Students are guided through the process, developing a feeling of how their minds work, how they interact with the text, what criteria they use to judge the appropriateness of a statement.

Interacting with other students in small discussion groups enhances the simulation and reinforces this learning. The purpose of the discussion is to verify the decisions made about the acceptability of the statements, citing evidence from the text. This discussion strengthens the learning by carrying students through the simulated process once again, but not in a redundant way because the purpose is different: to convince their fellow students of the appropriateness of their decisions.

**Interpretive level**    A person who can read at the interpretive level with reasonable independence is able to make connections among the information identified as important at the literal level of comprehension. As pieces fit together, the reader is able to induce or infer ideas out of the perceived relationships. Then he develops statements which are expressions of those ideas, those relationships. Thus, the reader is able to develop and express some sense of what the author means by what he says. This reasonably skilled, independent reader can be guided at this level of comprehension by questions which are either self-imposed or teacher-imposed because he has the skills necessary for responding to such questions. The questions reinforce the skill the reader already possesses.

For students who do not have the skills to respond independently to questions at the interpretive level, declarative statements are provided. These statements are created by teachers asking themselves the interpretive questions: "What does the author mean by what he says?" "What conclusions can I draw from this information?" "What is the author implying, and what inferences can I draw?" These and other questions are asked by the teachers as they study the information identified through literal comprehension. As the teachers respond to the questions, they write down the answers as declarative statements.

These statements are used to guide students' responses to the reading selection and they will simulate the interpretive level of comprehension if used properly. Students examine each statement and determine if it represents an idea which the author would support. They are asked, also, to cite evidence from the text which supports or rejects the statement as an expression of the author's ideas.

As students sort through the information to find support for accepting or rejecting an interpretive statement, they go through the same process the teachers went through when they created the statement in the first place. The difference is that the teachers *created* the statement (because they had the skills to do so) while the students find evidence to support the statement. The teacher has simulated the "putting together" process which readers must be able to apply in order to read interpretively. As students find evidence to support the statements, they develop a sense of how to create statements for themselves. They develop readiness for questions as guides to the interpretive level of comprehension.

This simulation is reinforced as students discuss their responses to the statements in small groups. The most important question the teacher can ask the students, the question they learn to ask one another, is: "What's your evidence?" When students accept or reject a statement, they must support their decision with evidence from the text, from the literal level guide, or from both. The discussion groups provide opportunity for this exchange; the statements which guide the students provide the vehicle for the learning.

**Applied level** People who read at the applied level of comprehension with reasonable independence are able to synthesize the author's ideas with their own ideas and experiences. They can formulate broad principles or generalizations which embrace both sources and can express those principles and/or generalizations in oral or written form. Reasonably skilled, independent readers can be guided at this level of comprehension either by self-imposed or teacher-imposed questions because they have the skills necessary for responding. The questions reinforce the skill they already possess.

For students who do not have the skill or independence for responding to questions at the applied level of comprehension, declarative statements are provided. These statements are created by teachers asking themselves the questions: "What is the significance of the author's ideas?" "How do the author's ideas relate to my own ideas and experiences relative to this topic?" "What generalizations can I draw by synthesizing the author's ideas with my own?"

As teachers ask themselves these and other questions, they write down the answers as a series of declarative statements. Often the statements take the form of familiar sayings or truisms. These are given to the students to guide their comprehension at the applied level.

These statements simulate the applied level of comprehension because they are the product of the applied level of comprehension. When students support the statements with evidence from both the author's ideas and their own experience and prior knowledge, they are going through the same process the teachers went through to create the statements in the first place. The difference is that the teachers *created* the statements (because they had the skills to do so); the students found evidence to *support* the statements. But in finding this evidence, they develop a sense of how to relate new and old ideas and how to develop statements which represent the product of that synthesis. They develop readiness for questions as guides to the applied level of comprehension.

The small-group discussion reinforces this simulation in the same way it reinforces the other levels of comprehension. Students ask one another for evidence to support or reject a statement. They go through the process once again of synthesizing ideas and information to support the generalizations. They have a pattern to follow and a basis for independent comprehension at the applied level.

### Patterns and Reasoning

Organizational patterns and reasoning are identified in Chapters 4 and 5 as two general processes by which students derive information and ideas from text materials. Each can be simulated for instructional purposes even as levels of comprehension are.

The basis for simulating patterns and reasoning is the same as it is for levels. Teachers apply the process themselves, whether patterns, reasoning, or levels. They give the product of their application to their students in some form of declarative statement. Students examine the connection between the statements and the information source. They make a judgement as to the appropriateness of the statements and cite evidence from the source to support their decision. If the statements are indeed the product of the process being taught, when applied to the information source, then citing evidence from the information source to support the statements is a simulation of the process which produced the statement in the first place. Since the connections can be explicit or implicit, the students experience applying the pattern at both literal and interpretive levels.

Four organizational patterns were discussed in Chapter 4. Each pattern describes how actions, conditions, events, objects, or individuals are related to one another as they are presented and discussed in the information source. The skilled reader is able to perceive factors which are related (objects, conditions, events, or actions) and the nature of that relationship (cause/effect or comparison/contrast, for example). She is then able to draw some generalizations from that perceived relationship, both with respect to its nature and its consequence.

Students who are not aware of either the organizational patterns or how to apply them in their reading need to be shown how to use them. As noted above, students are presented with material which connects information, ideas, or both from the information source in a fashion which characterizes the predominant organizational pattern used by the author of the reading selection. Students judge whether the connections presented in the material actually are made by the author (refer back to Chapter 4 to refresh your memory on how patterns guides are designed). In citing evidence to support their decision, they functionally experience the process of applying the pattern to their own reading. The process is simulated for them.

To deal with the consequences of the connections perceived among the ideas and information, students are given a set of declarative statements they can accept or reject, according to evidence from the text, their experience, or both. These statements are similar to the interpretive or applied levels of comprehension and they simulate these levels in the manner described on pages 80-82. The Part II sections of patterns guides on pages 90-91 illustrate this simulation.

Both "open" and "closed" reasoning are simulated for students through the use of declarative statements placed in reasoning guides. Teachers produce the guides by applying their own reasoning skills to the information source and the general concept under consideration. They write down the product of their reasoning in a format which students can manipulate, usually some form of declarative statement.

### No More Questions?

Taking questions away from teachers would be like taking all hand tools away from a carpenter. Questions are a part of teachers' standard equipment. One should not infer from the previous discussion of simulation that asking students questions is improper. Questions and questioning are important and obviously must be retained by all teachers.

The issue is not whether to use questions, but when to use them. If questions are used to teach students how to read material, they are being misused. If they are being used to reinforce skills which the students already have, they are being used well. Questions are of doubtful value only when they are used assumptively. When questions assume possession of skills not yet taught or learned, they are assumptive. You know, of course, that declarative statements which attempt to simulate a process can be assumptive too. When statements require a level of sophistication which students have not yet attained, they are assumptive.

As pointed out elsewhere (Herber and Nelson, 1975):

> It seems probable that for instruction in how to read with good comprehension, questioning is not the answer .... Using questioning to direct students' search for information or ideas assumes at least some competency and independence in the process essential for the search (pp. 513-514).

However,

> None of this is to suggest that questioning is poor teaching procedure in the absolute sense. Speeches have been given, conferences organized, papers, articles, and books written on questioning as an instructional device. Anyone conversant with education cannot doubt the appropriateness of questioning.
>
> The art and science of questioning is fundamental to good teaching. Well-informed questions can stimulate both critical and creative response from students as they interact with one another or the text material. Questions can be adjusted to the needs of students and their ability to respond, ranging from simple to profound, concrete to abstract. Good questions can reinforce the reading skills that students already have by providing practice on the application of those skills. Many teachers use study guide questions for that purpose. Good questions, accompanied by reinforcing feedback on the nature and quality of the responses, can raise the students' level of sophistication in their use of reading skills implicit in those questions. Many teachers provide students with study guide questions to serve as the basis for small group discussions to accomplish that purpose (p. 514).

What all of this suggests is *not* that the use of declarative statements should eliminate the use of questions for guiding students' reading. Rather, it suggests that the use of declarative statements should precede the use of questions for guiding students' reading. Once students develop a feel for how to respond to the resource material, they can move to response to questions.

> With that feeling as the base and the reference point, and with the confidence that comes from success, students then can respond more readily to questions that require the application of the skill in order to produce their own answers. The teacher can explain that the process is almost the same: they still look for relationships and they still think about what ideas those relationships represent (using a patterns guide, for example); but

now they develop their own expressions of those relationships. With the previous simulated experience providing a pattern to follow, they are in a much better position to produce such answers than if they had not had that experience (Herber and Nelson, 1975, p. 516.)

## Developing Independence

A major concern, naturally, is how students will develop independence if they are always given declarative statements to react to rather than questions. The answer, of course, is that students are not *always* given declarative statements to react to. There is a logical sequence present both in the relationship between declarative statements and questions and in the related consideration of just how much supporting information you provide students to insure their success. Again, the principle in operation is that it is easier to recognize that a stated idea is connected to an information source than it is to produce the statement in the first place as an answer to a question. The following sequence is based on that principle (Herber and Nelson, 1975):

1. The teacher prepares statements for students' reactions. References are added to indicate where students might look in the text to determine if there is information to support the statements (page, column, paragraph, if necessary).

2. The teacher prepares statements for students' reactions. No references are given.

3. The teacher prepares questions for students to answer. References are added to indicate where students might look in the text to find information which, when combined, might answer the question.

4. The teacher prepares questions for students to answer. No references are given.

5. Students survey the material, raise their own questions, and answer them.

6. Students produce statements of meaning, concepts, and ideas as they read.

Within each of these steps in the sequence a teacher can accommodate a range of ability and achievement by adjusting the sophistication levels of the statements or questions. One can see that steps one through four are teacher-directed; steps five and six are student-directed. Observation of instruction in our schools would find more teachers expecting steps five and six from students than providing steps one through four for students.

There is no *experimental* data which validates this sequence, only *experiential*. In the real world of the everyday classroom, things are not neat and tidy; sequences such as this have to be accommodated to that reality. This accommodation is rather simple. Teachers determine which units, out of all of the units to be covered in their curriculum, are most important. For these they prepare guides which simulate the appropriate reading or reasoning processes. If a sequence among these important units can be established, then the guides are prepared so that each successive unit is more sophisticated and requires more independence in the students' response to the statements.

For those remaining units of instruction, those interspersed among the most important ones, teachers guide their students with questions reflecting the level of independence achieved in the use of statements. For example, if the first unit is important, the guides may be designed to include statements with references to locations in the source where evidence to support or reject the statements might be found. The second unit, being less important and given less time for presentation and study, will incorporate guides composed of questions. But these questions include references to locations in the text where the reader can find information to answer the questions. Teachers point out the relationship between the two guides, explaining that the statements students write will be similar in their relationship to the information source as were the statements in the other guide in their relationship to their information source. There is, by this variation in the sequence toward independence, a built-in transfer of the competence from one setting to another.

## GROUPING

Who has not experienced the clarifying effect of talking out a problem with someone else? Who has not had the experience of discovering the answer to a question while in the process of trying to formulate the question in a discussion with other people in a small group? Perhaps you have had these experiences, but they happened more by chance than by design. If so, imagine the value of an environment where such experiences are part of the learning procedure, structured so as to occur with regularity. Would you guess that your learning experiences would be more exciting, perhaps even more beneficial? If you have taken part in such a learning environment, you already know that the answer to that question has to be affirmative.

### Purposes for Grouping

Any person favoring the use of intraclass grouping as part of instruction in a content area could produce a set of purposes for such organization and activity. What follows is a selective distillation of such lists which reflects the spirit, substance, and intent of this book.

**Student involvement** One of the problems identified in Chapter 2 was that of finding ways to help students become more actively involved in the learning process. As students progress through the grades they become, generally speaking, less and less actively involved in the learning process; they assume increasingly passive roles as they listen to lectures, watch media, read sources.

Their interaction with other students is mainly outside of class, on their own initiative. Purposeful, well-structured interaction among students in small-group discussions in content-area classrooms reverses this trend. Each student benefits and becomes a more active participant in the learning process.

**Learning environment** Small groups in a classroom can provide a good environment for risk-taking. Very little learning takes place without risk: risk of failure, risk of being wrong, risk of injury, risk of responsibility for follow-through if one is right, and the like. The basic issue at stake is one Dr. Harold Rankin addressed directly when he was superintendent of schools in James-ville-Dewitt, New York. At the faculty meeting before school opened one fall he said to his teachers and staff.

> I believe that you people have the right to fail! Not everything you try will work out as you hoped it would. Not everything you think will work actually will work. But some things will and those you will continue to use to the benefit of your students and yourselves. Things that don't work you will put aside; you don't have to make excuses or try to justify "poor data." You have the right to be wrong as you search for the best possible instructions for your students.

You will not be surprised to know that the faculty in this school district were interested in finding the best ways to help their students learn, nor will you be surprised to know that most of this faculty passed along to their own students this same attitude: namely, that they also had the right to "fail," that they had the right to be wrong as they engaged in their pursuit of ideas.

Teachers with this kind of attitude can make good use of intraclass grouping. It provides the setting within which these "rights" are exercised, where the "risks" are fun and the learning is exciting. As students participate in purposeful discussions in well-structured groups, they have opportunity to test new ideas—at least ideas which are new to them. A student who shares a logical inference from some experience or idea is running a risk. The inference may be an accepted part of the body of knowledge in the field she is studying but when that student has not previously read or heard of it, the inference truly is an exercise in original thinking, including all the risks of being wrong. Of course, to the person steeped in the discipline it is not an original thought, but to the person who had discovered it without outside intervention it is creative thinking. Our students constantly are developing such insights and we miss them if we don't have the proper vehicle for the discovery. Intraclass grouping provides a vehicle just by creating an environment for risk-taking and for testing ideas.

Imagine, then, the teaching and learning which can occur in these small groups. Students discover new points of view, new ways of dealing with problems, new perceptions of reality, new interpretations of old information, new confidence in old ideas, new excitement in having their contributions not only accepted but also respected both by the teacher and by fellow students.

**Accommodating students' needs**   As one reads the list of benefits in the preceding paragraphs, they may seem more appropriate to the advanced student. But this is an incorrect inference. All students, regardless of ability, benefit. So-called slow students derive as great benefit from intraclass grouping as do so-called average and so-called superior students. The nature of their insights, the quality of their discussion, the attention to the task, the accomplishment of the stated purposes will vary from level to level, but not always with the correlations we are conditioned to expect. Very often the so-called slow students reveal insights the so-called superior students overlook. The reason? Because the former group is not so encumbered with the need to know the "right" answer, the need to guess what is in the teacher's mind, as is the later group. With their greater freedom they often discover more exciting things. If you have taught students drawn from a range of abilities, you know this is true.

This is why, in the last six or seven years, the intraclass grouping connected with methods and materials advocated in this book has been heterogeneous. For most lessons, students are randomly assigned to groups, providing a range of achievement and ability in each. Students work together, helping one another as necessary, contributing as they are able. Each student draws on his or her own knowledge and capability and participates in the teaching and learning exchanges in the group. Each student is helped at his level of need; each contributes at her level of knowledge and insight.

Without engaging in elaborate schemes to individualize instruction, without spending enormous sums of money to purchase multilevel materials (assuming you can find them for your particular curriculum), without spending the countless hours designing activities for individual students, the needs of students can be accommodated. Individualization is *approximated* through intraclass grouping. When guide materials of the type discussed in this text serve as the structure and focus of the students' interaction in the small groups, this approximation of individualization occurs. The guide materials stimulate students' responses to the information sources. Their own previous experience, ability, achievement, and insight determine the level of sophistication at which they will respond to those materials. In the small-group environment, each student's response is an important contribution. In that environment, students learn from one another. It is not just one-way learning. In a classroom where helping one another to learn is important and is seen by students as one of their primary responsibilities, no one is shortchanged, no one is left out, no one is a freeloader, no one is overlooked. Utopia? No. Reality? If you let it happen.

Obviously it won't happen overnight. Students have to be taught how to work together in groups if these benefits are to be realized. This takes time and patience and it brings moments of despair, but they will learn if you want them to and if you work with them as though you expect it. This chapter suggests several ways to set up groups and to make certain they operate well.

**Multiplier effect**  Very often the best teachers in our schools are the students themselves. You know that's true if you have ever struggled with an explanation of some point in your curriculum and have had a student clarify it for the class with just a few, brief, succinct sentences. Intraclass grouping capitalizes on this phenomenon and multiplies the effect of the teacher.

The good executive makes use of the talent with which she is surrounded. When people are available who can perform tasks as well or better than she can, the executive preserves time and energy by devoting herself to just those things which only she can do and lets other personnel do the other things. Why not teachers? They are surrounded by students who are perfectly capable of helping themselves and one another—if they are given the tools and the opportunity.

The intraclass grouping provides the opportunity; guide materials of all sort provide the tools. The teacher's knowledge and talent are multiplied.

**Negative and positive**  Teachers unfamiliar with intraclass grouping are inclined to react more negatively than positively to suggestions that they incorporate the procedure into their own instruction. Often this is because their own experience with small-group discussions has been related to so-called sensitivity training or group therapy sessions of some sort. Many persons who have not actually participated in such small-group activity have negative feelings about it and transfer those feelings to any discussion of small-group work in their own classes. Many people who *have* participated in such small-group experiences also feel this way.

Our purpose here is not to judge the value of sensitivity training therapy. However, it is important to point out that the grouping discussed in this chapter and recommended throughout the book is *not* this kind of grouping. As William Fawcett Hill (1969) says, "If discussion groups are run along lines more appropriate to therapy groups, the validity of the . . . criticism [concerning the use of grouping in the classroom] must be recognized and dealt with." He further states that we must be aware of grouping procedures which emphasize " . . . the pleasure principle at the expense of the reality principle, and [which confound] . . . laissez-faire with democratic principles."

Hill also points out another misunderstanding of grouping and its purposes. Grouping is viewed as a frill, not as integral to students' learning or to the study of any portion of the curriculum which has "real substance." Intraclass grouping is treated as an extra which will be used if and when there is enough time for it. As Hill (1969) says,

> we . . . cannot help noticing that the majority of teaching is done by the traditional methods and in fact, many of the advocates of the discussion group desert the method any time that subject matter of any degree of difficulty must be thoroughly mastered. In short, the discussion method is usually reserved for such courses as Marriage and the Modern Family,

Understanding Modern Art, or Citizenship. Even the critics agree that the discussion group is good if the goal is attitude formation or opinion-sharing. The question that is of concern . . . is whether group discussion can be used effectively to meet stringent requirements of subject matter mastery. The position taken . . . is that mastery of difficult material can be achieved through the discussion group, but not through permissive and unstructured approaches (pp. 15-16).

The last clause in the last sentence is of critical importance and represents a point which has been dealt with throughout this book. The guide materials discussed in the previous chapters establish, among other things, purpose and structure for the groups.

The organization and operation of the group is important; but the decision to have your class divided into groups is the critical action on which the other actions turn. Abandoning grouping techniques in the face of time or content pressures is very much like abandoning the forehand you are learning from the tennis pro whenever you find yourself under pressure from your opponent in the match: you revert to what is natural, even though it may be less effective. However, by using intraclass grouping consistently over time, you and your class will become efficient and the process will become natural to you.

Hill (1969) summarizes the purposes for grouping when he says that a "good group is one where the process, or communication, problems are adequately handled and the potential of the members realized, so that the learning of the course material is enhanced" (p. 21).

### Types of Groups

Groups can be classified into three broad categories: training groups, work groups (Miles, 1967), work-training groups. Training groups are formed when students with comparable needs or strengths are to be instructed in an activity or concept. Work groups are formed when students with comparable strengths and interests have a specific task to perform that requires them to utilize skills they already possess.

A teacher can become quite frustrated if he does not keep these distinctions clearly in mind. He can form a training group and expect students to develop some product. When the group's purpose is to learn a specific skill or develop understanding of a specific concept, it is not realistic to expect it to develop a product using that skill or concept. Or he can give students a work task to perform and be frustrated because they have not developed new skills in the process. This is assumptive teaching, assuming that merely giving students a task will automatically develop in them new skills. If skills development is the desired product, the teacher should form a training group, not a work group.

Work-training groups combine the features of each of the component groups. Since the instruction in reading is functional and since the course content and related reading processes are taught simultaneously, students are placed together in groups both to be trained in the process and to develop a product which reflects their understanding of the course content. Students in these work-training groups represent a range of ability, achievement, motivations, and interests. But the training in the reading processes still can occur, as discussed. Since the training is functional, a product necessarily emerges.

Work-training groups are not assumptive if sufficient structure and guidance is provided for the participating students. As long as they know what is to be done and are shown how to apply it to the content being studied, the basic teaching principle is intact and the groups contribute importantly to its actualization: "The essence of good teaching is to show a person how to do what he or she is required to do."

### Operation of groups

Intraclass grouping of students can be as important to the success of their learning as the books they use. But this value is not derived by chance. There must be a vehicle to support the students' interaction in groups and they must have some idea of how to function in the groups to derive maximum benefit. Without the vehicle and the criteria, grouping is a virtual waste of time, a reasonably pleasant interlude in learning.

The guides which have been discussed throughout this book are excellent vehicles for group work. As students use these guides and participate in the group discussions, they have specific roles to perform and criteria for determining the relative success of their performance. Given the diversity of views found in the literature on grouping and group interaction, any list of suggested roles for group participants is rather arbitrary. Even so, it is useful to provide one for guiding students' participation in group discussions. Hill (1969) provides a useful list, along with the suggestion that all participants in a group be mindful of all of the roles and be able to function in each. "A member playing any one role consistently and persistently will be more of a hindrance than a help" (p. 33).

The labels for each of the roles Hill suggests seem self-explanatory, except for Number 7, which is elaborated upon below. You probably will want to read Hill's useful book, *Learning Through Discussion*, for greater detail.

### GROUP ROLES AND MEMBER SKILLS

A. Sequence of task roles specific to discussion of a topic
   1. Initiating
   2. Giving and asking for information
   3. Giving and asking for reactions
   4. Restating and giving examples

    5. Confronting and reality testing
    6. Clarifying, synthesizing, and summarizing
B. Overall task roles . . .
    7. Gatekeeping and expediting
    8. Timekeeping
    9. Evaluating and diagnosing
   10. Standard setting
C. Group maintenance roles . . .
   11. Sponsoring and encouraging
   12. Group tension relieving

By "gatekeeping" Hill means those activities which are associated with keeping a group aware of its purposes and operation, and its criteria for effectiveness.

**Criteria for members** Vacca (1973) incorporated intraclass grouping in his study of the development of students' achievement in the use of organizational patterns while reading social studies material in eighth-grade history. Drawing inferences from previous studies which also made use of intraclass grouping, Vacca established specific criteria by which students and teachers could judge the quality of the members' participation.

Vacca's criteria are as follows:

## OPPORTUNITIES AND RESPONSIBILITIES

### Group Interaction

1. Each member makes a serious effort to do the assignment.
2. Do each task in the order indicated, and in the manner indicated.
    — a. First on your own; then discuss with other members of your group

                                  or

    — b. Do the entire task with others in your group

                                  or

    — c. Do the entire task on your own, asking for help only when needed.
3. In group interaction, use the following procedure.
    — a. Each item is discussed, in order of appearance.
    — b. If a member disagrees on any item, he must *defend* his position and give specific reasons for the disagreement. Reasons may be from the text and/or from experience (depending on the task).
    — c. No one bosses or dominates or removes himself from the discussion.

4. Each member must participate and add something to the discussion. If one member refuses to participate or to perform the task, the whole group suffers in the self-assessment of performance.

In his study, Vacca had the teacher discuss the criteria with the students and establish a point system to reflect the extent to which the students met the criteria. At the end of each week, the students in each group judged their week's performance by the criteria and assigned themselves number 3, 2, or 1, indicating good, satisfactory, or poor, respectively. The teacher independently rated each group and then conferred with the group about the assigned rating. The teacher and members of the group then compared their ratings and sought to resolve their differences where they existed. The point value established by the discussion was the one then given to the group.

A color code was assigned to each value and individual students within each group received both the point value and the color received by that group. That color was entered for each person on a Learning Incentive Chart on Friday. The following Monday the students were reassigned, randomly, to new groups for the week. One of the first things students did was to check the color received the previous week by each of the other members who made up their new group. Any student with a color indicating poor adherence to the criteria by the group to which he had belonged the previous week was admonished by the others in the new group that a better job was to be done during the current week.

Aside from the interesting motivational effect of its application, the availability of such criteria helped students know how to function; they knew what was expected of them, what was expected of the other participants, what was expected of the teacher. Vacca concluded that the students' work in groups, using the organizational patterns guides he had designed for that purpose, had a clearly beneficial effect on their content achievement and understanding.

**Teachers' roles in grouping** Successful intraclass grouping doesn't just happen. Obviously important is the teacher's role, from being willing to "allow" intraclass grouping to occur to being willing to stand aside and be "carefully quiet" when students are immersed in the teaching and learning that takes place in effective groups.

What leadership options are open to teachers in the style or attitude they display while exercising their leadership role? Miles (1967) presents several options. Though these suggestions are related to the role of a leader within a group, they are equally appropriate in a discussion of the role of the teacher during the organization and functioning of various groups within the class.

AUTOCRATIC: Where the leader dictates the task, assigns workers to subtasks, and determines when the tasks have been completed satisfactorily.

BARGAINING: When a horse-trading approach involving rewards and punishments is central. The focus tends to be on the leaders agreeing to meet members' personal needs if they in turn will work on the official group task.

PATERNALISM: Where the leader supplies nearly all the functions—benevolently—and does not permit members to perform leadership acts.

LAISSEZ-FAIRE INACTION: Where the leader supplies no functions, and does nothing to help members supply them.

COOPERATIVE PROBLEM-SOLVING: Where the demands of the problems and the needs of persons are both central, and anyone who sees a missing function is expected to supply it.*

Obviously we must function with groups in the manner and style that is natural for us. Equally obvious is the fact that the *cooperative problem-solving* style is most consistent with the emphasis of this text. *Laissez-faire inaction* style is assumptive. *Paternalistic* style does not allow students to develop independence. *Bargaining* seems unnecessary.

Within these leadership styles, specific roles are open to the teacher. Miles (1967) suggests several roles which, interestingly, overlap the roles for group members suggested by Hill (1969). This is reasonable since a good group leader should engage in each of the roles of a member as she participates in the group and since each member of a group should engage in each of the roles of a leader as he provides leadership for the group.

INITIATING: Keeping the group action moving, or getting it going (for example, suggesting action steps, pointing out goals, proposing procedures, clarifying).

REGULATING: Influencing the direction and tempo of the group's work (for example, summarizing, pointing out the time limits, restating goals).

INFORMING: Bringing information or opinion to the group.

SUPPORTIVE: Creating emotional climates which hold the group together, making it easier for members to contribute to work on the task (for example, harmonizing, relieving tension, voicing group feelings, encouraging).

EVALUATING: Helping group to evaluate its decisions, goals, or procedures (for example, testing for consensus, noting group processes).**

*Matthew B. Miles, *Learning to Work in Groups,* New York: Teachers College Press, 1967, pp. 18-19.
**Ibid., pp. 9-20.

## BENEFITS FROM INTRACLASS
## GROUPING

Grouping provides for what Durrell (1966) calls "multiple recitation." When a teacher works with her class as a single group, each student has an opportunity to participate in the discussion only as often as the teacher calls on him. On the average it would be unusual for a student to recite more than twice in a given class period. However, when a student is a part of a small group, she has many more opportunities to participate in discussion. This allows each student to consider ideas and pursue questions in depth. Her peers' reaction to her ideas, and her defense of them, cause her to learn more thoroughly. She has more frequent opportunity to succeed than in the traditional class format.

Grouping within a class makes it more possible to approximate service to the individual differences of students. Group members are given a reasonable task; they have an opportunity to contribute and to receive peer approval; their achievement is recognized; they learn from others in the class. The more able students are not neglected through assumptions of competence; the less able students are not put off by low-level material which substitutes simplicity for substance.

It is very difficult to establish objectively the worth and contribution of intraclass grouping in content areas. Available measures are inadequate. To those who see little value in grouping, the explanations and evidence cited sound very much like biased rationalization. To advocates of grouping, such explanations sound sensible and perfectly reasonable.

Several things are certain:

1. There do not seem to be adequate measures of some of the apparent benefits of grouping.
2. Some benefits are not clearly apparent; they are indirect, subtle, intuitively perceived, and thus, difficult to quantify.
3. Some teachers and some students do not enjoy group work, others do.
4. Working in groups efficiently seems to be a learned activity, and students appear to improve in the quality of their interaction with practice.
5. Organizing one's class into groups for instructional purposes seems to be a learned activity and teachers appear to improve in their use of intraclass grouping with practice.
6. While there is relatively little objective data from direct measures of the effects of intraclass grouping which would indicate its superiority over more traditional types of classroom organization, there is little evidence to indicate its inferiority either. A pessimistic inference is that we don't know what we should do; an optimistic inference is that we have at least two options. It depends on your perspective. Do you say the glass is half full or

half empty? Do you say that no difference gives you two choices or nothing?

Estes (1970) and Rynders (1971) found no beneficial effects in the use of intraclass grouping. In fact, Estes suggests that the use of groups had a detrimental effect.

On the other hand, Vacca (1973), Berget (1973), and Walker (1975) all found that the use of intraclass grouping had a beneficial effect on students' learning. The more "field-based" studies by Herber (1976) as well as by Daughtrey and Davis (1972) support this positive result. Even though these last two studies did not directly study intraclass grouping as a process, the classroom instruction being evaluated in terms of students' achievement in reading and in content acquisition did incorporate such grouping. Participants in both studies reported their positive feelings about intraclass grouping and their belief—their "feeling"—that it contributed much to their students' learning.

Of interest are the results from Barron's (1971) longitudinal study in the area of biology. He found teacher-led, full-class discussion more productive than small-group discussion. But he also reported that the teacher who led the discussions did so in a manner which suggested that she had been strongly influenced by the interaction she had observed among students within small groups. She conducted the full-class discussions as though she were an active member of the group, assuming leadership of the group for purposes of focusing on a question, issue, or idea. She directed the discussion by getting students to interact with one another; she called on students for clarifying comments on questions raised or answers given; she participated as a member of a group rather than as an authoritarian leader. Thus, Barron's findings could be viewed as supporting the values of grouping more than the values of the traditional format. Again, evidence provides teachers with options, which, of course, are the spice of any life or activity.

### SUMMARY

This chapter presented three interrelated factors which contribute to reading instruction in content areas. Simulation involves the attempt to help students develop a feeling for the various reading and reasoning processes which we hope they will be able to use independently someday. Guiding is integral to simulation. It is "showing how" to develop that feeling, to apply those processes. This guiding is provided through materials designed especially for that purpose: guides for levels, patterns, reasoning, and vocabulary reinforcement and extension.

Intraclass grouping serves as the format through which the benefits of guiding and simulation are realized. With the course content providing the substance for discussion and the guides providing the structure for the interaction, intraclass grouping contributes much to students' achievement. And the mix of these three factors contributes much to students' affective well-being.

\*	\*	\*	\*	\*	\*

## REACTION GUIDE

*Directions*: In Part I of this guide are statements related to the topics of simulation and guiding. In Part II are statements related to grouping. For each statement, place a check on the first line if you agree with it and on the second line if you think it is supported by the chapter. Discuss the evidence for your decisions.

*Part I*

\_\_\_\_ \_\_\_\_ 1. If you can't show, tell.

\_\_\_\_ \_\_\_\_ 2. Students aren't supposed to know your subject until *after* you teach them.

\_\_\_\_ \_\_\_\_ 3. Independence is a relative state.

\_\_\_\_ \_\_\_\_ 4. Experiencing what can be, helps you deal with what is.

\_\_\_\_ \_\_\_\_ 5. Telling is not showing; assigning is not teaching.

\_\_\_\_ \_\_\_\_ 6. It is easier to curse the darkness than to light a candle.

\_\_\_\_ \_\_\_\_ 7. More is not always better nor is harder always strengthening.

\_\_\_\_ \_\_\_\_ 8. It is easier to test than to teach.

\_\_\_\_ \_\_\_\_ 9. It may be better to give than receive, but it takes more grace to receive than to give.

\_\_\_\_ \_\_\_\_ 10. The essence of good teaching is to show students how to do what you require them to do.

*Part II*

\_\_\_\_ \_\_\_\_ 1. Talking is usually more active than listening.

\_\_\_\_ \_\_\_\_ 2. Discussion is more profitable in a group than alone, and less suspect!

\_\_\_\_ \_\_\_\_ 3. Passivity may be a product of education.

\_\_\_\_ \_\_\_\_ 4. Discussion with focus and purpose is a clarifying experience; without them, it is a pooling of ignorance.

\_\_\_\_ \_\_\_\_ 5. Risk is relative, but not to the "risker."

\_\_\_\_ \_\_\_\_ 6. Respect is more rapidly earned when reasons for it are easily discernible.

_____ _____   7. More is learned by resolving differences than by comparing similarities.

_____ _____   8. When the teacher's mind is the criterion, students lose their own.

_____ _____   9. Too much of a good thing may not be.

_____ _____   10. Students may learn more from teacher's silences than from their utterances.

\* \* \* \* \* \*

## REFERENCES

BARRON, RICHARD. *The use of an iterative research process to improve a method of vocabulary instruction in tenth grade biology.* Unpublished doctoral dissertation, Syracuse Universiry, 1971.

DAVIS, ALLEN L. III, Edward Daughtrey, Virginia Brinson, and Kenneth Hall. *A study of the effectiveness of teaching reading in the content areas of English, mathematics, science, and social studies.* Norfolk, Virginia Public Schools: Department of Secondary Education, August, 1971.

DURRELL, DONALD D. *Improving reading instruction.* New York: Harcourt Brace Jovanovich, 1966.

ESTES, THOMAS H. *Use of guide material and small group discussion in reading ninth grade social studies assignments.* Unpublished doctoral dissertation, Syracuse University, 1970.

HERBER, HAROLD L. *Middle-school program for teaching reading in content areas.* East Syracuse-Minoa School District, Unpublished report, 1976.

HERBER, HAROLD L., & Joan Nelson. "Questioning is not the answer. *Journal of Reading,*" 1975, *18* (7), 512-517.

HILL, WM. FAWCETT. *Learning through discussion.* Beverly Hills, Calif.: Sage Publications, 1969.

MILES, MATTHEW, *Learning to work in groups.* New York: Teachers College Press, 1967.

RYNDERS, PETER. *The use of cloze procedure to develop comprehension skill in the intermediate grades.* Unpublished doctoral dissertation, Syracuse University, 1971.

VACCA, RICHARD. *An investigation of a functional reading strategy in seventh grade social studies.* Unpublished doctoral dissertation, Syracuse University, 1973.

WALKER, NORA. *An investigation into the effects of graphic organizers on the learning of social studies readers in the middle grades.* Unpublished doctoral dissertation, Syracuse University, 1975.

*nine*

# Instructional Framework

---

**VOCABULARY**

The following terms are important to an understanding of this chapter. Each is defined in context. Read through the list to identify those for which you have uncertain meanings. Then as you read the chapter, pay particular attention to their definitions. Also, make certain that the meanings attributed to the remaining words by their context in the chapter correspond to the meanings they hold for you.

directed reading activity
preparation
independence
review
purpose
transfer
horizontal transformation
functional analysis
content analysis

assumptive teaching
guidance
motivation
anticipation
expanded directions
transformation
vertical transformation
teacher preparation
resource analysis

The following terms have been used in previous chapters and are important to an understanding of this chapter as well. You may wish to review their definitions and the meanings attributed to them by previous contexts before reading this chapter.

structured overview
levels of comprehension
organizational patterns
word definitions
grouping
student interaction
concepts

guide
reasoning
vocabulary acquisition
word meanings
individualizing instruction
principles
details

## IDEA DIRECTION

Organization is the key to efficiency, especially in teaching. When you are responsible for teaching between thirty and forty students in a single class, you must be efficient to survive—therefore, organized.

This chapter presents the Instructional Framework as an organizational scheme to help you deal with the question of efficiency. It presents ways to select from the methods and materials which have been presented to create well-organized units of instruction and daily lessons. It is a flexible structure into which you can comfortably fit your own teaching style. Keep that fact in mind as you explore this Instructional Framework.

## READING DIRECTION

As you read this chapter you should recall the previously suggested methods and materials as instructional options. Each has a place in the Instructional Framework, although all cannot be used at one time. Consider where each fits and why. The reaction guide at the end of the chapter may help.

## INDEPENDENCE AND ASSUMPTIVE TEACHING

Several times this book has referred to assumptive teaching. Before you consider how to utilize its suggestions for helping students become better readers in your content area, you may find it useful to refresh your thinking regarding the dangers of assumptive teaching.

A third-grade teacher expressed concern about the experiences her students would confront when they entered fourth grade. Because of departmentalization and because of stronger emphasis on the content areas of the curriculum, fourth-graders were expected to function quite independently. They would receive relatively little instruction of a highly structured nature. The teacher's concern was how to prepare her students for this level of independent study. Her solution: "I put them on their own here in grade three!" Suggestions that students need to be guided in the development of independence in the use of skills were met with the rejoinder, "That's just spoon-feeding." The assumptive teaching continued.

Of course, when these third-grade students reach fourth grade, the fourth-grade teacher will prepare them for the independence required in the fifth grade. And what will be the preparation? Placing students on their own in grade four. Again, the response to suggestions for guiding students toward independence at their current grade level will be: "Spoon-feeding!"

Teachers from grades three through twelve have expressed the same sentiment with almost identical wording. To prepare students for the independence they will be expected to demonstrate at the "next" grade level, teachers withhold guidance in learning activities, avoid "spoon-feeding," and require independent performance at the current level. Teachers prepare fourth-graders for grade five, fifth-graders for six, sixth for seven . . . eleventh for twelve. Then, of course, teachers of high school seniors know that colleges require the capacity for independent study. What better preparation is there than to require students to function independently in the twelfth grade?

One wonders, not unreasonably, who shows students *how* to become independent readers! Obviously a great responsibility is placed on the shoulders of first- and second-grade teachers who, presumably, prepare students for a life of independent study. At each level the students' independence is assumed as they are "prepared" for the independence required at succeeding levels. Clearly the students are shortchanged, never being shown how to apply those skills which teachers at each level assume they can handle independently.

What is the teachers' role in this unfortunate sequence? If they assume students' independence, then their role is testing rather than teaching—testing to see how well students are performing with the skills they are assumed to possess, testing to see what knowledge they have acquired while exercising the skills in which, it is assumed, they have independent power. Teaching consists mainly of daily assignments on which students recite the following day in a teacher-led discussion. Teachers and the texts become mere information-dispensers, a role for which machines are better suited. In contrast, independence should be looked upon not as the means but as the end product of skills and content instruction.

Independence is a relative term. Teachers need to move students along the continuum with forethought and calculation. A design, a structure, within which students are led to potential independence is needed. If independent activity is expected and students have not been *shown how* to perform that activity, the teaching is assumptive. It neglects the critical factor in good instruction: that is, that students must be *shown how* to do whatever it is they are *expected* to do independently. With respect to any skill, independence is an ultimate state, not an immediate one.

Teachers can help students experience immediate success and ultimate independence if they provide a structure, or framework, within which students are guided through the process being taught, developing an understanding of both the process and the content to which the process is applied. "Teachers may feel that there is too much 'hand-holding' in this . . . approach. In a sense good teaching is hand-holding; it is literally leading the pupils through a process until such time as they can walk alone. Rarely does that time come abruptly" (Niles, 1964).

This chapter presents a structure that you can provide for your students. The structure is a lesson framework designed in reference to the act of reading. It incorporates what is to be accomplished prior to, during, and after the reading of a given assignment. Although many non-reading activities occur in any subject area and although it is possible to learn in ways other than reading, the purpose here is to focus attention on the reading phase of learning and on those elements of instruction which support this activity.

## STRUCTURE OF LESSONS

The structure through which such instruction is provided consists of three major parts: preparation, guidance, and independence.

### Preparation

An activity designed to promote learning—whether of content or process— is more effective if the participants are prepared to engage in that activity. Preparation has several components.

**Motivation** People seem to learn best those things in which they are interested. As interest is aroused, attention is more acute and minds are more receptive. As part of the structure for ensuring success in learning reading skills and subject content, motivation makes an important contribution. You probably have developed your own techniques for arousing your students' interest in a particular topic.

Any discussion of motivation raises the question of what happened to the students' natural curiosity. What makes it necessary for teachers to find ways to generate some interest in the curriculum they are studying? Chapter 7 recognizes that students naturally are motivated to learn and that motivation remains as students progress through school. The problem is that what students are motivated to learn often is not what the school requires them to learn. It may be easier to head off the loss of capacity to be interested than to try to instill interests after the capacity for interests has been damaged.

This is an important issue, practical and worthy of close study. Until we find ways to bring a closer relationship between students' natural interests and the schools' requirements, teachers will have difficulty arousing students' interests in specific units of study in content areas.

Techniques for motivation are as varied as the teachers who employ them. It is unrealistic and unnecessary to be prescriptive in this area. But consideration of motivation raises another issue: motivation involves not only arousing interest but also establishing purposes for learning.

Education being what it is, a person must study some things in which he or she has no particular interest. If the purpose for the study is evident, the time and energy expended will bring a reasonable return in knowledge gained and used. Assuming that students are not equally interested in all areas of intellectual endeavor, a content teacher will devise interest-arousing activities to capture their attention. Suggestions given in Chapters 6 and 7 are particularly germane. From these you can create situations which encourage students to make the emotional and intellectual investments in the lesson, as discussed on pages 180-81. Helping them become aware of their own prior knowledge concerning the topic under consideration has motivational value. The further exploration of that knowledge contributes to the purpose for the lesson.

**Background information and review** When students begin a new unit of study and read material related to that unit, they need a frame of reference for the new ideas they will acquire. Otherwise their idea intake will be erratic and will lack organization. They will recall isolated bits of information, which may or may not have bearing on what they have studied previously. They will find it difficult to draw generalizations from that information.

Background information refers to those major and minor concepts which identify, qualify, and support the specific unit to be studied. As part of their motivational procedure, teachers will draw upon students' experiences, asking them for information that will enlighten the class on specific points and prepare it for an in-depth study of the topic. Teachers will also draw on their own knowledge of the topic to provide information which arouses interest and sets the problem in bold relief.

Whether teachers draw from their own fund of knowledge or from students' experiences, their purpose is to provide a context into which new information can be fitted, subsequently enlarged into a major concept, and possibly explored in depth. Regardless of the teachers' styles, their intention is to prepare students to read an assignment successfully. Background information also aids the motivation factor. When students have little experience with or knowledge of a topic, their interest is minimal. Through teachers and fellow students, they can gain sufficient vicarious and actual experience to maintain their interest.

Review provides the true frame of reference into which students fit new ideas acquired through their reading and study. Review provides intellectual hooks on which to hang new ideas. Review has a narrower focus than "background information." The latter is assumed not to be part of the students' immediate understanding or direct experience; it is provided by the teacher to enrich the context for the new unit.

Review assumes previous experience which has bearing on the new unit. This experience is recalled and related to the new unit, enlarging and strengthening the context for the topics within the unit.

A student can experience learning difficulties if he or she does not have the benefit of review. If she does not go over previously learned information to speculate on its relative value and bearing on the new topic, her only recourse is to memorize isolated bits of information with little purpose or focus.

As discussed in Chapter 6 the structured overview is useful at this stage of the lesson. It serves to help students organize their prior knowledge in the reviewing process, developing a framework into which new information and ideas can be placed. The teacher, contributing also to the structured overview, provides background information by this device.

**Anticipation and purpose** The combination of *background information* and *review* creates a sense of anticipation in students, an "I'm-looking-for-something" attitude. Purposes for reading are established. They need not be dictated by the teacher; they can be evolved by students through the structure provided by the teacher.

Develop a purpose and it can be realized. Read without anticipation and you are reduced to word-calling. Students who look for ideas as they read will find them; but if they look for nothing, they find that too!

Two broad areas of purpose need to be established: (1) the ideas to be discovered; (2) the reading process to be applied. The structure provided by teachers should reflect their own preparation for the lesson: they determine the ideas important enough for the students to study. They encourage students to be receptive to those ideas as they read. They also determine how the students must read the material to develop those ideas, and they give students direction in the application of those skills. Consequently, as students read for the purpose of developing specific ideas, they do so with a conscious application of the appropriate reading process.

The discussions on pages 26-27 are applicable at this stage of the lesson structure. You will recall the points made about functional reading instruction, that content determines process. Here is where that principle applies. The information source is examined and a determination is made as to how it must be read in order for the concepts to be acquired. Chapters 3, 4, 5, and 6 suggest various processes which may be emphasized.

As noted above and suggested throughout the book, the teacher's analysis of the content to be taught is of primary importance to the success of reading instruction in content areas. In this chapter this important procedure is discussed more in detail.

**Direction** Once teachers establish how the student should read the information source being assigned, they develop directions for that reading. These directions may be in written or oral form. In either case, their purpose is to aid students in determining how to proceed with the reading of the source.

The thrust of this book has been on the development of materials and application of procedures that will guide students as they read required information sources. Through that guidance students acquire the content and develop a sense of the reading process essential to the acquisition of that content. In most cases the directions for such materials are in printed form. Obviously it is important for the students to have a clear understanding of how to perform the tasks implicit in the guide material.

It probably is obvious that the teacher should go over the directions with the students, insuring that they are aware of how to perform the tasks essential to the successful completion of the guide material. It is useful to do one or two of the items in the guide with the students to illustrate how the directions apply to the materials. Carefulness in directing students' use of the guides makes their use more productive in terms of skills and content learned.

Barron (1971) looked for ways to maximize the value of the guide materials. He developed what he called "expanded directions," using suggestions for instructions developed by Gagné (1970).

Barron's study related to vocabulary development in biology. The expanded directions were for vocabulary-development exercises. They involved three steps: (1) a teacher-led discussion of the relationship between the task to be performed and the broad goals of thinking and learning for that particular content area; (2) a teacher-led completion of a portion of the guide to be used by the students, accompanied by a description of ways in which they could provide evidence to support their responses to items in the guide; (3) an explanation of the requirement that their work would be finished only when each *attempted* response to items in the guide could be verbally justified.

The application of these steps will vary according to the reading process applied by the guide. Though you may at first feel you don't have time to go through these steps with your guide materials, you may discover that these steps save time in the long run. When students know what the task is and how it fits in with the learning and thinking goals of the course, they will probably derive greater benefit from it. Such a result is worth the necessary investment in time. Of course, as students become familiar with certain kinds of materials, they need only to be reminded of the purposes of the materials and how to complete them. The original investment of time will continue to pay dividends.

**Language development** Each subject has its own language, its own technical vocabulary. To study the subject, students must know the language which serves as the basis for communicating ideas within that subject. They do not develop an understanding of this vocabulary by chance, only by design. The design should include calculated exposure to the technical vocabulary of the subject and opportunity to use that vocabulary sufficiently often to ensure familiarity and facility with it. Through the design, meanings of words are reinforced and understandings of concepts extended.

When students deal with the technical vocabulary before reading a selection, they have a better understanding of the content than when the vocabulary is ignored or treated only superficially. Frequent exposure to and manipulation of the vocabulary develop and reinforce definitions and meanings of words and make learning more permanent.

Suggestions for vocabulary development found in Chapters 6 and 7 are applicable here. The use of the structured overview combines purpose setting and motivation with review of familiar words and the presentation of new words. Functional development of skills is enhanced during the teaching of selected words. Reinforcement of definitions is appropriate prior to reading the related selection. The activities discussed on pages 143 and 149 are applicable in this part of the Instructional Framework. Activities through which students generate word lists, as discussed on pages 178-80, also are applicable here.

Obviously more activities and alternatives are suggested than can be used in any single lesson. The suggestions should be viewed as resources from which one draws selectively, depending on instructional time available, students' needs, importance of the unit of study, and the like.

### Guidance

After the preparatory steps in the structure of lessons have been completed, students are ready to read. What do teachers do at this point? They make certain that students apply the skills for which they have been given direction and that they pursue the ideas embodied in the assigned materials. They guide the students in this experience, *not* assuming they already know what is being taught. This guidance has flexibility and latitude, however, because its purpose is not conformity but ultimate independence. Consequently, guidance must be sufficiently structured to give purpose and direction, but sufficiently open to allow personal strengths, preferences, and discoveries to emerge.

It is here that one uses the guides for levels or patterns or reasoning, which are discussed in Chapters 3, 4, and 5, respectively. As students read they are guided to develop and reinforce appropriate skills and content-related concepts.

**Development of processes** Guides for levels or patterns or reasoning are designed to show students how to apply skills as they read. Merely telling students what skills they should use is not sufficient, though it is essential. Suggestions such as the following are only a partial solution: "If we want [the student] to draw general conclusions from the material, then we must indicate this purpose before he reads it, preferably by giving him or helping devise questions which require general conclusions" (Durr, 1963).

Asking questions that "require" students to use a skill does not necessarily teach them the skill. Such procedures are assumptive. The two are quite different. *After* the skill has been taught and the student has had opportunity under some direction to develop familiarity with it, it is useful reinforcement to ask questions requiring use of the skill. But while it is being *taught*, some procedure other than merely asking questions requiring use of the skill should be used. The discussion of simulation (Chapter 8) is applicable here.

The guides should provide a structure which will give students a conscious experience in the application of the skill and, simultaneously, an understanding of the course content. They should provide for differences in ability and achievement among students in classes and ensure success in the assigned reading. Guides discussed in Chapters 3, 4, and 5 can be designed for these purposes.

**Development of concepts**  One of the problems listed in Chapter 2 of this book is "concept development." Learning in content areas is more than just the accumulation of facts. Teaching that depends for its success on students' ability to memorize and recall great quantities of detail educates students for the present and not for the future. Students are best served when teachers show them how to develop and organize concepts from the myriad of detailed information they encounter in any given subject.

As you will recall from the discussion of the guide materials for levels and patterns and reasoning, reading instruction in content areas involves both the acquisition of information and the development of concepts. The skills implicit in these processes and the concepts which are the product of their application are essential parts of the curriculum. The simultaneous development of content (concepts) and process (reading and reasoning skills) is the goal of such instruction, with neither being sacrificed to the other.

It is at this point in the lesson structure that guides discussed in Chapters 3, 4, and 5 should be applied.

### Independence

**Application of processes**  As has been mentioned previously in this book, there is a widespread concern that students need to develop and demonstrate independence in the use of reading skills in all subjects. This is an important concern, but independence is not produced merely by expecting or demanding it. It is produced by structuring lessons with such care that the students are clearly shown how to apply the skills and are guided for long enough to develop a "feel" for the skills. The discussion of the sequence toward independence in Chapter 8 is particularly applicable here.

The structure of lessons presented in this chapter does lead toward independence. It prepares students for a task and then carefully guides them as they perform it. Having developed a pattern of behavior, students will repeat it with fewer and fewer external controls until they are able to adapt and modify it to suit their personal style. True independence will then have been reached.

The road to independence is long. It is damaging to students for teachers to expect independence to be applied at the beginning of the instructional journey rather than found at the end.

**Application of concepts** A chemistry teacher was disturbed because his students could not "handle concepts" in his course. The statewide final examination required independent application of concepts developed throughout the course. The suggestion was made that he prepare guide materials showing the students how to develop and apply concepts, as they would be expected to do in the examination. He replied that to do so would take the time he needed to cover the course and would, therefore, jeopardize the students' performance on the examination. It was pointed out to him that since his students already were doing poorly because of their inability to "handle concepts," it would be to the students' advantage if he were to teach them how to develop the concepts they were expected to handle. He persisted that he could not afford the time; if the students could not handle concepts when they came to his class, "they didn't belong there." He was then asked, "What is it that you have responsibility to teach? If students must *already* know when they come to your class what they *should* know when they take the end-of-the-year examination, you really have nothing to teach them!" The conversation ended in stony silence.

Independent use of concepts is, indeed, a proper goal for teachers to hold for students. Various guides walk students through simulated experiences in the development and use of concepts. These successful experiences develop a behavior pattern that students can repeat when required to function independently. As students become more proficient, they begin to modify the pattern to suit their own special needs. True independence is then achieved. To repeat, independence is not the starting point but rather the end product of good teaching.

## STRUCTURE WITHIN LESSONS

The critical part of the structure *of* lessons is the structure provided *within* lessons: the guides for levels, patterns, and reasoning. These guides provide a model, a simulation, of the desired behavior. They assume the preparatory part of the Instructional Framework and point toward the ultimate independence which the Instructional Framework fosters. The structure within lessons is the part frequently omitted for reasons already discussed.

The structure within lessons has three elements: (1) manipulation of alternatives, (2) transfer and transformation, and (3) personalizing the process. Each is applied according to the students' sophistication in the use of the procedure being learned.

### Manipulation of Alternatives

Both skills and concepts have specific components. If students are to acquire a feeling for the skill or an understanding of the concept, it is necessary for them to manipulate the components of the skill or concept. Through such manipulation they see how the concept is formed or how the skill operates. The teacher can develop a guide (structure) which incorporates the components of the skill or concept as a set of alternatives that students must sort out. This sorting and arranging of the components develops a sensitivity to the relationships necessary for developing the concepts and a sensitivity to the process of forming and applying the relationships. The guide, then, becomes a simulator of the experience and understanding which is being taught.

When the guide follows the "direction" of the Instructional Framework, the simulation is a powerful learning experience. The alternatives which incorporate the components needed for the desired learning provide this simulation. Students discuss the differences they find when comparing their responses to the alternatives and the learning is reinforced. A pattern of behavior is started that will lead to independence. Such a structure is in direct contrast to that frequently observed in classrooms. All too often students are subjected to closed questioning, their mental activity is reduced to guessing what is in the teacher's mind; they are rewarded if the guess is correct, penalized for presenting other possibilities, even though valid.

The materials presented in Chapters 3, 4, 5, and 7 amply illustrate this aspect of the structure *within* lessons. Chapter 8, on simulation, discusses the need for students to manipulate the components of the concept being studied and the processes being applied.

When coupled with the preparation phase of the Instructional Framework, which includes specific direction on the use of the process, this material develops an awareness of how the process "feels" and of what information and ideas the student can acquire by using the process. Of special interest is the fact that this material can be used with below-average, average, and above-average classes. All three classes respond similarly, the differences being "in degree, not in kind." Experience supports Bruner's (1960) contention that "intellectual activity anywhere is the same, whether at the frontier of knowledge or the third-grade classroom .... The difference is in degree, not in kind." It also supports Bruner's (1960) position that

> The task of teaching a subject to a child at any particular age is one of representing the structure of that subject in terms of the child's way of viewing things. The task can be thought of as one of translation. General hypothesis that has just been stated is premised on the considered judgment that any idea can be presented honestly and usefully in the thought forms of children of school age, and that these first representations can later be made more powerful and precise the more easily by virtue of this early learning.

### Transfer and Transformation

The next phase of the structure within lessons is to account for transfer. After students have experienced success in reading the information source and in developing concepts while they are guided through the process, as suggested in Chapters 3, 4, and 5, they are ready to try the procedure without the aid of carefully structured guides. They will still need some coaching to transfer their competence from highly structured material to more independent application of the skill, and this coaching is part of attending to transfer. The teacher helps students recall prior instruction they have experienced relative to the particular reading or reasoning process in question. She discusses with them how the skill "worked" in those previous situations, then she discusses the appropriateness of that process to the situation they now face. She may then ask questions which will require the use of the previously learned process to stimulate the transfer and application of the process. (Review the suggested sequence on page 199.)

Recall of prior uses of a particular reading process and a discussion of its appropriateness to the new situation ensure transfer and lead students toward ultimate independence. The attention to transfer is profitable only when a behavior pattern or understanding has been sufficiently established and students have been sufficiently coached in its use so that they have something which can be transferred.

Note that the transfer discussed above occurs within a subject area, not from subject to subject. Skills learned in one setting under careful guidance are applied in a similar setting more independently. The students are transferring what they have learned in the structured situation to the independent situation. Transfer also takes place from subject to subject, but that process is better described by the term *transformation* than transfer.

Transfer of reading skills within a subject area does not seem to cause philosophical problems. As students progress from grade to grade within a subject, the skills learned in one grade are transferred to and used in the next grade. But some teachers question whether reading skills are transferable from subject to subject. Untold hours have been spent by well-intentioned teachers compiling lists of reading skills supposedly unique to particular subject areas. They believe some skills to be peculiar to specific subjects and appropriate to no other; therefore, such skills must be taught directly in the appropriate courses. They compile lists of skills which are presumably unique to each content area, assuming that if teachers have available the lists of skills appropriate to their subjects, they can better meet their responsibility to teach them.

A careful examination of such lists of skills raises serious doubts in the minds of most observers. It seems doubtful that each subject area really has as many skills unique to itself as has been suggested. One can conclude that the uniqueness lies more in semantics than skills: that different authors use different names for the same process. Very few skills are unique to one or even two areas. And this is even more true when one simplifies the reading process for instructional purposes as suggested in Chapter 2 and illustrated throughout this book.

Therefore, since few skills are unique to one content area, transfer should serve the development of most reading skills in all content areas. Skills taught in one area *should* serve students in all areas. And they will, if the essential factor is accounted for—*transformation.*

Transformation is the adaptation of a skill or process to meet the demands of material peculiar to a content area. The need for this adaptation is clear when we accept the view that reading skills required in one subject are generally applicable to all other subjects.

Does this mean that compiling lists of skills peculiar to each subject area is a waste of time? Yes, it means precisely that. *Very few* skills are unique to a single area. A more valuable exercise would be to consider how to adapt skills common to all areas (and this appears to include most reading skills) to suit the peculiarities of each subject. The concept of transformation more clearly delineates the responsibility of each content teacher for teaching his students how to read his subject matter. One must be aware, however, that there are two kinds of transformation: horizontal and vertical.

Horizontal transformation is adapting a given skill as one moves from subject to subject within the same guide, adapting it to meet the demands of information sources in each of the subjects. Though the same skill is applied, it has to be adapted because of the uniqueness of the material in each area. This is the significant point: it is not the skill that is unique, but the material to be studied. Because a different set of ideas, a different set of values, a different vocabulary are fed into this skill for each of the areas, students must adapt the process to meet the peculiarities of each subject.

The other type of transformation is vertical. The concepts and materials students are required to handle increase in sophistication at each grade level. As students move from grade to grade within a subject, they must be able to adapt their skills to handle the increased sophistication of materials to which their skills are applied.

To illustrate vertical transformation, consider the organizational pattern of cause and effect. Whether applied to simple or complex materials, the set of relationships is the same. The process is the same, but the levels of sophistication at which it is applied are quite different. Students moving from low, average, or honor status in grade seven to low, average, or honor status in grade eleven must learn how to adapt their skills to meet the increased sophistication required by the materials at each successive grade level. This is vertical transformation.

Neither vertical nor horizontal transformation can be assumed to occur, whether applied to levels of comprehension, organizational patterns, reasoning, or vocabulary acquisition. Students at all ability levels need to be shown how to adapt skills; they must learn how it feels to make the modifications and adjustments required by various subjects and grade levels.

### Personalizing the Process

For students truly to be independent, they must be free to perform tasks differently than they have been taught if their own method is efficient and produces the desired results. For example, students might discover another way to approach the task of reading for inference. If so, they should be allowed to adapt the skill to suit their personal style and need. To insist that students perform a task in precisely the same manner that the teacher prescribed is to produce automatons, not individual thinkers and learners. Certainly students must follow a required procedure in the first phase of the structure within lessons so that they are exposed to a pattern and learn how it works. They are then in a position to modify it. Without the first phase, students have nothing to modify and their "independent" modifications may not be modifications at all, but only the results of nondirected self-discovery, usually a much less efficient way to learn.

Ironically, teachers who reject the use of guides for levels, patterns, and reasoning because they require dependence, themselves foster dependence. They focus on informational recall and also insist that students perform tasks or make use of ideas in precisely the way they were taught. Yet only when students are allowed to develop a personal style with respect to any skill or understanding are they truly independent. The *structure within lessons,* part of the *structure of lessons* of the Instructional Framework, allows such development, but in a logical sequence. After students have been shown *how* to perform a task and how to transfer it to new but similar situations, they devise their own method and become truly independent.

## INSTRUCTIONAL FRAMEWORK
## AND THE DIRECTED READING ACTIVITY

Readers familiar with the literature about reading instruction may think the Instructional Framework (IF) is merely a renaming of the Directed Reading Activity (DRA). Such is not the case. The DRA was designed principally for the development of a reading lesson from a reading textbook, although it is also recommended for use in content areas. The IF is designed mainly for use with content texts, although it could be used with reading texts.

The DRA, like the IF, is a three-step procedure, but there are fundamental differences. The components of the IF were presented above. The phases of the DRA are: (1) building background and purpose by introducing new vocabulary, reviewing previous lessons where appropriate, drawing on students' experience background, previewing material to determine how it should be read; (2) silent reading and study to accomplish the established purposes; (3) follow-up questioning, testing, and discussion to determine understandings derived from content and process.

Both the IF and DRA are similar in their first phase. The major difference exists in the second phase. The IF guides students as they read and react, as they gather information and develop concepts. The DRA allows time for reading and encourages students to apply skills discussed in the first phase. However, the "structure within" the lesson is not provided in the DRA as it is in the IF. Therefore, the DRA assumes that a level of independence already has been attained by the readers. Phase three of the DRA builds on that assumption.

Phase two of the IF *guides* the student in the application of skills and the development of concepts. Then, in phase three, the IF allows for independent application of both skills and concepts. Both in phase two and three students have opportunity to explore ideas: under close guidance in phase two and through independent activity in phase three. In contrast, this activity is reserved to phase three of the DRA.

In effect, phase three of the IF incorporates phases two and three of the DRA. This makes phase two of the IF, the guided reading, a unique phase. The structure within lessons—phase two of the IF—stands apart from the DRA. It is the critical factor in teaching reading and course content simultaneously.

Many have been critical of the DRA, citing a number of objections. According to one critic:

> On the instructional front, all teachers must understand how reading as a cognitive process is akin to thinking. Reading must be taught in such a way that the precept of versatility becomes a reality . . . . Yet classroom practices, saddled by out-moded and ill-conceived directed reading activities presented and re-presented by stereotyped basic reader programs, violate these principles. Children can think. They can read critically and reflectively and creatively at all levels—if they are taught to do so. Efficient cognitive skills can be taught. However, in the all-too-typical schools the minimal, parrot-like demands placed upon children actually deprive them of opportunity to do so (Stauffer, 1967).

The Instructional Framework avoids the conditions that prompt such criticism of the DRA.

### Benefits

What benefits accrue to the students and the teacher using the Instructional Framework and, particularly, the structured materials that are recommended? They can be summarized under three headings: (1) individualization of instruction, (2) student interaction, and (3) functional assessment.

**Individualization of instruction** The teacher who is faced with a class ranging across several grade-equivalent levels of ability and achievement finds it difficult to meet the needs of each individual. However, phase two of the Instructional Framework offers hope.

Materials which provide the structure *within* lessons are designed to guide students in the development of specific skills and concepts. These guides can be constructed to accommodate differences in students' ability and achievement. Since a given skill or concept can be applied at many levels of sophistication, each student can respond to the selection, through the guides, at a level appropriate to his needs.

"Comprehending and recalling materials they [students] have read is much more than a matter of the right vocabulary load" (Durrell, 1966). It is a matter of adjusting the structure within which students are guided so that they can apply the skill at a level of sophistication appropriate to their capabilities at the moment.

It is virtually impossible to meet the needs of every individual in every classroom every day. However, one can approximate this goal by grouping students within a class.

**Student interaction** Emerson referred to people "who sit behind their eyes." How descriptive this is of students in a classroom where passive receptivity by students and active presentation by the teacher is the order of the day. If one were to classify the students' conscious state, one could label it the "conference state," placing it one step above the catatonic. This state is characteristic of people in situations where they are "talked to" and have little opportunity to actively respond. Symptoms are the glazed eye, the head fixed in position to face the speaker, the occasional nod and smile of automatic response. One finds these symptoms among adults who attend church, art lectures, presentations of philosophical treatises; it is particularly prevalent among teachers who attend faculty meetings, in-service sessions after school, and evening courses at the university. People do, indeed, often just sit behind their eyes, with much that is unrelated to the topic under consideration going on behind those eyes. Students in elementary and secondary schools are no different from adults in this respect.

Imagine the typical high school student who rushes to school each morning, enters his first-period class where he is talked to for forty minutes. He then has four minutes to get to his next class, where again he is talked to for another forty minutes. So it goes through the day until, if he takes five subjects, he has been talked to for a total of three and one-half hours and given little opportunity to respond as an active participant. If this continues year after year, students' intellectual curiosity is reduced until they are interested only in discovering what the teacher has in mind, what the teacher expects to be given back on examination papers. Then they deliver what is expected. Their natural curiosity is stultified.

The guides which help students acquire and apply skills and concepts also provide for student interaction, student involvement in the learning process. Students bring to these guides their present knowledge and experience and share both with other members of the group. Each student's contribution is accepted and respected as the content is explored and the skills developed and reinforced. Interaction encourages more interaction; students become actively involved in the learning process.

**Functional assessment** The best assessment is to observe student response to good instruction. It is functional assessment. When carefully guided and differentiated instruction is provided in a classroom, teachers have excellent opportunity to observe their students' daily progress. When a lesson is adjusted to their achievement levels, the teacher can continue to modify the requirements as she notes how well the students perform. Thus, content teachers conduct an ongoing analysis of their students' needs rather than an elaborate, formal testing program.

Obviously there is more to assessment than this, and the topic is explored more fully in Chapter 10. However, it is important to note that when students' differences are accommodated, there is an ongoing analysis of students' progress. Flexible instruction, current to the needs of students, provides the basis for functional assessment. Guided interaction among students within groups reveals to teachers many of the students' needs, and how the next lesson needs to be adjusted to include them.

## TEACHER PREPARATION

The Instructional Framework is based on the teacher's own preparation for the lesson. Each of the elements of the lesson requires thoughtful analysis of the content to be taught, the processes to be taught, the objectives to be attained. "Winging it" works occasionally when you are tired or when you don't have time to get really ready for the next day. But that is the exception rather than the rule, or you're in real trouble: with yourself, your students, and your administration (or you should be).

### Content Analysis

Basic to this careful preparation is the analysis of the content to be taught. Throughout this book references have been made to the importance of analyzing the content to establish a clear picture of the concepts to be taught and the reading processes to be emphasized.

Gagné (1970) suggests a set of relationships which can serve as criteria for the content analysis which precedes a lesson. He suggests that a body of knowledge is comprised of principles, concepts, and details. Through a process he calls "chaining," details are connected to formulate concepts; concepts then are connected to form principles.

It is useful for teachers in a subject area periodically to examine their curriculum to identify the principles it embodies, then determine if these principles are logical extensions of the relationships which exist among the concepts taught in the curriculum. In like manner, it is useful to determine if the concepts are logical extensions of the relationships which exist among the details taught in the curriculum.

As this is true for the entire curriculum, so it is true for specific lessons or units of instruction. Teachers should identify the principle being emphasized, the concepts from which the principle is developed, and the pertinent details from which the concepts are developed.

If you have read Chapters 3 and 4, you will quickly see the connection between Gagné's suggestions for organizing a curriculum and the processes the reader can use to develop an understanding of information sources in the curriculum. Although all the suggested processes are related, the levels-of-comprehension construct seems most closely related.

A content analysis of the segment of the curriculum to be taught should be a consistent obligation that one discharges before preparing the Instructional Framework and all of its component parts. Clearly stating the concept or concepts to be learned makes it more probable that students will learn them.

## Resource Analysis

The textbook is but one source of information students and teachers use, but it is an extremely important one. This can be a cause of grief to both students and teacher if students have difficulty reading it. Because the focus of this book is on helping you find ways to help your students read better the textbooks you assign them, it is important to see how content analysis relates to resource analysis.

Subject-area teachers are well acquainted with content in their areas of specialization and know the major concepts their students should develop. They plan each new unit with those concepts in mind. They give reading assignments that will develop, reinforce, and extend students' understanding of these concepts. But here is where problems arise. Teachers attribute to a given selection in a text ideas which sometimes are not actually there. Drawing on their thorough knowledge of the content, teachers unconsciously supply information to fill in the gaps in exposition written and read by experts in their fields. As a result, teachers assume that students will develop certain understandings from their reading when, in reality, the components of those understandings are partially or completely missing from the text.

Teachers do not sense these gaps because they subconsciously supply the missing information. Students have neither the background nor conditioning to be able to supply the missing information. Indeed, students frequently are not sufficiently sophisticated in the subject to realize when there are gaps. As a result they may develop partial concepts, form confused impressions, and reach erroneous conclusions, which little resemble the major ideas their teachers assume they should acquire. In other words, students are occasionally set to the task of reading the text to discover ideas that, although they are in the teacher's mind, are simply not in the text.

This understandable phenomenon is constantly at work. When subject-area specialists re-examine their resource materials to determine the ideas they actually contain, they see clearly how they have "read into" these sources nonexistent information (in terms of literal content of the text).

The reason for such gaps in textbooks is understandable. Texts are written by scholars who have a high level of understanding in their discipline. They draw on this personal wealth of information as they write their texts. Frequently they make assumptions in the development of concepts, assuming for students a higher level of understanding than is warranted. These concepts seem so elementary to specialists that it hardly seems necessary to develop them. However, because students are uninitiated in the subject, or at least in the particular unit being read, assumptions made by experts become knowledge gaps for students.

So the teacher prepares to give the reading assignment by determining the ideas actually present in the material to be read. She plays the role of one who knows relatively little about the subject, placing herself in the position of a student who understands only those concepts which have been developed up to that point. As a hypothetical "student," the teacher has limited facility with the language of the subject and has neither extensive experience nor depth of understanding which comes from years of study. Endeavoring to push from her mind most of what she knows about the subject, the teacher looks at the reading selection and asks herself, "What ideas that students can perceive and use are actually here in this material?"

This is one of the most difficult tasks to ask of a content teacher. However, if she makes such an analysis, she finds it eliminates much frustration—her students' and her own. Her expectations of what concepts the students should obtain from their reading are based on knowledge of material actually in the text, not on assumptions of what should be there. Obviously, students respond to what is in the reading selection rather than to what teachers assume is there.

## SUMMARY

The Instructional Framework is a structure *of* lessons. Of critical importance is the structure *within* lessons, guides which simulate the application of skills and development of concepts for students. Within such structure students develop proficiency until they are able to function independently.

Individual differences among students in a content classroom can be served as students enjoy interaction within the structure provided by the guide. The interaction provides the basis for ongoing, functional analysis of students' needs.

Through the Instructional Framework, with its structure *of* and structure *within* lessons, desirable experiences are simulated. As students go through the simulated experiences they develop patterns of behavior that ultimately lead them to function independently.

\*     \*     \*     \*     \*     \*

## REACTION GUIDE

*Directions:* Of the several statements listed below, some are directly stated in this chapter, others implied. Place an "I" on the line before the items which represent inferences you can draw from this chapter. Mark with a "D" items which represent direct statements from the text.

_____ 1. Teachers generally neglect to prepare students to do their assigned reading.

_____ 2. The Instructional Framework and the Directed Reading Activity are not the same.

_____ 3. The DRA is appropriate for reading lessons.

_____ 4. Students read with greater comprehension when they have a purpose for reading.

_____ 5. The preparation phases of the Directed Reading Activity and Instructional Framework are essentially the same.

_____ 6. Content teachers are often reluctant to incorporate the Instructional Framework because it takes too much time away from the course.

_____ 7. There are strong feelings against the DRA as an instructional procedure.

_____ 8. Being guided in the use of a skill is much different than being tested to see if one has used it correctly.

_____ 9. Teachers can simulate the use of a skill so that students develop a "feeling for" it.

_____ 10. Teachers frequently engage in more testing of reading skills than teaching of reading skills.

_____ 11. Carefully structuring students' responses to show them *how* to respond is neither "hand-holding" nor "spoon-feeding."

_____ 12. A few "extra" moments spent preparing students for an assignment returns dividends in their increased achievement in reading and responding to the material.

_____ 13. There are some who believe students should set their own purposes for reading; to them, the IF is detrimental to their development of independence in the use of skills.

_____ 14. When a teacher says to his students, "By the way, be sure to read the next chapter for tomorrow!" as they leave the room, after the bell has rung, he is not adequately preparing students to read that assignment.

_____ 15. The structure, through which one provides guidance in the use of reading and reasoning skills, is very flexible and takes many forms.

*Generalization*

*Directions:* Check those generalizations you can support as a result of relating this chapter to your teaching and learning experiences.

_____ 1. An activity can be "taken apart" and its "pieces" studied separately.

_____ 2. Any skill is operational over a great range of sophistication.

_____ 3. When a person is *prepared* to function in a certain task, he does so with greater efficiency than when he is unprepared.

____ 4. Unless a teacher prepares a student for a reading assignment, the student will begin the task unprepared.

____ 5. Testing can also serve to teach, but testing is not generally thought of as teaching.

____ 6. Reading and reasoning skills can be "simulated" so that students can consciously experience how they "feel."

____ 7. There must be a structure *of* lessons as well as a structure *within* lessons in any subject.

____ 8. One can, but need not, jeopardize the substance of what is read by emphasizing the skills needed to read it.

____ 9. Testing and teaching can occur simultaneously when guided instruction is individualized.

### REINFORCING ACTIVITY

The previous eight chapters present methods and materials which fit into the Instructional Framework discussed in this chapter. Demonstrate your understanding of this fit by classifying the vocabulary for those chapters under the three headings listed below. Some words may fit under more than one heading, some under all, and some under none. Be ready to discuss the reasons for your decisions.

PREPARATION                    GUIDANCE                    INDEPENDENCE

\*    \*    \*    \*    \*    \*

### REFERENCES

BARRON, RICHARD. *The use of an iterative research process to improve a method of vocabulary instruction in tenth grade biology.* Unpublished doctoral dissertation, Syracuse University, 1971.

BRUNER, JEROME. *The process of education.* Cambridge, Mass.: Harvard University Press, 1960.

DURR, WILLIAM, "Improving secondary reading through the content subjects." In *Reading as an intellectual activity.* Newark, Del.: International Reading Association, 1963.

DURRELL, DONALD D. *Improving reading instruction.* New York: Harcourt Brace Jovanovich, 1966.

GAGNE, ROBERT M. *The conditions of knowledge.* New York: Holt, Rinehart & Winston, 1970.

NILES, OLIVE S. "Developing basic comprehension." In *Speaking of reading.* Syracuse, N.Y.: Syracuse University Reading and Language Arts Center, 1964.

STAUFFER, RUSSELL G. "Time for amendment." *The Reading Teacher,* 20, no. 8 (1967), 685.

*ten*

# Assessment

---

**VOCABULARY**

The following terms are important to an understanding of this chapter. Each is defined in context. Read through the list to identify those for which you have uncertain meanings. Then, as you read the chapter, pay particular attention to their definitions. Also, make certain that the meanings attributed to the other words in the list by their use in the context of the chapter correspond to your own meanings for them.

| | |
|---|---|
| assessment | informal assessment |
| standardized assessment | cloze |
| grading | review |
| aided recall | unaided recall |
| normal curve | |

Each of the following terms has been defined previously in this book. If you are not reading the chapters in sequence, you may need to examine the vocabulary lists for the chapters which precede this one for definitions of words for which you hold uncertain meanings.

functional assessment　　　　instructional framework
independence

## IDEA DIRECTION

One hardly can talk of teaching without talking of testing. Teachers want to know their students' potential for learning and their specific achievement in an instructional area of concern. They want to know how to determine that information most economically. Finally, they want to know how to report on students' progress and what label will most clearly communicate that progress.

Assessment involves all of this, and even more. This chapter will discuss possible responses to the concerns mentioned above—and more.

## READING DIRECTION

This chapter requires considerable flexibility in reading. First, it discusses the kinds of assessment available to teachers. Second, it gives an illustrative test to examine—or even to take. Third, it includes two review procedures in which you can engage to illustrate the points made about this aspect of assessment and which serve to give you a sense of what you have learned from this book. You will need to accommodate your skills to each of these phases and purposes.

---

## TYPES OF ASSESSMENT

Too much time is spent on formal testing in our schools. A common concern among teachers is that they do not have enough time to prepare lessons and to give the kind of instruction that would be profitable for their students. Yet these same teachers spend countless hours preparing and correcting tests; they spend too many class periods administering exams. If only half the time now devoted to testing were used for preparing those "better lessons," their instruction would be much better.

One reason for this excessive testing is an excessive compulsion for gathering information about students' strengths, weaknesses, interests, and accomplishments. There is a tendency to gather much more information than is needed or can be used to accomplish the purposes for which schools have been established.

There also is a tendency to believe that instruction of students cannot commence until all that information is in the teachers' hands. Nowhere is this belief more prevalent than in reading instruction. Frequently one finds that reading instruction has not started even by mid-November because "we are still testing" to determine the students' needs. Happily, teachers need not wait for data from tests to begin teaching if reading instruction is integrated with content instruction and if some of the following suggestions are adopted.

One way to achieve a better balance between what is needed and what is obtained is to change the type of assessment most commonly emphasized. There are really three types of assessment: functional, informal, and standardized. The last two dominate education; the first has not yet had its day.

### Functional Assessment

Functional assessment involves constant analysis of students' needs by observing how they respond to guided instruction. A teacher can account for achievement levels among his students as suggested on pages 62-65. He observes how students respond to instruction provided for these levels, noting what kind of success they experience. In subsequent lessons, the activities are adjusted according to the students' responses during the previous lesson. The assessment, therefore, is functional, occurring as part of the instruction and not as a separate operation. No formal data are collected; no scores are computed. Subjective judgment is the criterion, and it is effective.

Intuition, or subjective judgment, of the teacher is important in functional assessment. A teacher who has a "feeling for" his students can estimate their levels of achievement on a given activity with considerable accuracy. If he accounts for those levels by differentiating assignments, he is beginning the process of functional assessment. The next step is to observe students' responses and to adjust, intuitively, subsequent assignments according to that response. If the assignment was too difficult, involve the student in an easier one; if it was too easy, adjust it upward; if it was just right, continue at that level to reinforce for a period of time.

Given a sensitivity to students' needs and a willingness to be flexible, a teacher can engage in functional assessment while using lessons and materials described in this book. He will know more about the students' needs than if he relied on either informal or standardized assessment.

For example, activities recommended as appropriate for the preparation phase of the Instructional Framework can serve as vehicles for this functional assessment. Similarly, the activities related to levels of comprehension, organizational patterns, reasoning, and vocabulary development give a functional assessment of students' needs and progress as well as the simulation of the processes they are designed to teach. Thus, the time spent developing materials has a double return: instruction in the implicit processes; assessment of competence with the process.

Engaging in functional assessment, using the time saved to prepare tests that enhance learning, relying more on teachers' judgment, resisting outside and uninformed pressures—all put evaluation in the content classroom in proper perspective. With such perspective, evaluation consumes a share of instructional time more appropriate to its value.

## Informal Assessment

As already mentioned, assessment is misused if information is sought for its own sake and is not used to aid the student. By its very nature, functional assessment obviates this danger. Both informal and standardized testing, however, are subject to the danger, since they focus principally on skills and concepts for their own sake, rather than on their use and value and on the students' application of them.

Tests providing informal assessment are usually teacher-made. They are designed to analyze achievement on specific skills and understandings, often related to the subject area of the teacher making the assessment. The teacher identifies selections from material used in the subject and the types of skills and ideas they embody. She designs questions which require students to use these predetermined skills to obtain the answers. She determines students' levels of achievement from their responses on the informal tests, and plans subsequent instruction accordingly.

An increasingly popular means of assessing students' reading achievement in content areas is the *cloze* test, applied to subject matter tests. Representative passages from the text are reproduced with every fifth word omitted and a blank line of approximately fifteen spaces inserted in place of the word. Students are asked to read this "mutilated" passage and supply the missing word for each blank space, using the context of the original text which remains. Scores are derived by determining the number of blanks filled in with the exact word that appeared in the original material (Bormuth, 1968). Synonyms are not counted; only exact word replacements. Dividing the number of correct responses by the number of possible responses gives the accuracy scores in percentages. There is some disagreement among researchers as to the meaning of various accuracy scores; however, the following interpretation is considered reasonable. You can use it for your students and see how it fits, making adjustments as needed. The interpretation is: 57 percent or over indicates independent level; between 44 percent and 57 percent indicates instructional level; below 44 percent indicates frustration level.

Several cautions are in order. Remember that if students score at the independent level, they already have a decent grasp of your subject, and you should be thinking about enriching alternatives. If students score at the instructional level, that speaks to your job: to instruct them through the text and other means. If the students score at the frustration level, ask yourself if they would be frustrated if they were fully prepared for reading the material as suggested in Chapters 6 and 9. Perhaps that might shift their grasp of the material and the concept so that the level would be more instructional than frustrating. Finally, take the scores with a grain of salt. There is substantial research on the derivation of scores on cloze tests and their relationship to other measures of students' reading achievement, and the relationships are reasonably close. Be careful, however, not to throw out the text or the kids because the two don't match. Cloze, though useful, is only one indicator of reading difficulty. Students' response to your guided instruction certainly is as useful an indication, even if you can't attach a number to that response as readily as you can to cloze.

Informal assessment is much like functional except that informal assessment is a step separated from instruction. When the instruction meets students' needs, the information becomes obsolete because students' needs have changed. Hence, reassessment is necessary. It is much more efficient to omit the collection of data from the informal assessment and concentrate on functional assessment.

### Standardized Assessment

Standardized assessment should be considered basic to any program designed to build skills as well as concepts. Standardized tests have been validated on large samplings of the populations they were designed to assess. The reliability of such tests is well determined; we are relatively certain that a given test really assesses the kind of achievement it purports to.

Standardized tests indicate a general index of achievement for an individual in comparison with other students at that age or grade level. One should examine the tests used to identify the subskills which contribute to the total test score. This gives meaning to the total score and to an assessment of the performance of an individual.

## TESTING TO REFLECT TEACHING

A social studies teacher had been excited by the manner in which his students were participating in the lessons he had developed to integrate instruction in history with instruction in reading. He felt certain that the students were learning both the historical content and the reading process.

His optimism was shattered when he began to read through the tests students had turned in. In contrast to what he had observed during the lessons, the students seemed not to know anything the test was designed to measure. An analysis of his test, as compared with his instruction, quickly uncovered the problem. He had tested what he had taught, but at a level of sophistication far higher than the level at which he had taught it.

When the problem was pointed out to this teacher, he readily saw the reason for the students' failure, developed a more appropriate test, and found that the students did well.

Many teachers regularly make the same mistake this teacher made, and both students and teachers suffer as a result. When tests do not reflect *how* the students were taught, they are just as unreliable as if they failed to reflect *what* was taught. The need, obviously, is to develop tests which reflect both the *what* and the *how* of instruction. In the following discussion, the focus is on the *how*, with the assumption that each teacher will make certain of the *what*.

Making certain that a test reflects *how* the students were taught involves two factors: (1) level of sophistication; (2) degree of independence.

Most concepts studied in school can be approached instructionally at many levels of sophistication. In fact, a careful examination of the curriculum across grade levels within a given subject area will reveal the same basic concepts being emphasized over and over. If properly handled, this does not seem redundant to the students because at each successive grade level the concept is treated at a higher level of sophistication and abstraction. Naturally enough, the tests which assess students' grasp of these concepts should reflect the same level of sophistication and abstraction at which the instruction was given. This, of course, is nothing new to experienced teachers. It is logical and attempts usually are made to provide such consistency in teacher-constructed tests.

The problem of greater concern in the "how" of assessment is the degree of independence in reading required of students by the test instrument relative to the degree of independence required of students by the instruction. The social studies teacher who experienced the frustration with his students' response on his test had taught them using many of the procedures outlined in this text. He had provided them with guides of various sorts to accompany the reading of their information sources and they had worked on these materials in groups. The materials were designed to provide students with alternative statements to react to, justify, and discuss. The teacher gave them the "stuff" of the concepts and, by showing them how to manipulate it, he guided them in learning the content and the related reading and reasoning processes. But then he gave them an essay test, with nothing to manipulate. The level of independence in the use of reading skills which he required of them in the test was much greater then the level of independence he required of them in his teaching. He had not taught them how to function at the level at which he was testing them. Failure was a certainty.

This teacher fell victim to a common error. "Independence" is thought of in an absolute sense when it is really a relative state. He thought that tests should assess students' "independent" knowledge and he translated that to mean an essay test. But these students required a test that presented them with alternative statements that they could judge as to their appropriateness, given the tasks set forth in the test, statements through which they could demonstrate their understanding of the concepts they had studied. Students could have functioned independently with such a test, each one reflecting what he or she had learned. And for students instructed at such a level of independence, such a test would be valid and appropriate.

The relativity of independence has to do with the kind and amount of assistance built into the task being performed. The absoluteness of independence has to do with the intervention of other individuals to aid in the completion of the task. The two are often confused. Teachers frequently believe they are violating the absoluteness when they provide for the relativity. When you think about it, you know that they are wrong. One student can take a test which requires the manipulation in some way of a series of statements representing information and ideas she has studied. Another student can take a test which requires a response to a series of essay questions dealing with information and ideas he has studied. Each student takes the test independently, because no other person intervenes or provides aid while the test is being taken. The levels of independence in handling the information and ideas differ, however, and are reflected in the nature of the assistance built into the test itself.

Some teachers find this a problem because they have become so conditioned to thinking about independence only in the absolute sense. Thus, they think of it as being unfair if students take tests with such built-in aids. They say, "of course they will pass; how could they *not* pass if I provide everything for them to use to answer the questions." Well, they should pass the test if they have learned the material. That is not the point, unless the purpose of testing is to fail students. If the purpose is to demonstrate how well students do what and how you have taught them, then you should expect all of them to pass with flying colors. What that means for grading, also a problem, is discussed later in this chapter.

There is another aspect of independence which must be accounted for in assessment: the independence in students' thinking. The procedures outlined in this book encourage students to pursue ideas to their logical conclusions, to express ideas from insights which may differ from conclusions drawn by most of the other students or from the "answer key." A real problem is encountered when you try to design a test to measure students' learning without squelching the independent thinking you have tried to instill in your students. Of course, you can give them essay questions if they have attained that level of independence. Diversity of thinking can easily be expressed in that kind of format. But if students have not attained that relative level of independence, another way must be found. You need a test that gives them alternatives to manipulate through which they can demonstrate the insights they have developed, but a test which also holds open the option of creating their own alternatives for expressing their ideas.

The following test is an example of such an instrument. It covers the content of this text. It provides for the relative independence of students taking the test: it can accommodate absolute independence, in that a person can take the test without intervention from any other person; it can accommodate students who wish to express additional ideas or qualifications of ideas, but does not penalize students who do not pursue this option.

Such a test takes longer to prepare and longer to evaluate then more conventional tests. But if you depend more on functional assessment for determining students' needs and progress, you will require fewer informal tests and, consequently, will have more time to prepare tests such as this.

Name ———————————— Code Number ——————————

Final Examination          Teaching Reading in Content Areas

Directions: This test has six sections. Each section has ten statements you are to evaluate. The criteria for evaluating the ten statements in each section immediately precede the ten statements. Combine a letter representing a criterion in column A with a number representing a criterion in column B and place the combination on the numbered line preceding the statement you are evaluating. Do this for each statement.

When you move to a new section, you will shift to the new criteria and follow the same procedure.

More than one response is possible for most statements. Use the one you feel is best, most appropriate, or least offensive as the case might be.

Should you select *e* and/or 5 as your criterion (criteria) for a statement, write out your response on an $8\frac{1}{2}'' \times 11''$ sheet of paper and attach it to this text. Be certain to note the number of the statement to which you are responding. Also, be certain to separate the response you are providing for *e* from your response for 5. Use the following format:

(statement number)——————.
e. ——————————
5. ——————————
—————————— etc.

A good test-taking strategy is first to read the statements in a section and place a small check before those you accept. Then read the criteria and look for reasons you can use for your acceptance and rejection. When you find none, select *e* or 5, and write your own.

| A | B |
|---|---|
| a. Yes | 1. Reading, in the narrow sense, requires the ability to decode words and to determine their meanings. |
| b. No | |
| c. A reasonable position | 2. Skills can be taught functionally or directly. |
| d. An unsupportable position | 3. Vocabulary and curriculum structure means "principles, concepts, and details." |
| e. Other | 4. Every discipline has its own special language that students must know if they are to understand a subject. |
| | 5. Other: |

_____ 1. Each subject has a technical vocabulary.

_____ 2. Word attack skills are useful for reading resource materials in all subjects.

_____ 3. Proficiency in word attack skills make students independent readers.

_____ 4. The structured overview is useful for developing a sense of the structure of a unit.

_____ 5. Vocabulary reinforcement exercises can increase students' knowledge of the subject.

_____ 6. The structured overview sets up conceptual relationships.

_____ 7. The structured overview allows functional teaching of word analysis skills.

_____ 8. "Key concepts" relate to the structure of a curriculum.

_____ 9. Content teachers must assume *some* knowledge of vocabulary on the part of their students.

_____ 10. Students should be taught what they don't know of a technical language if they are expected to communicate in that language.

Section II

| A | B |
|---|---|
| a. An accurate assessment of the situation | 1. Teachers often teach intuitively. |
| b. A narrow view of the situation | 2. Interrelated ideas, once learned, can be recalled more easily than isolated and unrelated ideas. |
| c. Correct understanding of the purpose or practice | 3. Teaching "how" to do something requires some means by which the learner develops a feeling for what is to be done. |

   d. An incorrect understand-      4. Any activity or idea made up of sub-
      ing of the purpose or            components necessarily has a "struc-
      practice                         ture" by which it is identified.
   e. Other:                     5. Other:

_____ 11. Lessons evolve out of a teacher's own sense of structure.

_____ 12. Every curriculum has structure.

_____ 13. Memorization of overall structure is more useful to students than memorization of detail.

_____ 14. Structured lessons and guides stifle creativity.

_____ 15. Processes have a type of structure.

_____ 16. Guides are structured to simulate processes.

_____ 17. A lesson has identifiable parts.

_____ 18. It is difficult for teachers to identify the structure of their curriculum.

_____ 19. Behavioral objectives and lesson structure are incompatable.

_____ 20. A teacher cannot teach what he doesn't know.

*Section III*

            A                             B

a. Possible under certain      1. Functional development of skills al-
   circumstances             lows use of processes without knowl-
b. True                      edge of their labels.
c. False                  2. Students' response to structured ma-
d. Never possible            terials allows development of their
e. Other:                  skills and assessment of their levels of
                            sophistication.

                           3. Reading classes emphasize how to learn with any content, but content classes emphasize both how and what to learn as it relates to the discipline in question.

                           4. While reading requires reasoning, reasoning doesn't require reading; both need to be taught at all levels.

                           5. Other:

_____ 21. A dichotomy exists between process and content.

_____ 22. Reasoning and reading are essential processes for students' success in studying any curriculum.

_____ 23. Neither vertical nor horizontal transformation can be assumed, whether applied to levels or patterns.

_____ 24. Organizational patterns and levels of comprehension relate to the comprehension process.

_____ 25. Reading guides simulate comprehension processes.

_____ 26. Reasoning guides simulate reasoning processes.

_____ 27. Transformation occurs with reasoning as well as with reading processes.

_____ 28. Levels of comprehension are used rather than taught.

_____ 29. Guiding students' reading with reading or reasoning guides allows functional analysis of their skills needs.

_____ 30. A dichotomy exists between reasoning and reading processes.

*Section IV*

| A | B |
|---|---|
| a. Wishful thinking | 1. Content objectives are difficult to state formally. |
| b. Yes | |
| c. A debatable point | 2. Students can learn by chance or by design. |
| d. A widely accepted view | 3. Though all parts of a lesson are important, showing students how to do what they are required to do seems to be the most crucial part. |
| e. Other: | 4. An effective lesson has multiple parts, relative in importance, constructed by a knowledgeable teacher to attain specific objectives. |
| | 5. Other: |

_____ 31. Teachers generally are familiar with evaluation procedures.

_____ 32. Guiding students' response to materials is the most critical part of a lesson.

_____ 33. A "lesson" can be a one-day interaction with students or a multi-week exploration of a unit of the curriculum.

_____ 34. Independence can be taught but is not always learned.

_____ 35. Independence is sometimes learned without having been taught.

_____ 36. Any lesson has several components which must be interrelated according to students' needs and the purposes of the relationships.

_____ 37. A critical part of a lesson is the teacher's own preparation for it.

_____ 38. One cannot teach unless one knows what he wants his students to learn.

_____ 39. The structure *of* lessons provides the framework; the structure *within* lessons provides the guidance.

_____ 40. Testing and teaching can occur simultaneously when guided instruction is provided.

*Section V*

| A | B |
|---|---|
| a. Very important | 1. Small group discussions usually center on course content rather than on related processes, particularly when skills are developed functionally in response to reading and reasoning guides. |
| b. Yes | |
| c. Not when used properly | |
| d. No | |
| e. Other | |

2. Small groups of students engaged in unstructured, purposeless discussion rarely benefit from the experience as far as improvement of skills or development of understandings of course content are concerned.

3. Use of guided interaction in small groups is not the "traditional" method of teaching.

4. The needs of individuals can be met in small groups better than in large groups, and students can be shown how to develop some independence in learning.

5. Other:

_____ 41. Teacher flexibility is the hallmark of grouping.

_____ 42. Intraclass grouping approximates individualized instruction.

_____ 43. Learning is enhanced, not ensured, by intraclass grouping.

_____ 44. To outward appearances, intraclass grouping in a content class has more benefit for understanding of content than for learning of process.

_____ 45. To be effective, intraclass groups need a structure to guide their interaction.

_____ 46. Grouping helps shift the burden of learning from the teacher to the student, where it belongs.

_____ 47. Grouping isolates the teacher from the students.

_____ 48. Students learn from one another in groups.

_____ 49. Teachers should guide learning rather than impose knowledge.

_____ 50. It is easier to tell than to show.

## Section VI

| A | B |
|---|---|
| a. Always | 1. A teacher should not seek a normal distribution of scores on tests but a distribution skewed toward the top of the scale. |
| b. Never | |
| c. Yes | 2. There is a high correlation between expectancy and achievement. |
| d. No | |
| e. Other: | 3. Arbitrary and impersonal criteria destroy more potential than they develop competancy. |
| | 4. All tests, both teacher-made and standardized, should be both valid and reliable. |
| | 5. Other: |

_____ 51. The outstanding achievement of an able student is relatively no more significant than the outstanding achievement of a less able student.

_____ 52. Testing should enhance and crystalize learning.

_____ 53. It is unrealistic to give a "slow learner" an *A*.

_____ 54. One should assign marks by grade-level standards, not by teacher's whim or emotional interest in students' feelings.

_____ 55. Testing is frequently used to measure failure rather than success.

_____ 56. Tests should be built on the curriculum rather than on students' needs.

_____ 57. Failing low-achieving students—or at least giving them low grades—prepares them for the realities of life.

_____ 58. If you expect a student to fail, he will do so.

_____ 59. One should test what one teaches, both content and process.

_____ 60. One should test the way one teaches, with respect to structure and and guidance.

## ROLE OF REVIEW

Review is an important part of assessment because it really is self-assessment. The purpose of review should be to determine what one knows from all that one has studied and how readily available that knowledge is.

It is helpful to create situations where students can assess what they have learned and how firmly it is fixed in their minds. These experiences can be very productive if they are not graded and if they precede the administration of tests covering the content being reviewed. Well-organized review, prior to testing, can give students insight into what they do and don't know without threat of humiliation or fear of failure.

Two review procedures are suggested in this chapter. Both use the content of this book for illustrative purposes, allowing you to directly experience their value. The first procedure is called "focus." It uses the technical vocabulary of this book as well as broad topics which are, in fact, related to chapter titles. You are to relate specific terms to the broad topics, as you will note in the directions. Depending on your own understanding and insight, you will find several possible relationships for many of the words. Some of the words may seem silly if you have not yet developed an understanding of the related ideas in the text. If so, just remember that your students may feel the same way when they are in the process of developing understandings about your subject area. Be patient and think about the possibilities implicit in the relationship between each word and each topic. This process will help you review what you have learned thus far and also help you to organize that knowledge for subsequent recall and application. Do "focus" with colleagues, sharing reasons for your decisions as you complete the exercise.

## FOCUS

*Directions:* There are seven labels in Part I representing topics dealt with in this book. In Part II are thirty words that can be associated with these topics. On the line before each word write the letter or letters representing the topic or topics you would associate with that word. In Part III, add any other words you care to and identify the topic you associate with them.

*Part I*

| Levels of comprehension | Reasoning |
| Organizational patterns | Grouping |
| Lesson structure | Assessment |
| Vocabulary development | |

*Part II*

| | | | | | |
|---|---|---|---|---|---|
| ____ | 1. prepare | ____ | 11. within | ____ | 21. simulation |
| ____ | 2. guide | ____ | 12. of | ____ | 22. substance |
| ____ | 3. identification | ____ | 13. independence | ____ | 23. means |
| ____ | 4. analysis | ____ | 14. interaction | ____ | 24. sophistication |
| ____ | 5. elaboration | ____ | 15. criteria | ____ | 25. reinforcement |
| ____ | 6. synthesis | ____ | 16. s.o. | ____ | 26. extension |
| ____ | 7. how | ____ | 17. co-learner | ____ | 27. structure |
| ____ | 8. order | ____ | 18. functional | ____ | 28. need |
| ____ | 9. random | ____ | 19. statements | ____ | 29. overview |
| ____ | 10. why | ____ | 20. transfer | ____ | 30. investment |

The second procedure is called "triangular review." Materials for this review start on page 250, but should not be examined until after you read the description of and directions for the procedure.

Triangular Review involves both unaided and aided recall of information and ideas previously studied in a unit of study. It helps identify what has been forgotten completely or never learned. You know, of course, that after you have studied a topic some ideas can readily be brought to mind for discussions or for other applications. Other information or ideas are not so readily available, and you must be prompted in some way to recall them. Still other information or ideas may have been completely forgotten.

In Triangular Review, students are organized into groups of three. Two students in each group are given a checklist containing key words or phrases which represent information and ideas about a concept or topic studied in the unit of the curriculum being reviewed. The third member of the group is the one who will be reviewing her knowledge and understanding of the topic. She does not see the contents of the checklists but is given the topic which is being considered.

As soon as she is told the topic, the student engaged in the review begins to tell the other two students in the group all that she can recall about that topic. As the student mentions specific information or an idea represented by a word or phrase on the checklist, the two students place a check on the line before that word or phrase on their copies. When the student "runs dry" on this unaided recall, the two students work together to aid the student's recall of the information and ideas represented by the unchecked words and phrases. They phrase questions to help the student recall these items, expressing them in a way that does not give away the answer as part of the question. An $x$ is placed before those words and phrases recalled successfully by the student through this questioning. When the student engaged in the review can no longer provide responses to questions on specific items, the questioning stops and lines before those items are left blank.

The student engaged in the review then is given one of the two copies of the checklist and she can use it as the basis for subsequent study. The items preceded by checks represent information and ideas which are well in hand. Those preceded by the $x$ will need to be reviewed so that they can be brought to mind more readily. Those preceded by a blank require careful rethinking and further study since they are apparently not presently understood.

The student who gave his marked checklist to the student engaged in review receives a fresh copy of the same list for future reference. The two students who conducted the review were themselves involved in a review of their own knowledge. They had to think about the ideas and information represented by each of the words or phrases and decide whether or not the other student's responses were correct. It is a different kind of review, but nonetheless a review.

The three students are then given another set of checklists for a different topic. The roles are changed so that a different person among the three engages in the review while the other two conduct the review using the checklists. When that topic is completed, another set of checklists is distributed and the third person in the group engages in the review while the other two conduct it.

If you want to experience this kind of review, get together with two other people who are reading this book. Two of you should turn to the checklist on page 250. The third person should engage in the review. The topic should be announced to that person and the procedure outlined above should be followed. When that topic is finished, go on to the checklist on page 253 and finally to the checklist on page 189. Just remember not to look ahead to the remaining checklists before you use them for review or you'll spoil the process for yourself.

## ASSESSMENT AND GRADING

A science teacher once quit a program for low achievers because the students were doing too well! Principles expounded in this book were being used and several of her students were achieving at levels higher than students in the "regular" class. However, because they were in the so-called low-achiever class, they were not allowed to recieve higher than a $C$ on their report cards for any marking period. This teacher had to give examinations she knew would be too difficult for the students to bring down their average to the acceptable limit! Believing this to be immoral and terribly poor education, she quit in protest.

One deplores such situations—yet they are widespread. In many systems, students consigned to low-achiever classes are, by school policy, unable to attain more than a minimum passing mark, regardless of how well they do in the course.

Several arguments are given in favor of such a system. One is that we must have "standards" for the grades that are given and an $A$ should represent outstanding achievement. But according to what criteria? Is not the very best achievement of the least able student as outstanding as the very best achievement of the most able? Why should his accomplishment go unrecognized?

The answer, then, is to give an effort mark, a number that reflects the effort one has expended in attaining the mark given. Who among us, one needs to ask, would be content with F during their educational career? This says to students, "You are failing but we know you are doing your best!" There is some saying about being kicked while down . . .

But, then we hear, "This is life as it really is—the competitive world. In real life everyone doesn't get $A$. Given $A$s during their schooling, such students will be in for a shock when they get out and compete with people much more able than they." To the contrary: life is such that one gravitates into association with people of like capabilities, like interests, enthusiasms, skills, accomplish-

Checklist referred to on page 249:

## VOCABULARY DEVELOPMENT

_____ 1. Selection
_____ 2. Teaching
_____ 3. Word analysis

_____ Phonetic

_____ Structural

_____ Contextual

_____ Dictionary

_____ 4. Word recognition
_____ 5. Reinforcement
_____ 6. Multiple exposure
_____ 7. Word power
_____ 8. Criteria

_____ Key concepts

_____ Relative value

_____ Students' competence

ments. Certainly within that homogeneity there are ranges, but rarely are they so clear as we are led to believe. Why cannot there be $A$s within groups at those various levels? There are, if we know life as it really is.

But then we hear the argument that these students from less able ranks will think they are college material and want a scholarship to Harvard because of all their $A$s. Let them try, if they really do follow through. How many currently successful professionals would never have accomplished anything in life if they had been held to what appeared to be their potential for success while in elementary or secondary school? More than we can imagine. Moreover, we should not worry about this problem. Students know what's going on in the world. They measure themselves against students who "really have it" and know whether they are college material. They know that even though they are getting good marks in the courses they are taking, they probably would have problems with the work in the college preparatory courses.

A major objection to grading students according to the success of their response to the differentiated instruction given to them is potential complaints of the parents. Any number of systems, such as the following, can avoid this problem: numbers to indicate the track so that an $F$ indicated failure in the honors class rather than failure in spite of one's best efforts; colored report cards with the red, white, blue, and black designating various tracks; and so on.

Then, the final objection: a student from the slow class will quite likely be the valedictorian! Perhaps there *should* be one for each of the tracks—would there be anything wrong with that? For valedictorian of the entire population of a given grade, we can multiply into the averages a factor for the track in which the student took his courses—enter the factor of 5 for the honors, 4 for academic, and so on. Thus the overall valedictorian would be representative of intertrack competition, avoiding inaccurate grading of students in lower tracks in relationship to what they are really doing. Perhaps the best action would be to abolish the practice of identifying a valedictorian.

We are strongly influenced by the "normal-curve mentality." Success and failure must be balanced so that our students' test scores and course grades will fit a bell-shaped curve. In a heterogeneously grouped class, whether the grouping criterion is reading achievement or ability, the poor students are doomed to failure by such an attitude; at least, they are doomed to receiving very low grades. In schools with homogeneous grouping, the curve often is applied across classes so that whole classes are doomed to low grades or failure.

Such mentality substitutes statistics for instinctive judgment and common sense. Concern for being able to prove the validity of one's grading becomes more compelling than the concern for the students' achievement being accurately represented. The so-called averaging of grades is another expression of the same compulsion. The marks received within a marking period are averaged to derive the grade for that marking period; and all marking period grades are averaged to determine the grade for the year. What such grades designate is the average between ignorance and knowledge. Especially in subjects which are by their nature cumulative, with later learning depending on former learning, it seems illogical to pull down later grades, which demonstrate that learning has taken place by averaging in the earlier grades, which demonstrate that the student was still ignorant. A tenth-grade student received a 50 for the first marking period in biology. Even if he were to receive a 100 in each of the three remaining marking periods, the student's final grade could not be higher than 87.5. When this was challenged as illogical and unreasonable, given the cumulative nature of the curriculum, the teacher hid behind the excuse that "it is school policy to average the four marking period grades to derive the final grade." Would you think that a *B* would represent your achievement in a course if you had received an *F* as your first grade followed by three *A*s? Probably not.

This is not to say that teachers should be soft on grading. That occurred at the college level for a while but it benefited no one. Criteria still are needed; expectations still should be communicated; standards of quality still should be maintained. Showing students how to meet the standards and expectations while postponing the mark until they do meet them is not being soft. It is meeting one's responsibility with caring. In such caring there is great strength. Goethe said, "If you treat a man as he is, he will remain as he is. But if you treat a man as though he were what he ought to be and could be, then he will become what he ought to be and could be." Such expectation and caring should operate in the manner in which we tell students how well they are doing and in the help we give them so they can do better.

## SUMMARY

The recurring theme of this book is that the essence of good teaching is to show students how to do what you require them to do. This principle leads to students' success in accomplishing the objectives of the teaching. The principle assumes that the teacher not only expects that the students will be successful— hence, the "showing how"—but also cares whether or not they are.

Assessment procedures which are logical extensions of this principle and this attitude are positive in nature. They are consistent with the preceding learning experience both in content and process; thus, they are extensions of the learning experience. Results are used to further students' learning. The "normal-curve mentality" which accepts—yes, even demands—failure from some students has no place in such a program of instruction.

Checklist referred to on page 249:

### COMPREHENSION

    ——  1. Levels

    ——  2. Literal

    ——  3. Interpretive

    ——  4. Applied

    ——  5. Organizational patterns

    ——  6. Cause

    ——  7. Effect

    ——  8. Comparison

    ——  9. Contrast

    ——  10. Sequence

    ——  11. Listing

    ——  12. Guide

    ——  13. Structure

    ——  14. Sequencing

    ——  15. Statements

    ——  16. Questions

\* \* \* \* \* \*

## REACTION GUIDE

In Part I of this guide are ten quotations from the chapter. In Part II are seven expressions, statements, or sayings. Demonstrate your understanding of this chapter by matching quotations from Part I to the statements or sayings or expressions in Part II. Some quotations may fit several places. You may want to add more items to Part II. Compare your responses and your reasons with your colleagues.

### Part I

1. Too much time is spent on formal testing in our schools.
2. Teachers need not wait for data from tests to begin teaching.
3. Functional assessment . . . [is] . . . observing how [students] respond to guided instruction.
4. Assessment is misused if information is sought for its own sake and not to aid the student.
5. Be careful that you don't throw out the text or the kids because the two don't match.
6. Informal assessment is much like functional except that informal [is] separate from instruction.
7. The need . . . is to develop tests which reflect both the "what" and the "how" of instruction.
8. Independence is thought of in an absolute sense when really it is a relative state.
9. Review is self-assessment.
10. Expectation and caring should operate in the manner in which we tell students how well they are doing and in the help we give them so they can do better.

### Part II

_____ A. Solutions can cause problems too.
_____ B. Confusing trees with forests is a common failing.
_____ C. Purposes are obscured when ends and means are confused.
_____ D. If you're going to spend time, spend it on something important.
_____ E. Everyone needs help, in one form or another, on something or other.
_____ F. It is useful to know what you know you know.
_____ G. Meanwhile, . . .

## REINFORCING ACTIVITY

_Directions_: Listed below are ten pairs of words. Each pair is half an analogy. In the blanks to the right, write another pair of words to complete the analogy, drawing from whatever information or ideas you wish. For example, you might add "bound : free" to the pair in item 6; so you would have "aided recall is to unaided recall as bound is to free."

_____ 1. testing : teaching as

_____ 2. functional : informal as

_____ 3. assessment : evaluation as

_____ 4. marking : grading as

_____ 5. normal curve : standards as

_____ 6. aided recall : unaided recall as

_____ 7. guessing : knowing as

_____ 8. help : control as

_____ 9. wants : needs as

_____ 10. more : better as

\*   \*   \*   \*   \*   \*

## REFERENCE

BORMUTH, JOHN. "The close readability procedure." *Elementary English*, 45, no. 8 (1968), 429-36.

*appendix a*

# Reference Materials for the Chapters

## USING A PUSH FOR A BRAKE*

*Level I*

*Directions:* Check those items that you believe say what the author says. Sometimes exactly the same words will be used; sometimes they will not.

_____ 1. A lunar module doesn't fly, it falls.
_____ 2. A lunar module flies faster than a jet plane.
_____ 3. The force of a rocket engine pushes up as well as down.
_____ 4. The upward push from the LM's rocket engine acts as a brake.

*Level II*

*Directions:* Check those items that you feel represent ideas that the author presents. Be able to identify in the selection the information on which you based your choices.

_____ 1. A rocket engine will work where there is no air.
_____ 2. The only way to safely land a spacecraft is by using a rocket engine.
_____ 3. Rocket ships don't have brakes.
_____ 4. The only way to get to the moon is by falling there from outer space.

*See Chap. 3, p. 57.

*Directions:* Check those items you believe correctly use ideas in the reading selection. Be prepared to defend your choices.

_____ 1. Backing up is really going forward in reverse.

_____ 2. For every action there is an equal and opposite reaction.

_____ 3. Things are not always what they seem to be.

_____ 4. Problem solving makes use of the strange as well as the familiar.

## MATH—SOLVING WORD PROBLEMS*

*Problem:* Tom painted 12 shutters on his house. He used 1 1/5 quarts of paint for each shutter. How much paint did he use?

### Part I

*Directions:* Check all items that correctly identify information contained in the problem and what is to be found.

_____ 1. Tom owns a house.

_____ 2. The house has at least 12 shutters.

_____ 3. Tom used 1 1/5 quarts to paint all the shutters.

_____ 4. Tom used 1 1/5 quarts to paint each shutter.

_____ 5. What is to be found?

      _____ a. The size of the house.

      _____ b. How long it takes Tom to paint the shutters.

      _____ c. How many quarts of paint Tom used.

      _____ d. How much it costs to paint the shutters.

      _____ e. How much paint Tom used.

      _____ f. How much paint Tom bought.

### Part II

*Directions:* Check all items that correctly identify operations needed to solve the problem.

_____ 1. $12 \times 1 \, 1/5$

_____ 2. $1 \, 1/5 \times 12$

_____ 3. $6/5 \times 12$

_____ 4. $5/6 \times 12$

_____ 5. $12 \times 6/5$

*See Chap. 3, p. 59.

*Directions:* Check all items that identify mathematical concepts that are found in this problem.

_____ 1. In multiplication a product requires at least two factors.

_____ 2. Fractions and whole numbers can be multiplied together.

_____ 3. Multiplication of two factors gives a product.

_____ 4. Factors in multiplication can be whole numbers or fractions.

_____ 5. The commutative law operates in multiplication.

## ORGANIZATIONAL PATTERNS*

*Part I*

*Directions:* By direct statement or implication the author sets up specific relationships among events and ideas. Place a check on the numbered line before those you find in the selection. Be ready to give the supporting evidence for your choices.

_____ 1. noise / relevance                    _____

_____ 2. blaring records / printed truths      _____

_____ 3. sensitivity / productivity            _____

_____ 4. students' world / school world        _____

_____ 5. teachers' world / school world        _____

_____ 6. consumers / producers                 _____

_____ 7. personal / professional               _____

_____ 8. science / art                         _____

_____ 9. teaching / learning                   _____

_____ 10. reading / learning                   _____

*Part II*

*Directions:* Some of the relationships identified in Part I are cause/effect while others are comparison/contrast. On the line following each expressed relationship, write the name of the organizational pattern which characterizes that relationship. Be ready to give evidence to support your decision. Recall the previous guides we have used for each of these organizational patterns.

*Part III*

*Directions:* In light of the relationship between what you read and your own experiences, which of the following statements seem reasonable?

_____ 1. Students and teachers play school.

_____ 2. Relevance is related more to process than to content.

_____ 3. Formal education distorts participants' interests.

*See Chap. 4, p. 99.

_____ 4. Students' inner world is a source of enrichment for the teachers' professional world.

_____ 5. A higher correlation between teachers' personal and professional worlds would enrich education.

_____ 6. Communication ensures education.

### DILEMMA*

*Directions:* Check each of the following statements that you can support both with ideas from the poem and from your own ideas and experiences. Be ready to discuss this evidence with others in your group.

_____ 1. Purposes are clear when one lives by absolutes.

_____ 2. Uncertainties are the product of the mind, more imagined than real.

_____ 3. Though one searches for true meaning to life, one never finds it because one has only limited access to truth.

_____ 4. One is better off not thinking about life's purpose and meaning.

_____ 5. Even though you may never find the answer to your problems and/or questions, it is comforting to know that somewhere the answer does exist.

_____ 6. Life is unavailable to those who don't have the key.

## BALANCE OF POLITICAL POWER

### Structured Overview

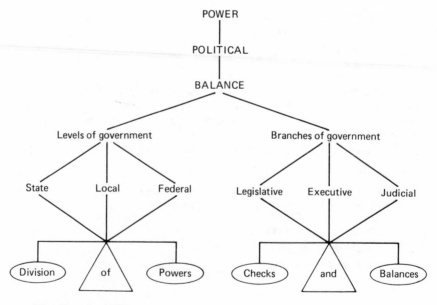

*See Chap. 5, p. 126.
**See Chap. 6, p. 152.

# WORLD EXPLORATION*†

## Structured Overview

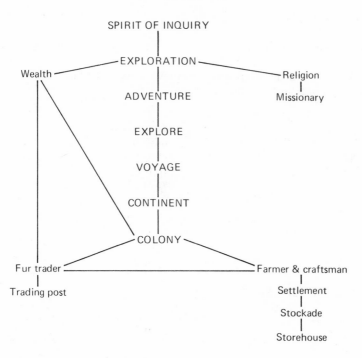

### Reinforcement Activity I

*Directions:* To solve the following puzzle, look at the definitions below. Think of a word which fits a definition and has the same number of letters as the number of spaces provided in the corresponding line. Write the word on the line. Do this for each definition. After you have completed the exercise, look at the first letter of each word. You will find that as you read down the letters spell one of your vocabulary words.

1. _ _ _ _ _ _ _ _   _ _ _ _ _
2. _ _ _ _ _ _ _ _ _
3. _ _ _ _ _ _ _
4. _ _ _ _ _ _ _ _
5. _ _ _ _ _ _ _ _ _ _

1. A machine that produces printed copies automatically.

2. The service and worship of God.

3. To search for new places and things.

*Courtesy of Michael Andrews
†See Chap. 6, p. 169.

4. A fence of tall poles set close together in the ground.

5. Town or city within a colony.


## Reinforcement Activity II

*Directions:* In each of the sets below three of the words are related. Circle the word that is *unrelated.* On the line at the top of the set, write the word or phrase that explains the relationship existing among the remaining three words. Some of the words are used in more than one set.

1. _____

   nation
   colony
   settlement
   wealth

2. _____

   stockade
   voyage
   adventure
   explore

3. _____

   fur trader
   trading posts
   storehouse
   religion

4. _____

   printing press
   print
   press
   missionary

5. _____

   missionary
   religion
   continent
   voyage

6. _____

   continent
   nation
   colony
   printing press

7. _____

   wealth
   fur trader
   trading post
   continent


## Reinforcement Activity III

*Directions:* Below you will find sets of two words each. In the first set the two words have a definite relationship. Under the first two words of each set is a single word and then a blank. Next to the blank are three words or phrases; on the blank write the one that relates to the single word as the first two do to each other.

1. continent / nation
   colony /_____(religion, explore, settlement)
2. religion / missionary
   trading post /_____ (printing press, voyage, fur trader)
3. adventure / voyage
   printing press /_____(storehouse, colony, print)
4. wealth / storehouse
   stockade /_____(colony, wealth, adventure)


## Reinforcement Activity IV

*Directions:* In column B there are definitions for the words listed in column A. Match each word and its definition. Place the letter of the definition on the line in front of the word it defines.


|        A              |        B              |
|-----------------------|-----------------------|

A

_____ 1. nation
_____ 2. stockade
_____ 3. colony
_____ 4. continent
_____ 5. voyage
_____ 6. missionary
_____ 7. religion
_____ 8. explore
_____ 9. fur trader
_____ 10. trading post
_____ 11. storehouse
_____ 12. settlement
_____ 13. printing press
_____ 14. adventure
_____ 15. wealth
_____ 16. print
_____ 17. press

B

A. a person who buys furs with other goods instead of money

B. places where Indians could trade their furs.

C. a place where goods are stored

D. a town or village within a colony

E. a machine that produces printed copies automatically

F. a country under one government

G. a fence of tall poles set together in the ground

H. a large region claimed and governed by another country

I. one of the seven great bodies of land on the globe

J. a trip or journey

K. priests or ministers sent to a country to teach a religion that is new to the people

L. the service and worship of God

M. to search for new places and things

N. an experience involving danger and unknown risks

O. all property that has money value

P. a copy made by forcing paper against an inked surface

Q. a machine by which a shape of a body is taken

## MOTION AND FORCE*†

### Structured Overview

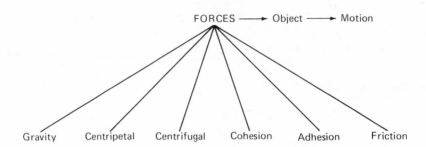

### Vocabulary Development Exercise I

*Directions:* To solve this puzzle, look at the definitions below. Think of a word which fits the definition, has the same number of letters as the number of spaces provided in the corresponding line, and has the given letter in the same position as indicated. Write the word on the line. The first one is done for you.

1.                f o r c e
2.      _ _ _ _ r _ _ _ _ _ _    _ _ _ _ _
3.  _ _ _ _ _ i _ _
4.      _ _ _ _ c _ _ _
5.  _ _ _ _ _ t _
6.  _ _ _ _ _ _ i _ _ _ _ _
7.            _ o _ _ _ _ _ _
8.  _ _ _ _ _ n

1. A push or a pull that produces or changes motion.
2. The force that pulls on an object being whirled around in a circle.
3. The force that holds particles of different kinds of substances together.
4. The smallest particle of a compound that has the properties of the compound.
5. A force that attracts all objects toward the center of the earth.
6. Balance.
7. The force that holds particles of the same kinds of substance together.
8. Movement.

*Courtesy of Greta Afton
†See Chap. 6, p. 169.

## Vocabulary Development Exercise II

*Directions:* In each of the sets below, three of the words are related. Circle the word that is *unrelated*. Compare your answers with those of the members of your group. Be prepared to explain the relationship existing among the remaining three words.

1. _____
   gravity
   opposite
   attraction
   force

2. _____
   friction
   center of gravity
   equilibrium
   equal

3. _____
   resistance
   friction
   movement
   energy

4. _____
   action
   reaction
   energy
   opposite

5. _____
   centripetal
   molecules
   centrifugal
   orbit

6. _____
   repel
   attraction
   adhesion
   cohesion

7. _____
   gravity
   weight
   equilibrium
   attraction

8. _____
   motion
   cohesion
   energy
   object

## Vocabulary Development Exercise—Analogies

*Directions:* Below you will find sets of two words each. In the first set the two words have a definite relationship. Under the first two words of each set is a single word and then a blank. Next to the blank are three words; write on the blank the one that relates to the single word as the first two do to each other.

1. force / movement
   gravity /_____(energy, weight, attraction)
2. electrical / energy
   centripetal /_____(force, attraction, forceful)
3. friction / resistance
   gravity /_____(reaction, cohesion, attraction)
4. lubrication / friction
   energy /_____(mass, resistance, inertia)

5. attraction / cohesion
   resistance /＿＿＿＿＿(adhesion, friction, oppose)
6. weight / mass
   cohesion /＿＿＿＿＿(cohere, adhesion, attraction)
7. inertia / mass
   speed /＿＿＿＿＿(weight, time, force)
8. weight / resistance
   mass /＿＿＿＿＿(gravity, inertia, force)
9. action / reaction
   centripetal /＿＿＿＿＿(attraction, centrifugal, energy)

## GREAT MOMENTS FROM OUR PAST*†

> When they tie the can to a
>     union man,
> Sit down! Sit down!
> When the speed-up comes,
>     just twiddle your thumbs,
> Sit down! Sit down!
> When the bosses won't talk,
>     don't take a walk,
> Sit down! Sit down!

This is a song that thousands of workers were singing in 1937. They were taking part in a new kind of strike—the sit-down. These workers would not leave the factories when they went on strike. Instead, they just sat down. They stayed inside the factories until the strike ended. Here is the story of the first one.

Workers at the General Motors factories in Michigan were angry. They earned only about $1,000 a year. And there was a speed-up on the assembly line. Workers had to work very quickly. It put them under a great strain.

Soon the workers began to join a new union. It was the United Auto Workers. But officers of General Motors would not meet with the union. In January, 1937, the union called a strike. The workers just put away their tools and sat down.

At night they slept on the floors of new cars. Food was passed to them through windows. They carefully guarded the company's property. And no drinking was allowed.

General Motors officers said the workers had no right to stay on company property. Union officers said they had a right to support their families.

General Motors shut off the heat in the factories. It was winter, and the men were cold. But they wouldn't leave. Police tried to rush into one factory. Workers drove them back. The police came back with tear gas. The workers drove them back again by turning fire hoses on them.

*Reprinted by permission from *Scholastic Scope.* © 1968 by Scholastic Magazines, Inc.
†See Chap. 7, p. 177.

The strike went on for weeks. Finally, a court ordered the strikers to leave the factories by three o'clock on February 3. The National Guard was called in to back up the court order. But the workers said they would not leave. Then Governor Frank Murphy ordered General Motors and the union to hold peace talks. Meanwhile, the workers got ready to fight.

Three o'clock came on February 3. But there was no battle. Governor Murphy would not order the National Guard to attack. He did not want any blood spilled. President Roosevelt also asked for a peaceful settlement. A week later the settlement came. General Motors agreed to bargain with the United Auto Workers. It agreed to do something about the speed-up. It was a big victory for the auto union, and for unions everywhere.

*appendix b*

# Sample Instructional Materials

The text has described and illustrated various instructional options by which content-area teachers can improve their students' vocabulary development, comprehension, and reasoning achievement. This section presents additional illustrations of these options. These guide materials emphasize vocabulary development and reinforcement, levels of comprehension, organizational patterns and reasoning, either singly or in combinations. They are taken from lessons actually taught to students at the grade levels indicated.

For each set of materials, the organizing idea is identified—as are the instructional options, the grade level at which the materials were used, and the subject area being taught. Note, once again, that the same processes are applicable across subject areas and grade levels within subjects. Note also—as illustrated in the social studies material—that the same general organizing idea can be used to teach specific social studies content at various grades or even at the same grade.

| | |
|---|---|
| *Area:* | Science (Your Skeleton) |
| *Grade:* | Fifth |
| *Organizing Idea:* | The body is protected by the skeleton and, in the skeleton, the vertebrae serve a special function. |
| *Instructional Option:* | Levels of comprehension |

### YOUR SKELETON*

*Level I*

*Directions:* Check the items you think say what the author says. Sometimes the exact words may be used. Other times other words may be used.

*Larry Maxwell

_____ 1. The skeleton does very important work.

_____ 2. The spinal column is made up of the vertebrae.

_____ 3. Making the body grow is the most important job of the skeleton.

_____ 4. The heart and lungs are protected by the ribs.

_____ 5. Without the vertebrae you could not stand up straight.

### Level II

*Directions:* Check the items that represent ideas you think the author means. Be ready to show why you did or did not check an item.

_____ 1. The skull and skeleton protect the inner parts of the body the way a helmet and pads protect the body of a football player.

_____ 2. Your body can't grow in height unless your skeleton does.

_____ 3. Man is a vertebrate.

_____ 4. All human beings have skeletons in their bodies.

_____ 5. Your ribs form a cage only when your heart or lungs are in danger.

### Level III

*Directions:* Check the items you think are correct. You may use the article to support your answer, but you do not have to.

_____ 1. You can't tell a book by its cover.

_____ 2. The correct tools are needed to do a job correctly.

_____ 3. You can't put a square peg in a round hole.

_____ 4. The more something is protected, the greater value it has.

_____ 5. You don't buy a hammer if you need a saw.

| | |
|---|---|
| *Area:* | Science (Weather) |
| *Grade:* | Sixth |
| *Organizing Idea:* | Temperature *changes* cause air movement which causes *change* in the weather. |
| *Instructional Options:* | Prediction |
| | Reasoning |

### MOVING WITHOUT TOUCHING*

Do you think it is possible to make the pointer move on the scale *without touching it*? Would it move up or down? Let's try some ideas and make some predictions. For each idea, predict if the pointer will go up, down, or not move. Use these marks: + for up; − for down; 0 for no movement.

_____ 1. Blow down on the paper.

*Reproduced by permission of TRICA Consultants, Inc., Homer N.Y., 1977.

\_\_\_\_ 2. Blow straight across the paper.

\_\_\_\_ 3. Blow up on the paper.

\_\_\_\_ 4. Pass a cardboard quickly across the top of the paper.

\_\_\_\_ 5 Pass a cardboard quickly across the bottom of the paper.

\_\_\_\_ 6. Bring a cardboard down quickly and stop it just above the paper.

\_\_\_\_ 7. Bring a cardboard up quickly and stop it just under the paper.

\_\_\_\_ 8. Place some ice just above the paper.

\_\_\_\_ 9. Place a lighted bulb just under the paper.

\_\_\_\_ 10. Other:

### IDEAS ABOUT AIR MOVEMENT

Here are some ideas which may have something to do with the movement of air. Check those that you can support from our experiments.

\_\_\_\_ 1. Warm air rises.

\_\_\_\_ 2. Cold air rises.

\_\_\_\_ 3. Warm air falls.

\_\_\_\_ 4. Cold air falls.

\_\_\_\_ 5. Warm air expands.

\_\_\_\_ 6. Cold air expands.

\_\_\_\_ 7. Warm air contracts.

\_\_\_\_ 8. Cold air contracts.

\_\_\_\_ 9. Warm air is heavier than cold air.

\_\_\_\_ 10. Cold air is heavier than warm air.

\_\_\_\_ 11. When air rises, other air moves in to take its place.

\_\_\_\_ 12. Air movements can cause changes in the weather.

Now look on page 200 in your text and see if the authors agree with you. Circle the numbers of all statements where they agree with you. Be ready to tell why you think they do.

| | |
|---|---|
| *Area:* | Science (General) |
| *Grade:* | Eighth |
| *Organizing Idea:* | Energy which is transferred from one object to another so that it is stored is called potential energy. |
| *Instructional Options:* | Reinforcement of meanings of words<br>Organizational patterns (cause/effect)* |

*Ibid.

## ENERGY*

*Directions:* Follow the directions given to you by your teacher.

| | | |
|---|---|---|
| _____ energy | _____ work | _____ mass |
| _____ meter | _____ time | _____ distance |
| _____ force | _____ lift | _____ position |
| _____ weight | _____ height | _____ influence |
| _____ input | _____ output | _____ gravity |
| _____ gravitational | _____ potential | _____ stored |
| _____ f X d | _____ gain | _____ loss |
| _____ transfer | _____ spinigig | _____ track |
| _____ sinkers | _____ thread | _____ meter |
| _____ centimeter | _____ axle | _____ equipment |
| _____ components | | _____ variables |

- - - - - - - - - - - - - - - - - - - - - - - - - - - - - - - - - - - -

SUPPLIER          RECEIVER          SYSTEM

## ENERGY

*Part I*

*Directions:* On each line below are two words or phrases which are separated by a slanted line (/). Check the numbered line if the first word or phrase stands for a *cause* of what the second word or phrase stands for (*effect*). The numbers in parentheses ( ) refer to the page and paragraph in your textbook where you should read to find the answer. The numbers in the brackets [ ] refer to figures which show answers. Discuss each item with others in your group. Remember: We don't know if you are right or wrong until we hear your reason.

_____ 1. slanting track / rolling spinigig (84-1) [8-1]

_____ 2. slanting track / rising sinker (84-1) [8-1]

_____ 3. rolling spinigig / rising sinker (84-1) [8-1]

_____ 4. work on spinigig / work on sinker (85-1) [8-1]

_____ 5. lifting spinigig to top of track / ability to do work (86-2)

_____ 6. lifting object / potential energy (86-3 & 86-4)

_____ 7. released energy / work is done (86-3)

_____ 8. exerting force / give potential energy (89-3)

_____ 9. loss of potential energy / gain of potential energy (91-1)

_____ 10. transfer of energy / gain and loss of energy (91-1 & 91-2)

_____ 11. energy / work (93-2)

_____ 12. influence of gravity / potential energy (93-3)

*Ibid.

**269**

*Directions:* Think of the work you did in *Part I* of this guide as well as the experiments you have done related to potential energy. Read each of the following statements and check each one you think you can support. Discuss your choices and share your evidence.

_____ 1. For every cause there is an effect.

_____ 2. Energy can be transferred but not lost.

_____ 3. Much work can be done just by using the laws of nature.

_____ 4. What goes up must come down.

_____ 5. Reading a book is like creating potential energy.

| | |
|---|---|
| *Area:* | Biology (Pregnancy and Birth) |
| *Grade:* | Tenth |
| *Organizing Idea:* | The satisfactory development of an embryo is dependent upon a series of events that fall into a correct order. |
| *Instructional Options:* | Reinforcement of definitions of words |
| | Organizational patterns (time order) |

## GROWTH AND DEVELOPMENT
## OF AN EMBRYO: I*

*Directions:* Listed below are the definitions of twelve words which relate to the growth and development of an embryo. Read the definition of each, then write the word in the space which corresponds with the number of the definitions. The first letter of the word is provided. The number of blank spaces indicates the number of letters in the word. You may wish to use your texts and also the notes you took from the discussion of the vocabulary related to this topic.

1. F _ _ _ _ _ _ _ _ _ _ _

2. P _ _ _ _ _ _ _ _

3. C _ _ _ D _ _ _ _ _ _

4. C _ _ _ D _ _ _ _ _ _ _ _ _ _ _

5. E _ _ _ _ _

6. F _ _ _ _

7. U _ _ _ _ _

8. E _ _ _ _ _ _

9. M _ _ _ _ _ _

10. E _ _ _ _ _ _

*Ibid.

11. I _ _ _ _ _ _ _ _ _ _ _
12. P _ _ _ _ _ _ _ _ _ _ _

1. Uniting of male and female sex cells.
2. Period of time during which a fetus is developed.
3. Development of many cells from one cell.
4. Production of different kinds of cells during cell division.
5. Developing organism within the female structure.
6. Developing embryo after the third month of pregnancy.
7. Muscular, pear-shaped structure in which the embryo and fetus grow and develop.
8. Outer layer of the three primary cell layers.
9. Middle layer of the three primary cell layers.
10. Innermost layer of the three primary cell layers.
11. Process of the egg becoming embedded in the uterine lining.
12. A female sex hormone which influences the lining of the uterus.

## GROWTH AND DEVELOPMENT
## OF AN EMBRYO: II

*Directions:* Here are twelve sets of sentences identifying events or actions which take place in the formation and growth of an embryo. For each set, identify the one event or action which precedes the others in the set. Circle the letter of your choice. Use your text as a source for making decisions. Numbers in parentheses give page numbers for where to look in the text.

When you have finished, the choices you have made should show the sequence of the actions and events by which an embryo is developed.

1. Which occurs first in the formation and growth of an embryo? (346)
   a. Pregnancy begins.
   b. Sperm meet and join with egg.
   c. Production of progesterone is continued.
2. Which occurs second in the formation and growth of an embryo? (346)
   a. Production of progesterone is continued.
   b. Pregnancy begins.
   c. Cell division begins.
   d. Lining of uterus is maintained.
3. Which occurs third in the formation and growth of an embryo? (346-48)
   a. Production of progesterone is continued.
   b. Embryo moves from oviduct to uterus.
   c. Lining of uterus is maintained.
   d. Cell division begins.
4. Which occurs fourth in the formation and growth of an embryo? (346-48)
   a. Embryo moves from oviduct to uterus.

b. Cell division begins.

c. Lining of uterus is maintained.

5. Which occurs fifth in the formation and growth of an embryo? (346-48)

a. Implantation occurs.

b. Embryo penetrates lining of uterus.

c. Cell division begins.

d. Embryo moves from oviduct to uterus.

6. Which occurs sixth in the formation and growth of an embryo? (346-48)

a. Embryo penetrates lining of uterus.

b. Embryo moves from oviduct to uterus.

c. Implantation occurs.

7. Which occurs seventh in the formation and growth of an embryo? (346-48)

a. Embryo penetrates lining of uterus.

b. Implantation occurs.

c. Cell differentiation begins.

d. The chorion is formed as an embryonic membrane.

8. Which occurs eighth in the formation and growth of an embryo? (346-48)

a. The chorion is formed as an embryonic membrane.

b. Cell differentiation begins.

c. Implantation occurs.

9. Which occurs ninth in the formation and growth of an embryo? (346-47)

a. Three primary cell layers form in the embryo.

b. Primary cell layers differentiate into all of the tissues, organs, and organ systems.

c. Cell differentiation begins.

d. The chorion is formed as an embryonic membrane.

10. Which occurs tenth in the formation and growth of an embryo? (346-47)

a. Cell differentiation begins.

b. Three primary cell layers form in the embryo.

c. The chorion is formed as an embryonic membrane.

11. Which occurs eleventh in the formation and growth of an embryo? (346-47)

a. Primary cell layers differentiate into all of the tissues, organs, and organ systems.

b. Cell differentiation begins.

c. Three primary cell layers form in the embryo.

12. Which occurs twelfth in the formation and growth of an embryo? (346-47)

a. Three primary cell layers form in the embryo.

b. Primary cell layers differentiate into all of the tissues, organs, and organ systems.

c. Cell differentiation begins.

## GROWTH AND DEVELOPMENT
## OF AN EMBRYO: III

Directions will be given orally by the teacher.

_____ 1. Single cells can become complex organisms.

_____ 2. There must be some death to produce life.

_____ 3. Organisms are influenced by their environments.

_____ 4. An organism needs more than life to live.

_____ 5. Both physical and emotional factors are involved in reproduction.

_____ 6. The development of any complex product requires the application of a fixed sequence of actions and conditions.

---

| | |
|---|---|
| *Area:* | Social Studies (Bicycle Safety) |
| *Grade:* | Fifth |
| *Organizing Idea:* | Visibility is part of safe bicycle riding and there are a variety of ways for cyclists to make themselves visible. |
| *Instructional Option:* | Levels of comprehension |

### BICYCLE SAFETY*

*Level I*

*Directions:* First read these statements. Now read the selection. As you read, put a check next to the statements that say what the author says. Sometimes the author's exact same words are used. Sometimes other words are used.

_____ 1. Night riding is not safe.

_____ 2. You should be able to be seen for a whole block.

_____ 3. Bikes must have lights on the back and the front.

_____ 4. Bicycle shops sell headlights and taillights.

_____ 5. You can strap a battery light to your leg.

_____ 6. White or yellow clothes show up in the dark.

_____ 7. Fluorescent material glows in the dark.

_____ 8. You can sew reflectors to your clothes.

*Level II*

*Directions:* Check the statements that tell what the author means. Be able to find information in the selection to show that you are right.

_____ 1. The safest time to ride a bicycle is in broad daylight.

_____ 2. Many countries have bicycle safety laws.

_____ 3. A bicycle shop is a good place to find safety equipment for your bicycle.

_____ 4. An important part of bicycle safety is lighting yourself and your bicycle.

_____ 5. Lights, reflectors, and white clothes will help others to see you at night.

*Marcia Kropf

*Level III*

*Directions:* Check the statements that use ideas from the reading selection and ideas from your own experiences. Be able to support your answers.

_____ 1. The life you save could be your own.

_____ 2. Better safe than sorry.

_____ 3. Only fools do not observe the rules.

_____ 4. A stitch in time saves nine.

_____ 5. Wear white at night; it may brighten your life.

---

| | |
|---|---|
| *Area:* | Social Studies (American Factory System) |
| *Grade:* | Fifth |
| *Organizing Idea:* | The development of the American factory system created undesirable social and environmental consequences. |
| *Instructional Option:* | Levels of comprehension |

## AMERICAN FACTORY SYSTEM*

*Level I*

*Directions:* Read the following statements carefully. Check the statements that say what the author says. Some statements use the same words. Others use similar words.

_____ 1. Factories made the air and water dirty.

_____ 2. As the number of factories increased, pollution also increased.

_____ 3. Soot rose from factory smokestacks.

_____ 4. Factory owners did not think about cleaning up the air and water.

_____ 5. People complained of sore eyes and bad smells.

_____ 6. Unskilled workers had difficulty finding jobs.

_____ 7. Rats lived in the shabby neighborhoods.

_____ 8. Living conditions in cities caused sickness and unhappiness in families.

_____ 9. Air and water grew dangerously dirty.

*Level II*

*Directions:* Read the following statements carefully. Check those statements you feel tell what the author means. Be prepared to support your choices with information from the reading selection.

_____ 1. Pollution led to unhealthy living conditions.

_____ 2. Cities became overpopulated with unskilled workers.

*Donna Yackel

_____ 3. Cities became bad places to raise a family.

_____ 4. Unskilled workers suffered most from the unfavorable living conditions in cities.

_____ 5. The once good quality of water and air declined.

### Level III

*Directions:* Read the following statements. Using ideas from the reading selection and things you know about the factory system, check those statements you can support.

_____ 1. Progress is sometimes its own worst enemy.

_____ 2. Good intentions sometimes bring poor results.

_____ 3. Scientific advance has taken its toll on nature.

_____ 4. Yesterday's progress is today's problem.

_____ 5. Industry has made its profit at the expense of our environment.

_____ 6. At one time, a city was a pleasant place to live.

| | |
|---|---|
| *Area:* | Social Studies (Survival) |
| *Grade:* | Sixth |
| *Organizing Idea:* | *Survival* requires food, shelter, and clothing; these basic needs can be obtained by money, goods, and services. |
| *Instructional Option:* | Levels of comprehension |

### SURVIVAL*

### Level I

*Directions:* Check the statements which say what the author says in the story. The statements may use the same words as the author. They may use different words but say the same thing. Be ready to give reasons for your choices. Page numbers of where to look in your text are given in parentheses.

_____ 1. There are many differences among people. (1)

_____ 2. All people have the wish to survive. (2)

_____ 3. All people need food, clothing, and shelter. (2)

_____ 4. Different people eat different food. (3)

_____ 5. Different people wear different clothing. (4)

_____ 6. Different people have different kinds of shelter. (5)

_____ 7. Some people use money to buy what they need. (6 and 7)

_____ 8. Some people use goods to *barter* for what they need. (6 and 8)

_____ 9. Some people meet their needs by giving a service to other people. (6 and 9)

_____ 10. People have differences but they meet their needs the same way. (10)

*Reproduced by permission of TRICA Consultants, Inc., Homer, N.Y. 1977.

*Directions:* Check the statements which give ideas you can find in the story. Be ready to give reasons for your choices.

     1. Even if you wear very nice clothes, you won't live long if you don't eat.

\_\_\_\_ 2. A person does not have to have money to survive.

\_\_\_\_ 3. A little seems like a lot to someone who has nothing.

\_\_\_\_ 4. A person with an extra piece of clothing always can eat.

\_\_\_\_ 5. Money, goods, and services can buy each other or can buy food, clothing, or shelter.

*Level III*

*Directions:* Check the statements which give ideas you find in the story and in your own experiences. Be ready to give reasons for your choices.

\_\_\_\_ 1. You have to give something to get something.

\_\_\_\_ 2. What people want is not always what they need.

\_\_\_\_ 3. Life would be boring if everyone and everything were the same.

\_\_\_\_ 4. People who have should help people who have not.

| | |
|---|---|
| *Area:* | Social Studies (Trojan War) |
| *Grade:* | Sixth |
| *Organizing Idea:* | Even though *conflict* takes many forms, there is a similarity in principle with respect to causes, effects, and evidence. |
| *Instructional Option:* | Modified organizational pattern (cause/effect) |

**CONFLICT***

*Part IA*

*Directions:* Check the words or names which identify people who participated in the conflict. The numbers in the parentheses tell you where to look in your text. The first number is the page; the second is the column. Be ready to give evidence to support your answers.

\_\_\_\_ 1. Europe (142, 2)

\_\_\_\_ 2. Asia (142, 2)

\_\_\_\_ 3. Troy (142, 2)

\_\_\_\_ 4. Archaeologists (142, 2)

*Ibid.

_____ 5. Aegean world (143, 1)

_____ 6. Mycenae (143, 1)

_____ 7. Greece (143, 1)

_____ 8. Agamemnon (143, 1)

_____ 9. Homer (143, 1)

_____ 10. Schliemann (143, 2)

_____ 11. Paris (144, 1)

_____ 12. Helen (144, 1)

### Part IB

*Directions:* Here are twelve sets of words or phrases. Each set shows a separation between words and/or phrases. Each set represents a possible cause/effect relationship expressed or implied by the author. Place a check on the list before each cause/effect relationship you can support from the text in some way. Be ready to identify your evidence. The numbers in parentheses give you an idea of where to look in the text.

_____ 1. Conquered and destroyed / built again (142, 2)

_____ 2. Troy became trade center /Troy became rich and powerful (142, 2)

_____ 3. Riches and power / making of tools and weapons (142, 2 & 143, 1)

_____ 4. Passing time / developing civilization (143, 1)

_____ 5. Greeks won / Troy destroyed (143, 1)

_____ 6. No proof / disbelief (143, 2)

_____ 7. Dream / discovery (143, 3)

_____ 8. Discovery / knowledge (143, 2)

_____ 9. Love / war (144, 1)

_____ 10. Strength / victory (144, 1)

_____ 11. Trickery / defeat (144, 2 & 145, 1)

_____ 12. Freedom / homecoming (145, 1 & 145, 2)

### Part II

*Directions:* Check the statements which you can support from the text and/or from your own ideas and experiences. Be ready to give the reasons for your choices.

_____ 1. When one group improves itself, another group may suffer.

_____ 2. The reasons for conflict almost never change, and nor does the evidence that it took place.

_____ 3. It is easier to destroy than to build.

_____ 4. Smart weakness can defeat dumb strength.

_____ 5. People seem not to learn from history.

| *Area:* | Social Studies (Siege of Vicksburg) |
|---|---|
| *Grade:* | Eighth |
| *Organizing Idea:* | Even though *conflict* takes many forms, there is a similarity in principle with respect to causes, effects, and evidence. |
| *Instructional Option:* | Modified organizational pattern (cause/effect) |

### CONFLICT*

*Part I*

*Directions:* Here is a list of words or phrases or clauses that have something to do with the Civil War, particularly the Siege of Vicksburg. On each numbered line place the letter(s) of the following words which tell how the words or phrases or clauses relate to *conflict*. Your teacher will explain the numbers in parentheses.

A. Type or Form        B  Participant        C. Cause        D. Effect

_____ 1. General Grant. (1, 1)

_____ 2. Vicksburg was a great, fortified stronghold. (1, 1)

_____ 3. Grant decided on a risky scheme. (1, 2)

_____ 4. Grant's men crossed the river so that they could fight on dry land. (1, 2)

_____ 5. The Union navy. (1, 3)

_____ 6. Grierson destroyed railroad supply lines. (1, 5)

_____ 7. Sherman attacked above Vicksburg. (1, 6)

_____ 8. The union troops captured, looted, and burned Jackson. (1, 7 & 2, 8)

_____ 9. Pemberton's army was trapped in Vicksburg. (2, 9)

_____ 10. Grant decided on a siege of Vicksburg. (2, 10)

_____ 11. Civilians suffered in the siege. (2, 11)

_____ 12. The fortifications of Vicksburg were too strong to destroy. (2, 12)

_____ 13. Vicksburg surrendered to Grant on July 4, 1863. (2, 13)

_____ 14. The North had won an important victory at Vicksburg. (2, 14)

*Part II*

Directions for this material will be given to you orally.

_____ 1. Conflict makes use of many kinds of weapons. (List your evidence.)

_____ 2. People fight harder when they think they are right than when they think they are wrong. (List your evidence.)

*Ibid.

_____ 3. When one group improves itself, other groups usually suffer. (List your evidence.)

_____ 4. It is easier to destroy than to build. (List your evidence.)

_____ 5. The real causes of conflict are the same now as they have been for many centuries. (List your evidence.)

_____ 6. War brings both advancement and destruction. (List your evidence.)

| | |
|---|---|
| *Area:* | History (United States) |
| *Grade:* | Tenth |
| *Organizing Idea:* | Even though *conflict* takes many forms, there is a similarity in principle with respect to causes, effects, and evidence. |
| *Instructional Option:* | Modified organizational patterns (cause/effect) |

## PERSPECTIVE ON CONFLICT*

### Part I

*Directions:* Listed below are five words, each preceded by a letter. Following those words are twenty-six numbered lines, each containing words or phrases or clauses. On each numbered line place the letter(s) of the word(s) that tell how the words or phrases or clauses are related to conflict. The numbers in parentheses tell you where to look in your text. The first is the page number; the second is the column.

A. Types    B. Forms    C. Participants    D. Causes    E. Effects

_____ 1. Secession (334, 2)

_____ 2. Constitutional amendment (334, 2)

_____ 3. Lincoln sent relief expedition to Fort Sumter (334, 2)

_____ 4. Wrestling (334, 2)

_____ 5. Davis authorized military forces to act (334, 2)

_____ 6. Little more talk (335, 1)

_____ 7. Outbreak of patriotism (335, 1)

_____ 8. Suppress rebellion (335, 1)

_____ 9. Similar wave of feeling in the South (335, 1)

_____ 10. Border states (335, 1 & 340, 2)

_____ 11. The last of old wars and the first of the new (335, 1)

_____ 12. Chivalrous respect for the enemy (335, 1)

_____ 13. Telegraph, observation balloons, ironclad ships, trenches (338, 2)

_____ 14. Civilians and soldiers (338, 2)

*Ibid.

_____ 15. Scorched Earth Policy (338, 2)

_____ 16. Blockade of Southern ports (339, 2)

_____ 17. Southern exports and imports shrank (339, 2)

_____ 18. Merrimac, Virginia (339, 2), and Monitor (340, 1)

_____ 19. Preyed on Northern shipping (340, 1)

_____ 20. Merchant Marine suffered a blow (340, 1)

_____ 21. Fall of Fort Henry (341, 1) and capture of New Orleans (341, 2)

_____ 22. Grant's guerrilla warfare (341, 2 & 343, 1)

_____ 23. Confederacy split in two (343, 2)

_____ 24. Strategies of Lee and Jackson (343, 2)

_____ 25. Confederate failures at Antietam and Gettysburg (343, 2)

_____ 26. Their cause was lost (343, 2)

### Part II

*Directions:* Respond to each of the following statements as indicated in the teacher's oral instructions.

_____ 1. Man's inventiveness is stimulated by the need for destruction.

_____ 2. Whereas right is usually might, might may not be right.

_____ 3. The weapons of conflict are limited.

_____ 4. It is easier to destroy than to build.

_____ 5. The least obvious forms of conflict may be the most dangerous and long-lasting.

_____ 6. Conflict is avoided by compromise and resolved by destruction.

_____ 7. When one group improves itself, another group usually suffers.

_____ 8. The real causes of conflict remain essentially the same, even though the types, forms, and participants may change.

_____ 9. Other:

| | |
|---|---|
| *Area:* | World History (World War I) |
| *Grade:* | Tenth |
| *Organizing Idea:* | Even though *conflict* takes many forms, there is a similarity in principle with respect to causes, effects, and evidence. |
| *Instructional Options:* | Vocabulary presentation<br>Reinforcement of meanings<br>Organizational pattern (cause/effect) |

## A CHECKLIST ON CONFLICT*

*Directions:* Here are two lists of words, one labeled "General" and the other labeled "Specific." Place a check on the line before all words that you can relate in some way to *conflict.* Be ready to give general and specific reasons for your choices.

*Ibid.

| *General* | *Specific* |
|-----------|------------|
| —— nations | —— African colonies |
| —— people | —— Asian colonies |
| —— anger | —— Germany |
| —— military | —— France |
| —— agreement | —— Morocco |
| —— goods | —— imperialism |
| —— alliance | —— English |
| —— territory | —— Russia |
| —— trade | —— powder keg |
| —— money | —— nationalism |
| —— seize | —— militarism |
| —— raw material | —— minority groups |
| —— physical | —— Austria-Hungary |
| —— protect | —— Turkey |
| —— customs | —— choosing sides |
| —— religious | —— Central Powers |
| —— independence | —— Allied Powers |
| —— borders | —— system of alliances |
| —— political | —— Archduke Francis Ferdinand |
| —— assassination | |
| —— rival | |
| —— murder | |
| —— threaten | |
| —— support | |
| —— economic | |

## A STORY OF CONFLICT

*Part I*

*Directions:* If the first word or phrase on a line stands for a cause of the second word or phrase, place a check on the numbered line. Be ready to identify your supporting evidence. The numbers refer to the paragraphs in which the related information can be found.

—— 1. hidden anger / tension (1)

—— 2. fear of common enemy / nations joining forces (1)

—— 3. desire for same territory / anger with competition (2)

—— 4. frustrated wishes / readiness for war (2)

—— 5. desire to expand / imperialism (2 & 3)

—— 6. pride in accomplishments / spirit of nationalism (3)

—— 7. need for protection / spirit of militarism (3)

_____ 8. desire for independence / spirit of nationalism (4)

_____ 9. recovery of lost territory / plotting restoration (5)

_____ 10. different interest in Balkans / common concern over Balkans (6)

_____ 11. assassinated royalty / excuse for war (8 & 9)

_____ 12. readiness for war / probability of war (9 & 10)

### Part II

Directions for this material will be given to you orally.

_____ 1. Conflict makes use of many kinds of weapons. (List your evidence.)

_____ 2. People fight harder when they think they are right than when they think they are wrong. (List your evidence.)

_____ 3. When one group improves itself, other groups usually suffer. (List your evidence.)

_____ 4. It is easier to destroy than to build. (List your evidence.)

_____ 5. The real causes of conflict are the same now as they have been for many centuries. (List your evidence.)

_____ 6. Conflict brings both advancement and destruction. (List your evidence.)

## IDEAS ABOUT CONFLICT

*Directions:* Here are six sets of words related to your study of *conflict* and World War I. There are five words in each set. For each set, cross out one word and tell how the remaining four words fit together. There may be more than one combination.

1. _____

money
trade
goods
material
rival

4. _____

anger
people
alliance
seize
support

2. _____

economic
political
religious
physical
personal

5. _____

nationalism
imperialism
militarism
freedom
slavery

3. _____

protect
agreement
customs
territory
independence

6. _____

causes
effects
participants
actions
conditions

| | |
|---|---|
| *Area:* | American History (Post Civil War Industrialization) |
| *Grade:* | Eleventh |
| *Organizing Idea:* | Nostalgia has an effect on history. |
| *Instructional Option:* | Organizational pattern (comparison/contrast) |

### INDUSTRIALIZATION*

#### Part I

*Directions:* Listed below are sets of comparisons. Check each set you can find in the *Newsweek* article. This exercise can be done while you are reading the article or after you have read the article. Some of these comparisons are at the literal, some at the interpretive level.

_____ 1. nostalgia / tranquility
_____ 2. dissent / photography, statistics
_____ 3. urban life / rural life
_____ 4. thoroughness / skimming
_____ 5. bad old days / good new days
_____ 6. history / nostalgia
_____ 7. animals / pollution
_____ 8. transportation / progress
_____ 9. survival / Guilded Age
_____ 10. loneliness / crowding
_____ 11. religion / alcohol
_____ 12. abuse of drugs / human conflicts
_____ 13. children, youth / drugs, labor
_____ 14. education / medicine
_____ 15. hope for the future / content with the present / reminiscent of the past
_____ 16. cleanliness / health

#### Part II

*Directions:* Listed below are several statements which may or may not reflect applications of the comparisons you identified in Part I of this guide. Write the number(s) of comparisons you selected from Part I on the lettered line before those items to which you believe they apply. Some lines may have more than one number; others may have none. Some statements are at the interpretive level, some are at the applied level of comprehension.

_____ 1. Reflection tends to minimize the errors of the past.
_____ 2. Pictures speak louder than words.

*Catherine A. Burgess

_____ 3. The worst loneliness is the loneliness in a crowd.

_____ 4. We've come a long way, baby!

_____ 5. Things are never as bad as they seem.

_____ 6. We have overcome!

_____ 7. A byproduct of progress is chaos.

_____ 8. Cleanliness is next to godliness.

_____ 9. There is hope for the future.

### Part III

*Directions:* This guide has as its purpose the development of a comparison and contrast of the life in post Civil War America and the America of today (contemporary America). These two Americas are in many ways quite different, but are also in some ways the same. Identify the items in the following list as those facets of life that would be found in post Civil War America (*A*), contemporary America (*B*), or could be found in both (*A, B*). Indicate your response by placing the letter or letters referred to above before the appropriate statements.

_____ 1. child labor

_____ 2. pollution

_____ 3. traffic congestion

_____ 4. drug control

_____ 5. photography

_____ 6. indoor plumbing

_____ 7. crowded dwellings

_____ 8. dangers of alcohol

_____ 9. medical education guidelines ·

_____ 10. nostalgia over the past

| | |
|---|---|
| *Area:* | Mathematics (Word Problems) |
| *Grade:* | Sixth |
| *Organizing Idea:* | Distance, time, and rate are used in various combinations of two in order to explain the third. |
| *Instructional Option:* | Levels of comprehension |

### WORD PROBLEMS*

Joe has been traveling on a passenger train for 18 hours. The average speed of the train is 56 miles per hour. How many miles has Joe traveled on the train?

### Part I

Check all items which correctly identify information contained in the problem and what is to be found.

*Reproduced by permission of TRICA Consultants, Inc., Homer, N.Y., 1977.

_____ 1. Joe likes to ride trains.

_____ 2. The train traveled 56 miles each hour.

_____ 3. The train averaged 56 miles each hour.

_____ 4. The train traveled 56 miles.

_____ 5. Joe traveled 18 hours each mile.

What is to be found?

_____ a. The number of cars in the train.

_____ b. The average speed of the train.

_____ c. How much it cost Joe to ride on the train.

_____ d. How far Joe has traveled.

_____ e. How many miles Joe has traveled.

_____ f. How many miles Joe has traveled during his eighteen hours on the train.

### Part II

Check all items which correctly identify operations needed to solve the problem.

_____ 1. One train multiplied by 56 hours.

_____ 2. Eighteen hours multiplied by 56 miles per hour.

_____ 3. Fifty-six miles per hour multiplied by 18 hours.

_____ 4. One person multiplied by 18 hours.

$$-or-$$

_____ 5. Trains times miles per hour.

_____ 6. Miles per hour times number of people.

_____ 7. Miles per hour times hours.

_____ 8. Hours times miles per hour.

_____ 9. Rate times time.

_____ 10. Time times rate.

$$-or-$$

_____ 11. $18 \times 1$

_____ 12. $56 \times 18$

_____ 13. $1 \times 56$

_____ 14. $56 \times 1$

_____ 15. $18 \times 56$

### Part III

Check all items which identify ideas about mathematics found in this problem.

_____ 1. Multiplication of two factors gives a product.

_____ 2. In multiplication a product requires at least two factors.

_____ 3. Multiplication is like repeated addition.

_____ 4. The commutative law operates in multiplication.

_____ 5. Rate of travel times time of travel equals distance traveled.

Joanne ran a quarter of a mile in one minute. A mile contains 5,280 feet. How many feet did she run?

*Part I*

Check all items that correctly identify information contained in the problem and what is to be found.

_____ 1. Joanne ran 5,280 feet.

_____ 2. There are 5,280 feet in a mile.

_____ 3. One minute contains 5,280 feet.

_____ 4. Joanne ran 1/4 of a mile.

_____ 5. Joanne ran more than a mile.

_____ 6. Joanne ran less than a mile.

_____ 7. Joanne's feet hurt.

What is to be found?

_____ a. The number of feet in a mile.

_____ b. The distance Joanne ran.

_____ c. The number of feet Joanne ran.

_____ d. The number of feet Joanne must run to make a mile.

_____ e. The number of feet in a quarter of a mile.

*Part II*

Check all items which correctly identify operations that could be used to solve the problem.

_____ 1. 5,280 feet multiplied by 1/4

_____ 2. 5,280 feet multiplied by 4

_____ 3. 5,280 feet divided by 4

_____ 4. One minute multiplied by 4

_____ 5. .25 multiplied by 5,280

_____ 6. 4 divided by 5,280

—or—

_____ 1. $5,280 \times .25$

_____ 2. $1/4 \times 5,280$

_____ 3. $4 \times 5,280$

_____ 4. $5,280 \div 4$

_____ 5. $4 \div 5,280$

Check all items which identify ideas about mathematics suggested by this problem.

_____ 1. You can use different mathematical operations to solve the same problem.

_____ 2. Parts of a whole can be expressed either as fractions or decimals.

_____ 3. 1/4 = .25

_____ 4. Multiplying by 1/4 gives the same answer as dividing by 4.

_____ 5. Division "undoes" multiplication.

---

| | |
|---|---|
| *Area:* | Mathematics (Word Problems) |
| *Grade:* | Eighth |
| *Organizing Idea:* | The area of multiple rectangular regions can be computed by merely combining the areas of single regions that make up the whole. |
| *Instructional Option:* | Levels of comprehension |

### WORD PROBLEMS—RECTANGULAR REGIONS*

*Problem:* Lorenzo and Maria are buying sod for their backyard and connecting dog run. Here is a sketch of the area.

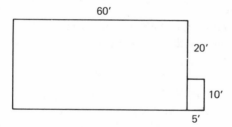

If sod costs $.75 a square foot, how much will it cost to cover the area with sod?

*Part I*

Check all the items which correctly identify information contained in the problem and what is to be found.

_____ 1. Lorenzo and Maria are improving their property.

*Ibid.

_____ 2. Their dog run is square.

_____ 3. The dog run is smaller than the yard.

_____ 4. The back yard is rectangular.

_____ 5. The back yard is square.

_____ 6. Lorenzo and Maria have a dog.

_____ 7. A square foot of sod costs less than a dollar.

What is to be found?

_____ a. The cost of the sod for the dog run.

_____ b. The cost of the sod for the yard.

_____ c. The total cost of the sod.

_____ d. The cost of each square foot of sod.

_____ e. The size of the house.

_____ f. The color of the house.

_____ g. The area of the dog run.

_____ h. The area of the yard.

_____ i. The length of fence around the dog run.

*Part II*

Check the following items which identify operations needed to solve this problem.

_____ 1. Length multiplied by width.

_____ 2. Length multiplied by width added to length multiplied by width.

_____ 3. Square feet multiplied by cost per square foot.

_____ 4. Area times cost.

_____ 5. Length times width plus length times width times cost.

_____ 6. Length times width times cost plus length times width times cost.

_____ 7. $1 \times w = A$

_____ 8. $1 \times w \times \$ = cost$

_____ 9. $(30 \times 60 \times \$.75) + (5 \times 10 \times \$.75) =$

_____ 10. $(30 \times 60) + (10 \times 5) \times \$.75 =$

*Part III*

Check the following statements that express ideas about mathematics found in your problem.

_____ 1. Areas of quadrilaterals can be found by multiplication.

_____ 2. Areas of rectangular regions can be found by multiplication and addition.

_____ 3. Areas of quadrilaterals can be found by addition.

_____ 4. Finding the cost of covering an area is a two-step process.

_____ 5. Other.

*Area:* Literature ("old age sticks" by e.e. cummings)
*Grade:* Seventh
*Organizing Idea:* *Conflict* between old age and youth is constant.
*Instructional Option:* Organizational pattern (comparison/contrast)

### THIS POEM SAYS . . . *

*Part I*

*Directions:* Listed below are pairs of comparisons which were either stated by the author or could be interpreted as something the author meant. Check each pair that you can find in the poem.

____ 1. Old age says *no* / youth says *yes.*
____ 2. Old age advises / youth rebels.
____ 3. Old age puts up stop signs / youth yanks them down.
____ 4. Old age forbids / youth is daring.
____ 5. Old age grumbles / youth laughs and sings.
____ 6. Youth is experimental / old age has experience.
____ 7. Old age is independent / youth is still dependent.
____ 8. Youth ignores / youth continues to grow older.

*Part II*

*Directions:* Listed below are several statements which you may or may not be able to apply to the comparisons you chose from Part I of this guide. Write the numbers of comparisons you selected from Part I on the line before the lettered statement to which you believe they apply. You may use one number more than once.

____ 1. Eventually every young person grows old.
____ 2. Being young often means being carefree and careless.
____ 3. With age comes wisdom, patience, and understanding.
____ 4. Good advice is rejected until needed.
____ 5. The generation gap is often simply a communication gap.
____ 6. The process of growing old and assuming responsibilities is often painful.
____ 7. As we grow older, we begin to understand and accept the opinions of those responsible for our existence.
____ 8. Being young means living for the moment with no thought of tomorrow.
____ 9. The battle between generations will continue to be waged.

*Agnes Jeanette Willhite

| | |
|---|---|
| *Area:* | Literature (Poetry Unit) |
| *Grade:* | Eighth |
| *Organizing Idea:* | *Time* has both quantitative and qualitative dimensions and every person experiences both dimensions differently. |
| *Instructional Options:* | Presentation of definitions of words |
| | Modified levels of comprehension |
| | Reasoning |

### TIME*

*Directions:* Each of the following statements may present ideas related to time. Place a check (√) on the first line if you agree with the statement. Be ready to discuss reasons for your choice.

___ ___ 1. Nothing is slower than time wished away; nothing is faster than time held dear.

___ ___ 2. People work for today and dream for tomorrow.

___ ___ 3. Time is a fence to be climbed, a chain to be broken.

___ ___ 4. What you do with your life is more important than how long you live.

___ ___ 5. Different people experience the same thing differently.

### POEM: "THE SPRINTERS" BY LEE MURCHISON. PAGE 273 IN *COUNTERPOINT IN LITERATURE,* SCOTT, FORESMAN, 1967

Can man beat time? Will time always be faster? What feelings come as people struggle against time?

1. Before you read this poem, note the definitions of these words below.
   pummeling: pounding rapidly
   pistoning: pushing with great force
   outpace: to move faster than someone or something else
   mock: to make fun of something or someone

2. One person in the group should read the poem aloud to the rest of the group. They may listen and follow along or just listen.

3. Some of the items listed below refer to runners; others refer to watchers; others, to time. Decide to which category each item belongs, then place the letter of that item under the heading where it best belongs.

   a. gun explodes them      d. try to smash

   b. fly in time's face      e. the beat that runs

   c. the ticking glass      f. the beat that streaks away

*Reproduced by permission of TRICA Consultants, Inc., Homer, New York, 1977.

g. tireless                          j. grace-driven stride
h. pound the stands                  k. mocks the clock
i. loving him                        l. bands which lock us in

*RUNNERS*                  *TIME*                  *WATCHERS*

_____                _____                _____
_____                _____                _____
_____                _____                _____
_____                _____                _____
_____                _____                _____

4. Now check those ideas you think the poem supports. Be ready to give reasons for your answers.

    _____ a. Time is a barrier to be broken.
    _____ b. No matter how fast man moves, time is always faster.
    _____ c. People love winners more than losers.
    _____ d. Records are made to be broken.
    _____ e. A kind of violence and wildness is part of any attempts to do the impossible.

5. Look again at the set of statements about time that you discussed before reading this poem. Place an *x* on the second line before each statement if you think the author of your poem would agree with it.

**POEM: "EIGHT O'CLOCK" BY A. E. HOUSEMAN.
IN *COUNTERPOINT IN LITERATURE,*
SCOTT, FORESMAN, 1967.**

How does a man feel when his last hour on earth is over? What is the mood as the last hour passes by? Read this poem to experience one poet's description.

1. Before you read this poem, note the definitions of these words:
   sprinkle: to throw down
   strapped: to be bound tightly
   noosed: to have a rope around one's neck
   nighing: coming close to something or someone
2. One person in the group should read the poem aloud to the rest of the group. They may listen and follow along or just listen.
3. Some of the items below refer to information given in the poem. Others refer to information or ideas the author *implies* (that is, he means it but doesn't say it). Decide to which category each item belongs and place its letter under the correct heading below. Some *may not* belong to either.

   a. The clock strikes every quarter hour.

b. The clock strikes all four quarters before striking the hour.

c. The man stood listening to the clock strike.

d. A man was cursed by his luck.

e. A man was facing his last hour on earth.

f. A man was hanged.

g. A man was tied and had a rope around his neck.

h. A man was looking forward to his death.

i. The whole town was aware of the execution.

*STATED*                                    *IMPLIED*

———————                          ———————
———————                          ———————
———————                          ———————
———————                          ———————
———————                          ———————

4. Now check the following ideas that you think this poem supports. Be ready to give reasons for your answers.

_____ a. Time gives to those who live and takes from those who die.

_____ b. Man can take time away from other men but can never give it.

_____ c. No matter how it arrives, the last moment of time will come.

_____ d. People do not always feel sorry for what they have done.

_____ e. Time cannot be stopped.

5. Look again at the set of statements about time that you discussed before reading this poem. Place an *x* on the second line before each statement if you think the author of your poem would agree with it.

**POEM: "THE DAY" BY THEODORE SPENCER.**
**ON PAGE 270**
**OF** *COUNTERPOINT IN LITERATURE,*
**SCOTT, FORESMAN, 1967.**

Does time remain the same? Read this poem and see what the poet seems to think.

1. Before you read this poem, note the definitions of words below.
   shrank: past tense of shrink; to become smaller
   limped: past tense of limp; to walk favoring one leg

2. One person in the group should read the poem aloud to the rest of the group. They may listen and follow along or just listen.

3. After the poem has been read, show the comparisons the author made by drawing connecting lines among the three columns of words listed below:

| day | minute | children |
| day | week | young men |
| day | hour | old men |
| day | year | dead men |
| day | month | lovers |
| day | forever | boys |

4. Now check the following ideas you think this poem supports. Be ready to give reasons for your answers.

____ a. Young time is short.

____ b. Old time is fast.

____ c. No time is endless.

____ d. What people actually experience is the opposite of what you might think they should.

____ e. The longer life is, the shorter time seems to be.

____ f. Time affects how people move.

5. Look again at the set of statements about time that you discussed before reading this poem. Place an $x$ on the second line before each statement if you think the author of your poem would agree with it.

| | |
|---|---|
| *Area:* | Literature ("The People, Yes") |
| *Grade:* | Tenth |
| *Organizing Idea:* | The coming into maturity involves the human quest for knowledge: first of the way of the world; then ultimately of one's own needs and desires. |
| *Instructional Options:* | Structured overview |
| | Structural analysis |
| | Reinforcement of definitions of words |
| | Reinforcement of meanings of words |

### QUEST FOR KNOWLEDGE*
#### Structured Overview

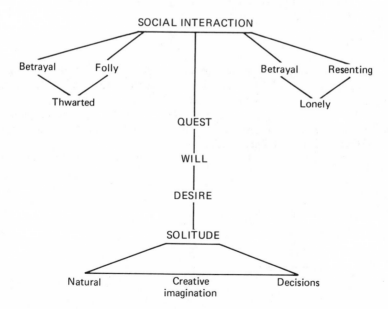

*Marjorie Dubrow

## ROOT WORDS

*Directions:* Some new words in this poem are made from root words you may know. For example: the word *learning* is made from the root word *learn*. Seeing the root word in a new word can help you read the new word.

These new words are made from root words:

| betrayal | imagination | resenting |
| creative | decisions | lonely |

Listed below are the root words from which the new words are made. The definitions of the root words are also listed. Using the short blank to the left of the root word, match the root word to its definition by indicating the definition number. Then write the new word in the blank to the right of the root word.

_____ betray _____ (betrayal)

_____ create _____ (creative)

_____ resent _____ (resenting)

_____ imagine _____ (imagination)

_____ lone _____ (lonely)

_____ decide _____ (decision)

1. to make a mental image of, suppose, think, create

2. by oneself, lonesome, isolated

3. to make up one's mind, arrive at a judgment or choice

4. to lead astray, to deceive

5. to bring into being, make, originate

6. to feel or show a bitter hurt at something from a sense of feeling injured or offended

## WORD PUZZLE

*Directions:* To solve this puzzle, look at the definitions below. Think of a word that fits the definition from the vocabulary list, has the same number of letters as the number of spaces provided in the corresponding line, and has the given letter in the same position as indicated. Write the word on the line. The first one is done for you. (Note: The first word is not on the vocabulary list. All other words are vocabulary words.)

1. <u>s e e k</u>

2. <u>n</u> _ _ _ _ _

3. _ <u>o</u> _ _ _

4. _ _ <u>w</u> _ _ _ _

5. _ _ <u>l</u> _ _

6. _ <u>e</u> _ _ _ _

7. _ _ _ _ _ _ d _
8.         _ _ _ g _ _ _ _ _ _ _
9.              _ _ e _ _

1. to try to get or find out by asking or searching
2. of or arising from nature; innate
3. a foolish action or belief
4. to be hindered, frustrated, or defeated
5. the power of making a reasoned choice or decision; a strong and fixed purpose
6. a strong wish or craving; a longing for
7. the state of being alone
8. creation of the mind; creative power
9. to go in search of something; a hunting or pursuit

## WORD MEANING AND ASSOCIATION

*Directions:* Five sets of words appear below with four words in each set. Circle three words in each set that have some relationship to one another. In the space provided, briefly describe the relationship among groups of words. If you feel there is more than one combination for each set of main words, please indicate it.

*Description*

1. change       resentment       imagination       protection

     GROUP ONE:                                        _____

     GROUP TWO:                                          _____

2. natural             rich            creative              easy

     GROUP ONE:                                          _____

     GROUP TWO:                                          _____

3. knowledge         quest           lonely               will

     GROUP ONE:                                          _____

     GROUP TWO:                                          _____

4. solitude           folly           decisions          growth

     GROUP ONE:                                          _____

GROUP TWO: _____

5. desire              betrayal          thwart          seek

GROUP ONE: _____

GROUP TWO: _____

## WORD MEANING

*Directions:* You often understand the meaning of a new word from other words you know in the sentence. Read the following sentences. Circle the word or words after the sentence that mean the same as the italicized word. Be careful! Some of the words have more than one meaning. Some of them may look like other words you know.

1. Where there's a *will*, there's a way.
   a strong purpose              a legal document
2. A friend's *betrayal* can cost a person his trust in others.
   deception                     secret information
3. The problem with being faced with a choice is that you have to make a *decision*.
   send out an order             make up your mind
4. Because people need to feel wanted, they *resent* things that make them feel they're not important.
   regret                        feel hurt or angry at
5. He's such a *natural* clown!
   related biologically          having certain qualities innately
6. It was his *folly* to buy tickets to yesterday's show!
   a dance revue                 a foolish undertaking

---

*Area:*                   Literature ("By the Waters of Babylon" by Stephen Vincent Benet)

*Grade:*                  Tenth

*Organizing Idea:*        History repeats itself in a cycle from "primitive" to "civilized," but people stay the same—never satisfied and continually fighting. Unless wisdom comes as fast as scientific progress, the cycle will continue.

*Instructional Option:*   Organizational pattern (sequence)

## BY THE WATERS OF BABYLON*

### Part I

*Directions:* Read each of the sentences taken from "By the Waters of Babylon." Try to put each in chronological order as it happened in the story. Then, on the second space, write *past, present,* or *future* to tell if it happened before, during, or after the time of John's visit to the great Dead Place in the

*Rosamond J. Waters

story. Consider the events in relation to our time. On the third space write past, present, or future to tell when they would logically happen in relation to our own time.

| Number in Order | Story Time | Our Time | |
|---|---|---|---|
| 1. _____ | _____ | _____ | Everywhere went the gods, on foot and in chariots—there were gods beyond number and counting and their chariots blocked the streets. |
| 2. _____ | _____ | _____ | The Forest People could have killed me without fight, if they had come upon me then. |
| 3. _____ | _____ | _____ | He gave me the metal to hold—I took it and did not die. |
| 4. _____ | _____ | _____ | It is forbidden to cross the great river and look upon the Place of the Gods— this is most strictly forbidden. |
| 5. _____ | _____ | _____ | We are not ignorant like the Forest People—our women spin wool on the wheel, our priests wear a white robe. |
| 6. _____ | _____ | _____ | When gods war with gods, they use weapons we do not know. It was fire in the sky and a mist that poisoned. |
| 7. _____ | _____ | _____ | Nevertheless we make a beginning . . . there are the books and the writings. |
| 8. _____ | _____ | _____ | And always, as they labored and rested, as they feasted and made love, there was a drum in their ears—the pulse of the giant city, beating and beating like a man's heart. |
| 9. _____ | _____ | _____ | Perhaps, in the old days, they ate knowledge too fast. |
| 10. _____ | _____ | _____ | I saw them with wisdom beyond wisdom and knowledge beyond knowledge. And yet not all they did was well done—even I could see that—and yet their wisdom could not but grow until all was peace. |
| 11. _____ | _____ | _____ | They ran about like ants in the streets of their city. |
| 12. _____ | _____ | _____ | I do not know the customs of rivers— we are the people of the Hills. |

### Part II

*Directions:* After reading "By the Waters of Babylon," use your own experience and knowledge and, keeping Part I in mind, check the statements you agree with.

1. It is better to lose one's life than one's spirit.
2. Too much knowledge is a dangerous thing.
3. When knowledge exceeds wisdom, tragedy results.
4. People always think the "good old days" were better than the present.
5. People always think things will be better tomorrow.
6. People tend to respect their ancestors and "great" men of the past more than men of today.
7. People are afraid of what they don't know about.
8. Many religious rites and customs stem from sensible practices.
9. No one looks upon God and lives.
10. People fight and kill each other no matter how "civilized" they are.
11. Even though we know our fate, we keep on with actions that will harm us.
12. History repeats itself.

---

| | |
|---|---|
| *Area:* | Literature (Short Story and Poem) |
| *Grade:* | Tenth |
| *Organizing Idea:* | Most people are concerned about their fate, and through reality and imagination they try to gain some perspective on what it will be and what will make it so. |
| *Instructional Options:* | Presentation of definitions of words<br>Reinforcement of meanings of words<br>Reasoning |

## PERSPECTIVE ON FATE*

*Part I*

*Directions:* Here are several pairs of words. Based on the experiences you have had with the words related to each pair, place an *S* on the line between them if their meanings are similar. Place a *D* on the line if their meanings are different.

1. remarkable    _____ unusual
2. oppressive    _____ very burdensome or severe
3. sketch        _____ a drawing
4. convey        _____ to suggest an idea
5. sustain       _____ to put down
6. vague         _____ certain
7. palpable      _____ able to be touched or felt
8. reverie       _____ quiet
9. rouse         _____ to waken

*Reproduced by permission of TRICA Consultants, Inc., Homer, New York, 1977.

10. impulse     —— sudden action or idea
11. elephantine     —— very large
12. intrusion     —— breaking into
13. flaw     —— a break or defect
14. portrait     —— a picture
15. exhibition     —— a show
16. carnation     —— a flower
17. uncanny     —— mysterious, unnatural
18. plausible     —— unbelievable
19. inscription     —— words written on something
20. coincidence     —— a chance happening
21. altered     —— changed
22. admiration     —— to think well of something or someone
23. prosperous     —— successful
24. improbable     —— not very likely
25. stifling     —— smothering, to be short of air

### Part II

*Directions:* Follow the directions which will be given to you orally.

—— —— 1. It is more satisfying to see where you have been than to wonder where you are going.

—— —— 2. There is nothing more powerful than *belief,* whether it be right or wrong.

—— —— 3. Decisions are the hinges of destiny.

—— —— 4. Expectation creates reality out of imagination.

—— —— 5. "I am the master of my fate;
I am the captain of my soul."
        —Henley (*Invictus*)

—— —— 6. Action without thought can lead to disaster.

—— —— 7. Even though you are careful when you make important decisions, you may still feel anxiety.

—— —— 8. Man's perspective is temporal even though his destination is eternal.

# Bibliography

**TEXTBOOKS**

AUKERMAN, ROBERT. *Reading in the secondary school classroom.* New York: McGraw-Hill, 1972.

BURMEISTER, LOU. *Reading strategies for secondary school teachers.* Reading, Mass.: Addison-Wesley, 1974.

DECHANT, EMERALD. *Reading improvement in the secondary school.* Englewood Cliffs, N.J.: Prentice-Hall Inc., 1973.

EARLE, RICHARD. *Teaching reading and mathematics.* Newark, Del.: International Reading Association, 1976.

ESTES, THOMAS. A scale to measure attitudes toward reading. *Journal of Reading,* 1971, *15,* 135-38.

ESTES, THOMAS, and JOSEPH VAUGHN, *Reading and learning in the content classroom.* Boston: Allyn and Bacon, Inc., 1978.

FARR, ROGER. *Reading: What can be measured.* Newark, Del.: International Reading Association, 1969.

GOODMAN, KENNETH. Behind the eye: What happens in reading. *Reading: Process and program.* Urbana, Ill.: National Council of Teachers of English, 1970.

HAFNER, LAWRENCE. *Improving reading in the secondary school.* New York: Macmillan, 1974.

HENRY, GEORGE. *Teaching reading as concept development.* Newark, Del.: International Reading Association, 1974.

HERBER, HAROLD, and RICHARD BARRON, eds. *Research in reading in content areas: Second year report.* Syracuse University: Reading and Language Arts Center, 1973.

HERBER, HAROLD, and JOAN NELSON. Questioning is not the answer. *Journal of Reading,* 1975, *18,* 512-17.

HERBER, HAROLD, and JAMES RILEY. *Research in reading in content areas: Fourth report.* Syracuse University: Reading and Language Arts Center, 1978.

HERBER, HAROLD, and PETER SANDERS, eds. *Research in reading in content areas: First year report.* Syracuse Univeristy: Reading and Language Arts Center, 1969.

HERBER, HAROLD, and RICHARD VACCA, eds. *Research in reading in content areas: Third report.* Syracuse University: Reading and Language Arts Center, 1977.

KARLIN, ROBERT. *Teaching reading in high school.* Indianapolis: Bobbs-Merrill, 1977.

KENNEDY, L., and R. HALINSKI. Measuring attitudes: An extra dimension. *Journal of reading,* 1975, *18,* 518-22.

LAFFEY, JAMES, ed. *Reading in the content areas.* Newark, Del.: International Reading Association, ERIC-CRIER, 1972.

ROBINSON, H. ALAN. *Teaching reading and study strategies.* Boston: Allyn and Bacon, Inc., 1975.

SANDERS, NORRIS. *Classroom questions: What kinds?* New York: Harper and Row, 1966.

SHEPHERD, DAVID. *Comprehensive high school reading methods.* Columbus, Ohio: Charles E. Merrill, 1973.

SMITH, RICHARD, and THOMAS BARRETT. *Teaching reading in middle schools.* Reading, Mass.: Addison-Wesley Publishing Co., 1974.

THELEN, JUDITH. *Improving reading in science.* Newark, Del.: International Reading Association, 1976.

THOMAS, ELLEN LAMAR, and H. ALAN ROBINSON. *Improving reading in every class.* Boston: Allyn and Bacon, Inc., 1977.

VAUGHN, JOSEPH. A scale to measure attitudes toward teaching reading in content classrooms. *Journal of Reading,* 1977, *20,* 605-9.

### JOURNALS

Journals published by the International Reading Association are the main source of good articles about teaching reading in content areas: *The Journal of Reading; The Reading Research Quarterly; The Reading Teacher.* Also useful are *The English Journal* and *Language Arts,* both published by the National Council of Teachers of English. Good articles are to be found in volumes since 1970.

Several other publications occasionally include good articles on this aspect of reading. These publications are listed below, along with representative articles. Periodic perusal of these publications is very productive.

### ARITHMETIC TEACHER

HATER, M. A. Building reading skills in the mathematics class. *Arithmetic Teacher,* 21 (December 1974), 662-68.

## BUSINESS EDUCATION FORUM

SCHULTHESIS, R. A., and K. NAPOLI. Strategies for helping poor readers in business subjects. *Business Education Forum,* 30 (November 1975), 5-6+.

SCOTT, J. C. Reading rate: A neglected factor in the basic business classroom. *Business Education Forum,* 28 (April 1974), 32.

## CLEARING HOUSE

CRISCUOLO, NICHOLAS. Five creative approaches to reading in New Haven middle schools. *Clearing House,* 49 (November 1975)113-15.

DUKE, CHARLES, and ANNE POWERS. Reading in the content area. *Clearing House,* 48 (December 1973), 221-26.

HANNY, ROBERT. A process for decoding how to teach. *Clearing House,* 49 (February 1976), 279-81.

HARRIS, LARRY. Reading: What can be done. *Clearing House,* 48 (December 1973), 217-21.

LAMBERT, LARRY, C. LAMAR THOMPSON, and CHARLES WEINER. Structural communications: An instructional strategy for the language arts. *Clearing House,* 49 (October 1975), 64-67.

OLMO, BARBARA. The process of transfer and the transfer of process. *Clearing House,* 49 (October 1975), 81-82.

PENDERGRASS, R. A., and DIANE WOOD. Facilitating discussions: Skills for teachers and students. *Clearing House,* 49 (February 1976), 267-70.

ROSEWELL, PAUL T. We all teach reading. *Clearing House,* 48 (December 1973), 213-17.

SHUMAN, R. B. School wide attack on reading problems. *Clearing House.* 49 (October 1975), 76-80.

SKINNER, S. BALLOW. Cognitive development: A prerequisite for critical thinking. *Clearing House,* 49 (March 1976), 292-99.

SWICK, KEVIN J. Utilization of analogies to teach critical thinking skills. *Clearing House,* 49 (December 1975), 180-82.

TOBACK, A. S. Secondary teachers can teach reading. *Clearing House,* 49 (February 1976), 248-49.

WEBER, E. J., and W. J. BROWN. High school reading success story. *Clearing House,* 49 (April 1976), 349-50.

## EDUCATIONAL LEADERSHIP

CORNBLETH, CATHERINE. Student questioning as a learning strategy. *Educational Leadership,* 33 (December 1975), 219-22.

SMITH, C. B. Teaching reading in the secondary school. *Educational Leadership,* 33 (April 1976), 509-12.

## FORECAST HOME ECONOMICS

DIEFFENDERFER, R. I. Teaching reading through crafts. *Forecast Home Economics,* 19 (February 1974), 14-15.

## HIGH SCHOOL JOURNAL

COOPER, C. R., and A. R. PETROSKY. Reading strategies and teaching implications for secondary schools from the psycholinguistic model of the reading process. *High School Journal,* 59 (November 1975), 91-102.

DUPUIS, M. Diagnostic teaching for every teacher. *High School Journal,* 59 (November 1975), 65-76.

PALMER, W. S., ed. Teaching reading in the secondary school: Practices and perspectives symposium. *High School Journal,* 59 (November 1975), 49-102.

SMALL, ROBERT. Preparing to teach a novel. *High School Journal,* 57 (February 1974), 190-203.

SWITZER, THOMAS. Something old and something new: The social studies in transition. *High School Journal,* 57 (March 1974), 240-49.

## INSTRUCTOR

HOOPER, H. Why do daredevils challenge Niagara? content reading. *Instructor,* 85 (May 1976), 46-9+.

KENNEDY, D. Cloze procedure: Use it to develop comprehension skills. *Instructor,* 84 (November 1974), 82.

SHARKNAS, JENEVIE. Helping kids make inferences. *Instructor,* 85 (March 1976), 71-74.

SILVER, JAMES. Social studies: There's more than meets the eye. *Instructor,* 85 (November 1975), 108-9.

WOLFE, R. Houses teach reading. *Instructor,* 84 (March 1975), 120.

## JOURNAL OF EDUCATIONAL PSYCHOLOGY

LEVIN, J. R. Inducing comprehension in poor readers: A test of a recent model; visual imagery organizational strategy. *Journal of Educational Psychology,* 65 (August 1973), 19-24.

## JOURNAL OF EDUCATIONAL RESEARCH

VACCA, R. T. Development of a functional reading strategy: Implications for content area inclusion. *Journal of Educational Research,* 69 (November 1975) 108-12.

## JOURNAL OF SPECIAL MENTAL RETARDATION

CAPLAN, R. I. Curriculum design in math for parents and teachers of reading disabled children. *J. Sp. Men. Retard.* 11 (Spring 1975), 204-8.

## JOURNAL OF NEGRO EDUCATION

RUBIN, D. Inner-city high school teachers as teachers of reading: A possible solution to the drop-out problem. *Journal of Negro Education,* 43 (Summer 1974), 337-47.

## MAN, SOCIETY AND TECHNOLOGY

SANACORE, J. Effective use of the industrial arts textbook. *Man, Society and Technology*, 34 (May 1975), 264-65.

## REVIEW OF EDUCATIONAL RESEARCH

HARTLEY, JANUS, and IVOR K. DAVIES. Preinstructional strategies: The role of pretests, behavioral objectives, overviews and advance organizers. *Review of Educational Research*, 46 (Spring 1976), 239-65.

## READING IMPROVEMENT

BLOSSOM, G. A. Tolleson school reading project: Use of glossaries. *Reading Improvement*, 10 (Winter 1973), 30-31.

CORLETT, D. Evaluation of reading in the classroom: Group informal inventories. *Reading Improvement*, 11 (Winter 1974), 20-22.

CRISCUOLO, P. Reading observation checklist. *Reading Improvement*, 11 (Winter 1974), 59-61.

INGERSOLL, G. M., and P. JOHNSON. Attitudes and reading comprehension: A preliminary investigation. *Reading Improvement*, 11 (Fall 1974), 52-56.

SANACORE, J. Sources for teaching reading in the content areas. *Reading Improvement*, 11 (Spring 1974), 54-57.

## SCHOOL SCIENCE AND MATH

ESLER, W. K., and K. MERRITT. Teaching reading through science experience stories. *School Science and Math*, 76 (March 1976), 203-6.

## SCIENCE EDUCATION

LAWSON, A. E., et al. Levels of intellectual development and reading ability in disadvantaged students and the teaching of science. *Science Education*, 59 (January 1975), 113-25.

## SCIENCE TEACHER

BANCHERI, L. P. Operation READS: Reading embracing all disciplines at Sewanhaka. *Science Teacher*, 41 (March 1974), 36-37.

CORNELIUS, D. W. Individualized testing for content reading. *Science Teacher*, 41 (October 1974), 40-42.

GAGE, T. How can we help kids read science textbooks? *Science Teacher*, 41 (December 1974), 37-40.

HASKER, G. W. New approach to reading difficulties. *Science Teacher*, 41 (September 1974), 42.

TELFER, R., and D. MOORE. Improving reading in individualized science. *Science Teacher,* 42 (June 1975), 22.

WARREN, R. A. Helping poor readers in secondary science. *Science Teacher,* 42 (May 1975), 42.

## SOCIAL STUDIES

DAVIS, ARNOLD. Reading maps: A much needed skill. *Social Studies,* 65 (February 1974), 67-71.

DOLGIN, ANN B. How to match reading materials to student reading levels. *Social Studies,* 65 (November/December 1975), 250-52.

DUSHER, RAYMOND. How to help social science students read better. *Social Studies,* 66 (September/December 1975), 258-61.

FEELEY, THEODORE II. The cloze and the maze. *Social Studies,* 66 (November/December 1975), 253-57.

McFARREN, G. ALLEN. The pendulum swings back: Structure to process. *Social Studies,* 65 (December 1974), 295-96.

MAKELA, LEE. A place for the novel in the East Asian survey. *Social Studies,* 66 (July/August 1975), 154-56.

PAJAK, EDWARD. A corkboard map or timeline: A new dimension for the classroom bulletin board. *Social Studies,* 66 (September/October 1975), 230-31.

PUGLISI, DICK. The concept of structure revisited. *Social Studies,* 66 (November/December 1975), 204-7.

RICE, ARTHUR. Using quotations in teaching social studies. *Social Studies,* 66 (November/December 1975), 265-66.

SOLVY, D. A. Teaching of reading in social studies. *Social Studies,* 66 (March 1975), 80-82.

TREZZA, FRANCIS. Social studies in the '70's . . . and beyond. *Social Studies,* 66 (November/December 1975), 162-63.

TURNER, T. N. Making the social studies textbook a more effective tool for less able readers. *Social Education,* 40 (January 1976), 38-41.

# Index*

*special thanks to Donna Alvermann